FOR THE COLOR OF HIS SKIN

THE MURDER OF YUSUF HAWKINS AND THE TRIAL OF BENSONHURST

JOHN DeSANTIS

INTRODUCTION BY ALAN M. DERSHOWITZ

PHAROS BOOKS
A SCRIPPS HOWARD COMPANY
NEW YORK

First published in 1991.

Library of Congress Cataloging-in-Publication Data:
DeSantis, John.
For the color of his skin: the murder of Yusuf Hawkins
and the trial of Bensonhurst / by John DeSantis.
p. cm.
Includes index.
ISBN 0-88687-621-4: $18.95
1. Murder—New York (N.Y.)—Case studies.   2. Hate
crimes—New York (N.Y.)—Case studies.
3. Bensonhurst (New York, N.Y.).
4. Hawkins, Yusuf.   5. New York (N.Y.)—Race
relations—Case studies.   6. Brooklyn (New York,
N.Y.)— Race relations—Case studies.   7. Trials
(Murder)—New York (State)—Kings County.
I. Title.
HV6534.N5D47   1991
364.1'523'0974723—dc20   91–16557   CIP

Printed in the United States of America

Pharos Books
A Scripps Howard Company
200 Park Avenue
New York, N.Y. 10166

10 9 8 7 6 5 4 3 2 1

Pharos Books are available at special discounts on
bulk purchases for sales promotions, premiums,
fundraising or educational use. For details, contact:
Special Sales Department
Pharos Books
200 Park Avenue
New York, NY 10166

For my mother, Leah Tarulli DeSantis
Who taught me to look
at both sides of everything
And makes sure that I still do

CONTENTS

FOREWORD

IKE the prosecution of those charged with the murder of Yusuf Hawkins, this book raises more questions than it answers. There are still conflicting stories about why thirty to forty young men were gathered in a Bensonhurst schoolyard on the night of August 23, 1989. But there can be little doubt that the act which led to the murder of an innocent and unassuming black teenager, the firing of four shots from a .32-caliber revolver, was motivated by the race of the victim. We can also be certain that seven young white men were arrested and charged in connection with that murder, and that most of them were found not guilty of the most serious crimes by juries made up of many different ethnic roots. There are those who say that this was proof that our jury system works, and that justice was done. That opinion is not shared by some prosecutors who worked on the case, or by the grieving family of Yusuf Hawkins, or by the families of Keith Mondello, John Vento, and Joseph Fama, who are currently serving time in prison.

There are many nuances in this case and the public reaction to it that were not adequately addressed throughout the news coverage in print and broadcast media. Although it is sometimes said that when the media reports on the media it's because they have run out of things to report on, that is not the case here. The news media's reaction to this case, coupled with its choice to ignore other stories that have also affected black communities in New York and elsewhere, was responsible in part for the polarization that already existed when the fatal gunshots were fired on that hot August night.

The Bensonhurst case brought reporters into neighborhoods that usually don't receive their attention, and there is a benefit from this. Contacts have been made that might not have been made before, and it even appears now that more attention is being paid to crimes in black communities once ignored by the press.

My own education in this regard, as a result of covering the case, is one of the reasons I wrote this book. If nothing else, perhaps now a thorough understanding of both sides of the controversy can be had by anyone who cares to know what was really happening during that most troubled summer.

There are a number of people whose assistance made this book possible, and who should be thanked. The Hawkins family and the Mondello family, the Reverend Al Sharpton, the New York City Police Department and Eric Shawn of WNYW television, Phillip Messing, formerly of the New York *Post*, Patricia Hurtado of New York *Newsday*, David DePetris and Stanley Meyer, Stephen Murphy, Matthew Mari, Jacob Evseroff, Sarina Scavone, Russell Gibbons, Harold Ayala and Linda Nipitello, Carmen Mercado, and Maimonedes Hospital are just a few.

Individuals, some of them prosecutors, defense attorneys' staff members, residents of Bensonhurst, police officers, and even some of the defendants in the case were willing to share information on condition of anonymity and added to the insight and understanding that have made this work possible.

Lieutenant Raymond O'Donnell and Sgt. Mary Wrensen of the NYPD Public Information Division were especially helpful.

Invaluable assistance during the writing of this book was also provided by Curtis W. Hollis, and during my initial coverage of the case by Gerry Mullany of United Press International.

This was an ambitious project for a first-time author, and my editor at Pharos Books, Sharilyn Jee, gave unselfishly of her experience and abilities, with a liberal dose of patience and understanding.

My agent, Bobbe Siegel, is owed a debt of thanks for her hard work and unflagging enthusiasm. And finally there are all of those people, some of whose names I never knew, who answered my questions as I covered this case and wrote the book, black and white New Yorkers who shared their opinions, feelings, and fears with me in order to guide me on a true course.

FOREWORD

I no longer live in New York City full-time, but am doing the work I love best, reporting on the people who are part of the world around me. But even as I look around the small Catskill Mountain community where I now spend most of my time and where this book was completed, I see small, petty examples of intolerance and even bigotry. In this community and others like it, I hope that the story told on these pages can serve as a lesson that prejudice against people of any group can bring nothing but pain and suffering in the long run, to the immediate victims and to everyone else around them.

JOHN E. DeSANTIS
Shandaken, N.Y.
April 13, 1991

INTRODUCTION

If William Shakespeare were alive today he would not be writing about the Montagues and the Capulets. He would be chronicling the tensions between Bensonhurst and Bedford–Stuyvesant. His protagonists would not be princes like Hamlet but unlikely hero-villains like the Falstaffian Reverend Al Sharpton. The killing of Yusuf Hawkins by a group of white kids in Bensonhurst is a tragedy of our times.

The question of whether the murder of the quiet black teenager was a "racially motivated" crime oversimplifies a complex contemporary issue. At one level, of course, the crime *was* racially motivated; had Hawkins been white he would never even have been noticed as he walked through the mostly Italian neighborhood of Bensonhurst. At another level, Hawkins was killed because he was seen as a dangerous and unwanted outsider. There can be little doubt that those who organized the bat-wielding crowd which eventually cornered Hawkins and his friends were laying in wait for drug-dealing blacks and Hispanics who were believed to be coming to Bensonhurst to "kick some white ass." Hawkins and his friends were in the wrong place—and of the wrong race—at the wrong time. Hawkins was the victim of mistaken identity, but the reason for the mistake was the color of his skin.

There are no flawless heroes here (as there rarely were in Shakespeare's complex tragedies), only victims, villains, court jesters, and two large choruses of townsfolk. One compelling message of this book is that when racial and political tensions are high no one really seeks justice. The Sharpton crowd did not want refined, legalistic distinctions drawn among the kids who surrounded Hawkins—the ringleader, the one who fired the fatal shots, the one who provided the gun. Sharpton wanted vengeance against "the thirty" who were all equally guilty of murder in his view. Nor did the Bensonhurst chorus seek individualized justice; they wanted everyone acquitted. Both sides proved the point that *racial justice* is an oxymoron: As soon as one begins to think about justice in terms of race or ethnic groups, the first casualty becomes *individual* justice, which is the only kind of justice deserving that noble title.

Nor is racial or political justice conducive to fair and effective law enforcement. This book chronicles the political nature of both the prosecution and the defense in these cases. When prosecutors try to placate angry mobs and vocal activists they forgo their important role as the front-line protectors of individual rights and individual justice. Whatever arguments can be made for affirmative action in employment and university admissions, there can be no just affirmative-action approach to law enforcement. Equal individual justice is the mandate both of our constitution and of jurisprudence. In this case too many lawyers heeded the voices of racial politics and too few looked to considerations of fairness, equity, and individual justice. This should not be surprising since political careers are made and broken on cases like the Hawkins murder, especially in racially volatile areas like Brooklyn where this tragedy began.

I know both Bensonhurst and Bedord-Stuyvesant well, having grown up in the neighborhood adjoining the former and gone to high school in the neighborhood adjoining the latter. As an Orthodox (and therefore visible) Jew, I was taunted both by the Italian kids of Bensonhurst and by the black kids of Bed-Stuy. The leaders of both communities inspire strong ethnic pride in the residents and deep-seated suspicion and distrust of outsiders, especially outsiders of different color. These perceptions are palpable when an outsider walks through either neighborhood.

This is not to suggest that the typical residents of Bensonhurst or Bedford-Stuyvesant are racists. The Hawkins tragedy involved only a small number of residents of each community who reflect the extremes of ethnocentricity. Kids who would gather with bats and guns to keep blacks—even black drug dealers who were "dating" one of "their" women—out of their neighborhood are not typical of Bensonhurst. Nor is Al Sharpton—who preaches a gospel of black superiority and white exclusion—typical of Bedford-Stuyvesant.

If there are any heroes of this tragedy, they are the anonymous jurors who seem to have taken seriously their important role of fact-finders and conscience of the entire community. Despite crass appeals to the white, black, and Hispanic jurors to do racial justice, they seem to have understood their job as doing individual justice to particular defendants based on their individual complicity and culpability. That does not mean they did perfect justice. The ringleader seems to have gotten off somewhat lightly. But this may have been the fault of prosecutors for having indiscriminately charged so many people with "acting in concert" for a shooting that seems to have been unplanned.

In the end, the most vocal of neither neighborhood were completely satisfied by the legal outcomes in the Hawkins case. But that is how it should be in a case as difficult and complex as this one. The role of our legal system is not to satisfy neighborhoods, it is to apply the law fairly and dispassionately. That may be a great deal to ask when passions run as high as they do in racially explosive situations like the Hawkins killing. But consider the alternative. We certainly do not want justice by mob rule, as Al Sharpton would give us. Nor do we want justice by the local—mostly white—police as existed in Brooklyn and other urban enclaves for many years.

The world is changing, and with it our legal system. The Al Sharptons of the world have had both a positive and negative impact on justice. They have insisted—to their credit—that black life be valued as highly as white life. They have put the issue of discrimination against blacks in our justice system high on the political agenda. And they have made it impossible to hide from view the many injustices that still disgrace our legal system. But their proposed remedies are often as bad as the maladies to which they correctly point. Substituting racial injustice against whites for racial injustice against blacks is no solution. Nor is justice by slogan or by demonstration.

Our legal system must be made color-blind. Justice must be the same in cases involving crimes committed by whites against blacks as it is in cases of crimes committed by blacks against whites. Prosecutors must understand that it is not their proper role to take sides in ethnic and racial conflict. They must be perceived as—and they must actually be—neutral enforcers of criminal law, without regard to the crowds, the voters, or the press. This is a tall order for elected prosecutors with political ambition. But it is central for preserving justice in this age of group rights, racial justice, and ethnic conflict.

Alan M. Dershowitz

THIRTY-TWO YOUNG

HORTLY after nine o'clock on the hot, humid evening of August 23, 1989, a red-and-white ambulance pulled up in front of Store Twenty-Four on New Utrecht Avenue in the Bensonhurst section of Brooklyn. Paramedic Pericles Leonardis headed directly for the refrigerator case. The stocky, dark-haired paramedic found the rows of frosty-cold iced-tea bottles and clamped a large hand around two of them.

His white uniform shirt was still clean, but the collar had wilted in the heat hours before, and beads of perspiration ran down his face.

The girl behind the counter rang up the sale, smiled, and asked if the ambulance crew had been busy.

"Nah, quiet," Peri replied. "Hopefully it'll stay that way, 'cause we've only got about an hour left to go."

Peri liked working in the Bensonhurst area. Although only a half-hour from Manhattan, the provincial, small-town atmosphere in the neighborhood reminded him of his own town on Long Island. After taking his change he returned to the ambulance, where his partner Ralph Fasano monitored the two-way radio. The New York City Emergency Medical Service Brooklyn South frequency had been silent for the past half-hour except for a few routine administrative transmissions and the announcement of a minor case out of their area.

Store Twenty-Four was centrally located within Peri and Ralph's response area, and they remained in the lot as they drank their iced teas. There was a rumble, and the radio transmission was drowned out by a Manhattan-bound subway train as it lumbered and squealed

1

above them on the elevated tracks over New Utrecht Avenue. As the train rounded a turn, showers of blue and white sparks lit up the darkness, and then it was gone.

Peri and Ralph were a classic Mutt-and-Jeff team, as different in personality and physical appearance as they were similar in their dedication and proficiency, according to other medical staffers who worked with them.

Tall, thin, twenty-eight, the bespectacled Ralph was deliberate and collected under the most trying circumstances. His low-key approach perfectly balanced that of the more excitable and gung-ho Peri, four years his junior.

The son of a heart surgeon who had immigrated from Greece, Peri had a burning desire to be wherever the action was. "He'd give you the shirt off his back, anytime, and let me tell you it would fit both of us" is one description of Peri offered by a supervisor.

In addition to his job as a paramedic, Peri was a volunteer fire-fighter at home on Long Island. His two hundred eighty pounds of sheer bulk and muscle came in handy at more than one emergency scene, and his enthusiasm boosted the morale of others when things got tough.

After finishing their iced tea the pair began the last leg of a sixteen-hour tour of duty. Their Ford Econoline van was one of two Advanced Life Support units operated by Maimonedes Medical Center. The hospital's three-year-old paramedic program had been created to provide needed prehospital care to an increasingly busy area. The ambulance was used for routine interhospital transports between Maimonedes and other facilities, especially during the day, but also responded to 911 emergency calls routed over the EMS radio frequency. The van's formal designation was ALS Unit Thirty-Two Young. *ALS* stood for Advanced Life Support, the three identified it as a Brooklyn unit, the two indicated its response area, and the *Young* was radio talk for the letter *Y*, which identified their particular unit.

The city maintains its own fleet of Basic and Advanced Life Support ambulances, but those from voluntary hospitals such as Maimonedes are directed through its dispatch system as well. A friendly rivalry exists between private medics like Peri and Ralph and the city's own emergency workers, but in most emergency situations petty differences are put aside and all personnel function well together.

Peri was pulling out of the convenience-store parking lot when a city ambulance broke in on the radio with an urgent message.

"We are en route to a report of a man shot at Bay Ridge Avenue and Twentieth Avenue, unconfirmed over the police radio," a voice said through the speaker.

"We're right there, just about," Peri said to Ralph, and began heading toward the location in case back-up was needed.

The responding city ambulance was manned by two Emergency Medical Technicians. Peri's and Ralph's paramedic certification authorized them to perform advanced procedures using more sophisticated equipment, and they knew from earlier transmissions that the nearest city paramedics were some distance away.

Peri and Ralph were also waiting for a confirmation of the job. New York's 911 system receives countless unfounded reports of shootings and other emergencies, sometimes placed by people who just want to hear sirens and see flashing red lights or used as a ploy to get quicker police or medical response to low-priority situations. The practice has also been used by criminals as a way of diverting police attention away from areas where a crime is planned.

As the ambulance cruised the residential street its headlights swept across a statue of the Virgin Mary on the lawn of one of the red-brick houses that lined the street. Moisture from humid air collected like tears in her glazed blue eyes.

The radio crackled to life again, confirming a man shot, and the peaceful street became a riot of red flashes and shrieking sirens as Peri hit the accelerator and sped down the street.

"Thirty-Two Young is backing up on that shooting!" Peri hollered into the microphone as the siren warbled through the grille. He braked at the intersection at Nineteenth Avenue, checking to the left.

"Clear on the right!" Ralph said and, as the rig jackrabbited ahead, he turned to the back and ran down a mental checklist of equipment that would be needed, collecting it the best he could while hanging on for dear life.

When they reached Bay Ridge and Twentieth several police cars were already there with the city ambulance, their roof lights cutting wide red swaths through the summer haze. Another police car arrived at the scene, hopping a curb as it screeched to a halt.

The EMTs had already begun their work. A curious mob had gathered around them despite police efforts to keep the scene clear.

"Come on, go home! Let's go," an annoyed young cop was saying to no one in particular as he waved his arms.

Ralph cut the siren but left the lights on as Peri, amazingly lithe considering his bearlike build, bounded out the driver's door, trauma kit in hand. He vaulted over the hood of a parked car and body-blocked his way through the rim of the crowd. An EMT was crouched near a brick wall adjacent to 2007 Bay Ridge Avenue, where a black teenager lay sprawled on the ground face-up. His white T-shirt was drenched with blood, his eyes fixed and glassy.

The EMT's partner held on to a limp dark-skinned arm as he checked for vital signs.

"What do we have?" Peri asked authoritatively.

"Gunshot wound. Faint pulse, but we just lost it," one of the medics replied.

Peri looked into the young man's deep brown eyes with their dilated pupils as he ripped off the blood-saturated shirt and searched for wounds. His bare fingers became sticky with the red wetness as he probed; there had been no time for protective gloves.

Ralph appeared at Peri's side and went to work inserting a long plastic tube down the young man's throat, easing it toward the lungs in an attempt to establish a clear airway, and then sealing the black ambubag over the nose and mouth. As one EMT began chest compression to force the still heart to pump, the other struggled to place the lower torso into mask trousers. These trousers fit over the victim's legs and, when pumped with air, restrict blood flow to the upper body, where it has a better chance of reaching vital organs. The two wounds Peri located were deep and, he thought, had probably caused considerable damage. One was in the center of the chest at the breastbone, the other just below the left nipple.

As Ralph felt the carotid artery through the victim's cool, moist neck, Peri tried to ascertain the wounds' depth and felt as if he was sticking his two fingers into a warm, moist bowling ball.

Emergency lights bounced off the brick wall where the four medics worked on the young man. As the growing crowd of white-sneakered young men in their Day-Glo shorts and shirts and girls with teased hair looked on, Ralph started up two intravenous lines. One contained a saline solution, the other was hooked to a bag of universal-donor blood.

Out of the corner of his eye Peri saw some men who looked like detectives closely examining a pair of baseball bats, made a mental note to check further for blunt trauma, and wondered what the hell had gone on. The kid was nicely dressed and didn't look anything like the gunshot-wound victims he normally picked up on the street. But then, again, you don't find too many black kids on Twentieth Avenue, he thought.

Finally stabilized, the limp form was scooped up on a metal-frame stretcher that was passed up to a gurney and tightly strapped in place. Cops and the medics half-rolled, half-carried the gurney to the city ambulance's back door. The large orange-and-white unit had more working room than the Maimonedes van. Ralph hopped in after the patient and continued working on him as Peri jumped behind the wheel of their own van to serve as an escort unit. As the van bolted to the first intersection, blocking any traffic that might come down the side street, Peri shouted into the mike over the piercing wail of the siren.

"This is Thirty-Two Young escorting your EMT unit to Maimonedes from Bay Ridge and Twentieth. Advise them to stand by for a male, approximately eighteen, with multiple gunshot wounds. Be advised patient is in cardiac and respiratory arrest, with no vitals. CPR is being done at this time."

In the cold white light of the city ambulance, Ralph squinted through his wire-rimmed eyeglasses, searching for another vein as carefully as he could in the rocking cabin. He started up two more IV lines while the EMT continued chest compressions.

The bumps and jolts of the speeding ambulance made the trip feel like a runaway roller-coaster ride, but in less than five minutes the back door opened into the glare of the hospital emergency dock. The stretcher was eased out of the ambulance and rushed into the emergency corridor. Peri and Ralph ticked off information to a nurse who trotted to keep up with the gurney while scribbling down as many notes as she could. With a slam of metal against double-portholed doors, the stretcher burst into the emergency room and was lined up alongside a table at the center of a buzzing hive of green-gowned personnel.

A respirator was hooked up to the boy's face, commencing its alternating *hiss-pfft* as a surgeon meticulously began his work while calling out orders above the hubbub.

"Scalpel."

"I need suction here, suction! Easy, get it in there. Move that light, the light over here!"

"Let's do this!"

Carefully and skillfully the surgeon made an incision through the chest while nurses tore away at clothing with scissors and knives that gleamed brightly under the surgical lights. The cardiac monitor above the table continued to emit a maddeningly unwavering high-pitched *be-e-e-e-p*.

The slightest hope rested on an even slimmer chance that the heart, unresponsive to the massive electrical defibrillator jolts, could manually be made to pump by squeezing the muscle itself.

Already insulted by the bullet wounds, the young chest was subjected to one more indignity and cracked open. When the cavity was opened, a torrent of liquid the color and consistency of cherry Kool-Aid cascaded onto the floor, staining the shoes and pants of the hospital workers and forming a large puddle below the table.

The fluids and universal-donor blood from Ralph's intravenous lines had not made their way into the collapsed veins as they were supposed to, but instead collected uselessly within the chest wall to the point where it was literally bursting with liquids.

A doctor leaned his head down and examined the heart. The bullet that had invaded its chambers and tumbled within them had reduced it to a shredded, useless mass of tissue that was beyond repair.

Peri, standing in a corner of the room, saw tired eyes between a green cap and face mask glance at the large digital clock. It was 9:48 P.M. The doctor wearily untied the face-mask and it dropped from his face.

The trauma room's racket was replaced by an eerie silence, broken only by the sound of the respirator doggedly pressing air into lifeless lungs. Then it too ceased, making the silence louder.

Orderlies and nurses began the grim task of cleaning the body and the trauma room floor as another surgeon loosely sewed the shattered chest closed. The room would have to be readied for the next emergency as soon as possible.

Peri and Ralph filed out with the EMTs, saddened that they were unsuccessful but satisfied that everything possible had been done. Everyone had pulled together, and each team praised the other for the collective effort.

Emergency workers speak of a "golden hour" for severe trauma cases. If the heart can be coaxed into beating on its own within sixty minutes of the time of injury, they believe, a chance of recovery still exists. Pericles Leonardis calls it "the race with the Reaper."

The victim had received all required prehospital care and was delivered to Maimonedes well within the golden hour, but it had not been enough, because there simply was no pump left to get going.

At the ambulance dock the medics returned each others' equipment, cleaning and sterilizing gear that would need to be used again. Two police officers walked up to Peri.

"DOA?" one of the cops asked. (*Dead on Arrival* usually indicates that someone was already dead on reaching a hospital. In New York City cop parlance the term is used to mean any deceased person.)

"Yeah," answered Peri. "So what was it?"

"We don't know," the other cop said. "It wasn't a robbery, and the kid's not from the neighborhood. They don't really know yet." It seemed to Peri that the officer was holding something back, and he thought about the baseball bats.

"If you need the paperwork, it's over with triage," Peri said, assuming the cops had not come to pass the time of day.

"Well, we need his shirt. Do you have it?" the cop asked somewhat

7

uneasily, the way police officers do when they think bosses are peeking over their shoulders.

Peri told them they didn't and directed the cops over to the city rig. The EMTs didn't remember seeing it on the ambulance at all and, after a quick search, determined it wasn't on board. A check of the trauma room failed to turn up the shirt either.

The medics knew that clothing worn by victims can be important forensic evidence in a homicide, and Peri assured the cops as they left that if the shirt turned up the precinct would be contacted.

Shortly after the departure of the officers a van arrived from the New York City Medical Examiner's office, and to Peri's amazement, took the body away. He couldn't remember ever seeing a corpse removed from a hospital so quickly. Somebody wants this kid autopsied in a hurry, he thought. As he turned over in his mind all he had seen he began to realize that this was not a routine homicide.

His tour completed, a tired Peri drove home to Long Island, thinking about the baseball bats, the incongruity of a black kid in a white neighborhood not known for its friendliness to outsiders, as well as the Medical Examiner's speed. It reminded him of December 1986, when he was an Emergency Medical Technician at a Queens hospital.

A black man had been brought in for treatment of injuries sustained from a beating by a marauding mob of youths armed with tree limbs, golf clubs, and bats. But he had not been the only victim. One of the man's companions, a younger black man, had been chased by the posse and, trying to escape them, had run across a busy parkway, straight into the path of an automobile traveling over fifty miles per hour. The impact was fatal to the young man, and the predominantly white neighborhood that had been the site of the incident, Howard Beach, had become infamous.

When Peri arrived home that night he called his good friend and supervisor to tell him about the shooting.

"I think it was racial," Peri said.

"What do you mean?" his friend asked.

"I mean, I think it was a racial killing. You know, another Howard Beach."

A HOUSE DIVIDED

NEW YORK City's borough of Brooklyn is larger in population and area than most cities in the United States. Located on the western end of Long Island, across the East River from the glitter and grime of lower Manhattan, Brooklyn was a city in its own right from 1834 until 1898, when it was incorporated into greater New York.

Automobile traffic from Manhattan passing over the obliging back of the Manhattan Bridge, one of three steel spiderworks spanning the river between Manhattan and Brooklyn, spills out onto a broad street called Flatbush Avenue, a black-topped and potholed spinal cord that begins at the foot of the bridge and ends at the Atlantic Ocean. Along the way it branches off into seemingly innumerable ganglia and neurons of back streets, avenues and alleys upon which reside one of the most ethnically, culturally, and economically diverse populations in the world.

The borough's multiethnic character dates back to its earliest history. The Italian explorer Giovanni da Verrazano was the first European to lay eyes on the Brooklyn shoreline—in 1524, when its only inhabitants were Native Americans. But Verrazano never left his ship, and the indigenous people remained undisturbed until Henry Hudson's sailors arrived in 1609, paving the way for eventual English settlement of an area known as Gravesend. The Dutch began moving in as well, and by 1698 Breuckelen (after a town in Holland) boasted a population of two thousand seventeen. The figure did not take into account the natives, who still lived there, but did include the Dutch, the English, and their African slaves.

In the centuries that followed immigrant groups from many nations passed through sections of Brooklyn in hopes of escaping the squalor and poverty of lower-Manhattan tenement rows. Some nationalities, such as the Italians and Jews of East New York, stayed only a generation or so and then went on to greener pastures. Others, such as the Poles of Greenpoint and the Russians of Brighton Beach, dug in and remained.

The best kielbasa this side of Warsaw can still be found on Greenpoint Avenue, and they still make homemade mozzarella cheese and other Italian delicacies in the Italian strongholds of Bensonhurst and Bay Ridge.

A few blocks from its Manhattan Bridge beginnings Flatbush Avenue is crossed by Fulton Street, a former Indian trail eventually named after the inventor of the steamboat. Fulton is now a commercial thoroughfare running through some of the toughest neighborhoods in the borough. One of these is the Bedford-Stuyvesant section. World War II veterans returning to the neighborhood's row-house blocks and seeking different surroundings moved their families to other places. Vacancies created by outgoing whites were filled by incoming families of blacks also seeking their piece of postwar prosperity and low rents.

Lack of employment opportunities endemically suffered by black Americans coupled with attendant poverty and substandard delivery of essential services soon turned Bedford-Stuyvesant and neighborhoods like it into crime-ridden slums.

During the 1960s many of the area's slum buildings were razed and replaced with multistory housing projects. The projects offered temporary cosmetic improvement, but the root causes of neighborhood problems were not demolished along with the old buildings, so crime and poverty remained.

Gunfire between rival drug dealers or sometimes between dealers and police is not an uncommon sound in the Bedford-Stuyvesant night, when the streets are awash with outlaws and toughs. Bedford-Stuyvesant was Dodge City Brooklyn-style, and psychologists now identify symptoms similar to combat fatigue in little schoolchildren, who are taught early to duck away from the windows when shooting starts.

The violence and crime of Bedford-Stuyvesant and other poor black neighborhoods are only part of the true character and personality of these blocks. In between the stores that stand shuttered by sheet-metal riot gates on Sunday mornings sounds of music and prayer emanate from dozens of storefront churches where men wear suits and women wear peacock hats that match brightly colored dresses.

Shattering the myth that people in such communities do little to effect positive change, a small trailer stands on the corner of Greene Avenue and Marcus Garvey Boulevard, not far from a veritable shopping center of crack houses, manned twenty-four hours a day by members of the Bedford-Stuyvesant Volunteer Ambulance Corps.

And behind the windows of projects like the Brevoort Houses mothers, fathers, and grandparents struggle quietly each day to keep their sons and daughters in school and away from the mean streets.

Bensonhurst, at the southern end of Brooklyn, stands in sharp contrast to Bedford-Stuyvesant, only eight miles away.

Italian immigrants and their sons and daughters made Bensonhurst their own when it was mostly farmland. Although Franklin D. Roosevelt High School on the lower end of the neighborhood boasts a student body that represents fifty-eight different nationalities, the Italian-American mark is stamped all over its tree-lined streets. The avenues with stores below and apartments above house some of the best cappuccino houses and Italian restaurants on the East Coast.

Street crime of the Bedford-Stuyvesant variety is rare in Bensonhurst. The closest thing to the Brevoort project are the Marlborough Houses, located more in nearby Coney Island than in Bensonhurst proper. Instead of crowded tenements and decaying brownstones with boarded-up windows, most of Bensonhurst's architecture consists of two-family brick houses built after World War

II. The houses overlook neatly trimmed lawns, many of them decorated with statues of saints and the Virgin Mary.

While Bensonhurst has its share of college graduates and profession-bound young men and women, like Bed-Stuy, there are also sinister problems lurking among its more disaffected youth, such as high dropout rates and drug abuse.

The corner boys of Bensonhurst, much like their blue-collar fathers, have deep-seated prejudices, especially regarding blacks. "They take all the good jobs, they take our women, they don't do anything except collect welfare" is the common appraisal.

By 1989, New York was a troubled city. The twin scourges of crack cocaine and AIDS were straining both law enforcement and health care resources past all reasonable limits. The gulf between the haves and the have-nots was wider than it had been in nearly a century. While largely uncharted resentment and anger at unyielding social conditions seethed and bubbled in black neighborhoods, well-documented and often-tolerated loathing and fear of blacks grew in the city's white enclaves as homicide statistics rose in minority communities. The resulting animosity and tension between the races had grown to a fever pitch by that summer, to a point where lives were endangered and even lost.

There is no way to adequately comprehend the root causes of racial tensions in New York and the nation without some understanding of the causal link between the institution of slavery and later socio-economic problems affecting African-Americans.

Many white Americans, particularly in the North, discount claims that the slavery issue has any bearing on contemporary social problems. But this attitude is seen as offensive and insensitive by some blacks.

"We were never brought here to this country to have equality and to share in the wealth of this country," says Nona Smith of the National Association for the Advancement of Colored People, which led the fight against early segregation laws in the South.

"We did a terrible wrong, and we have to find a way to compensate or rectify or acknowledge these wrongs. . . . If you consider what we went through, it takes a lot out of a people, and we are still the poorest. All the years! Nobody thinks about it. From taxes we paid, others benefited."

But many whites in Northern industrial cities feel that "reparations," even in the form of the simple acknowledgment that Nona Smith asks for, are not for them to offer.

"I wasn't there when my parents came over from Italy, but if you hear them talk they were crowded and pushed together . . . they were hungry, they were dirty and when they got here they weren't handled very gently," one Brooklyn woman says. "I never hurt anybody in my life, and I wouldn't hurt anybody in my life. What do I know about responsibility towards something I never did? I am tired of it. The slavery argument is a crutch . . . I wasn't even born then. How could you be guilty if you weren't there? And when did we ever have signs that had white only . . . white fountains, white toilets, in New York?"

There is an all-too-common view that slavery and later segregation were exclusively Southern institutions and practices. Some people point to the many Union soldiers who gave their lives on the battlefield "to free the blacks" during the Civil War as a means of exculpation.

But in cities like New York there was anger and bitterness at the economic suffering and loss of life the war wrought "just to free the niggers." During the time of the Civil War draft riots blacks in New York were persecuted, beaten, and sometimes killed because of anger at the war effort.

Even though Abraham Lincoln signed the Emancipation Proclamation that freed the slaves of the South, the U.S. Supreme Court would legalize segregation only a quarter-century later with the infamous Dred Scott decision. The doctrine of "separate but equal" became the law of the land.

The so-called Jim Crow laws, which mandated segregated cemeteries, restrooms, lunch counters and schools, remained until the landmark 1954 *Brown* vs. *Board of Education of Topeka* case, which led to the desegregation of Southern schools and paved the way for the civil rights movement, which effected change on a wider scale.

Signs are easily removed from bathroom doors, but not so long-entrenched attitudes and prejudices. Or the social and economic conditions that are blueprints for racial discrimination. De jure segregation—racial segregation mandated by law—was becoming a thing of the past in the South during the 1960s. De facto segregation—separation of the races through the effect of social and economic factors—became more entrenched in cities like New York as white parents, alarmed at the deteriorating state of the public school systems, began enrolling their children in private and parochial institutions of learning.

Well-meaning educators attempting to do something about the problem thought they had come up with a solution, which was to bus children to schools in other neighborhoods as a means of achieving racial balance and, hopefully, some measure of equality. But parents and children who attended the public schools in New York at the height of the busing controversy have expressed feelings which indicate that their perceptions of those different from themselves were undeniably warped by the busing experience.

Margaret Richman is a Queens grandmother whose eldest daughter was in third grade when the family learned about plans for "forced busing."

"The problem is I took this apartment because it was close to this school. Why should my third-grader be shipped out someplace? Concern about the integration wasn't my thing. I did not want my child on a bus because there was no reason for it . . . I had fears of an accident or other things. She was too young to be unsupervised."

Richman and other parents who took part in the protest insist they were not motivated by negative feelings toward blacks and point out that a number of black parents who opposed busing attended meetings and participated in some picketing of schools. "Our quarrel was not with the black parents, really," she said.

Rosemary Gunning, a former New York State assemblywoman,

recalls the bitterness engendered by the busing proposals and acknowledges that some parents were just plain antiblack. "There were some who were racists," she says. "But not most of the parents. They were afraid of their children going to some of the neighborhoods."

Eventually black children were bused in to predominantly white schools, but class differences and a variety of other conflicts made for classmates who were not always civil to each other. Some white adults who were children at the time recall being "shaken down" by bands of blacks, who also were alleged to have committed street crimes in white neighborhoods. Some blacks, on the other hand, recall being attacked by gangs of whites who did not want them in "their" neighborhoods.

In an address before the New York City Board of Education expressing opposition to the busing program, Mrs. Gunning recalls making a statement that she says she now sadly realizes was a prophecy: "These proposals are going to create a generation of race-conscious children."

There are many different kinds of New York City maps. Some show subway and bus routes; others break down the city into street grids to help tourists find world-famous landmarks more easily; others show it as a patchwork of police precincts. And there are the invisible maps drawn in the minds of people who live on its streets, that break the city down into turf—gang terminology for territory it controls. Turf wars over unwanted people in the neighborhood are legend in some places. Often the determining factor of a visitor's desirability has to do with race or nationality. Neighborhoods considered white enclaves are enforced as such, often with violence. Blacks respond in kind. These territorial stakes are tested and retested, with knives, fists, baseball bats, and sometimes firearms.

The type of crime most feared by the general public in America's urban centers in the late 1980s was not the internecine gang-type violence that erupted periodically. It was the sudden violence perpetrated against innocent victims on city streets, such as rape or robbery, that evoked the greatest anxiety. Americans became more aware of such crime through news sources, movies, and television shows. The news media increased crime reporting as law enforcement agencies increased their data-analysis capabilities and "law and order"-platform politicians spoke of the "crime wave" that gripped the nation.

In reality, the perceived crime wave never really existed. Comparative figures released by the United States Department of Justice in the spring of 1991 show, in fact, that violent crime victimization rates decreased drastically from 1973 through 1987. The assault figures reached a low of 22.3 victims per 1,000 persons nationwide aged twelve or older, and leveled off in 1989 at 23.0 per 1,000. (The figure is based on the National Crime Survey, which does not rely solely on what is reported to police.) Homicide, the most often reported crime, varies in rate over spans of time. From 1933 to 1958 the rate (based on the Uniform Crime Reports) dropped substantially, although it did pick up again around 1980. In 1988, however, the national homicide rate was 16 percent less than it had been eight years before. In New York City, the homicide rate did increase throughout the 1980s, but that increase has been attributed for the most part to increased violence among people in the drug trade.

Assessment of such crime reports and their methodology is best left to experts, but one incontrovertible fact stands out from the data. While the white population fears crime and particularly fears crime perpetrated by blacks, the victimization rate for blacks in almost every serious crime category is higher than that for whites, even though blacks make up less of the population. Higher numbers of robberies, assaults, and homicides are committed against blacks even though the simple assault rates for whites are higher. In 1989 fifty of every hundred murder victims were black.

Racially motivated crime was not new in the 1980s, but with fear of crime and consequently of blacks reaching an all-time high in American cities such crimes were being committed with startling frequency. Violence perpetrated against blacks because they were in an all-white neighborhood and "must be up to no good" was seen as justified by the fear factor.

The "get tough on crime" climate that was gripping the country was translated by some whites to mean "get tough on blacks," and incidences of violence against blacks continued to rise throughout the decade. While interracial violence was not the norm for traditional criminal activities (blacks are victimized by blacks over 80 percent of the time) this is not true for bias crimes: 177 so-called bias incidents were recorded in New York City during 1980. The number has been increasing steadily since: in 1989 there were 541. National figures on bias-related crimes were not kept by the federal government until 1991, although during the 1980s more municipalities began keeping their own records of such information.

There is some confusion about the interracial nature of bias crimes. Just because a crime is committed against whites by blacks, or vice versa, it is not necessarily motivated by racial bias. Other indications, such as words spoken by the perpetrator, a string of similar crimes in the recent past, or lack of other motive such as economic gain, are all taken into account to determine if a crime is truly a bias incident.

Many bias crimes are nonviolent, and figures include everything from painting of swastikas on synagogues to the burning of crosses on lawns. But violence, sometimes even homicide, is not unknown.

New York was the first American city to recognize that crimes committed because of the race, religion, or nationality of the victim needed special attention. In 1980 a panel was convened to discuss ways in which serious problems between Hassidic Jews and blacks in the Crown Heights section of Brooklyn could be dealt with. One recommendation was the creation of a Bias Incident Investigation Unit.

The Bias Unit detectives (whose scope was expanded in 1986 to include crimes committed because of sexual orientation) assist and guide precinct investigative units when the possibility exists that a crime is bias-related. Special steps are taken to ensure that justice will not be lax simply because the victim is of a minority group or is in some other way societally distinct.

The Bias Unit's first high-profile homicide case occurred in 1982, when a black New York City Transit Authority employee named Willie Turks was beaten to death in the mostly white Gravesend section of Brooklyn. The perpetrators, fifteen to twenty whites, accosted him after he crossed busy Avenue X to pick up a snack in a bagel store.

"Get the nigger" was the rallying cry as the gang stomped Turks and beat him with clubs.

Police could find no discernible provocation for the incident except that Turks was the wrong-color person in the wrong place at the wrong time.

In December of the same year a thin, bespectacled electronics expert named Bernhard Goetz shot four young black men after they demanded money from him on a New York City subway train. Goetz and his supporters, including some prominent blacks, maintained that the "vigilante shooting" was not racially motivated. The Police Department also determined that the shooting was "not bias-related," although many black activists thought differently.

Goetz admitted telling police he fired a shot into the back of one victim who lay prone on the subway platform after saying "You don't look so bad, here's another." Noting that Goetz had been a crime victim before, defense attorney Barry Slotnick asked a racially mixed jury to believe that his use of deadly force was justified.

Such actions are usually judged on what a "reasonable person" would do under the circumstances, rather than what an individual would do based on his or her own past experience, fears, or prejudice. In Goetz's case the "reasonable person" standard was out the window if the jury felt that, based on his fear of victimization because of situations encountered in the past, Goetz was justified in performing an act that was not what the law would usually hold "reasonable."

Goetz was acquitted of attempted murder charges but convicted of illegal possession of a gun, for which he served six months in jail. According to some activists, the acquittal was a declaration of open season on young black men, who could be shot dead on the street for the crime of being black and appearing scary to whites.

New York's racial attacks continued in 1986 and included the beating death of a black man in the Coney Island section of Brooklyn after his bicycle ran into a car driven by six whites. They were convicted and received jail sentences of up to twenty-five years.

Many of the blue-collar neighborhoods where such incidents occurred were places where violence was often used to settle disputes, even between people of the same race or ethnic origin. But a different standard seemed to apply when race was a factor, and that standard was often deadly. In New York and other cities, a pattern of individual acts of violence based solely on race was developing, resulting in deep divisions between blacks and whites. The depth of feeling was not initially recognized or addressed, except by the creation of more bias units in cities that found themselves the sites of more frequent racial attacks. Most racial killings that occurred during the 1980s were met with minimal public reaction from the African-American community. What reactions did occur received some attention, but they represented no threat to civil order. That is, until Howard Beach.

O N the night of December 19, 1986, three black men from the East New York section of Brooklyn developed car trouble, and walked down busy Cross Bay Boulevard in the Howard Beach section of Queens to find a telephone, which they located at the New Park Pizzeria. They also found trouble in the form of a gang of white youths who challenged their presence.

"What are you niggers doing here?" one of the whites asked. Words were exchanged, and the whites left. Before long they returned with reinforcements.

Armed with baseball bats, tree limbs, and golf clubs, a gang of close to a dozen whites chased the black men through the normally quiet streets shouting "Let's get the niggers" and "Why don't you niggers get the fuck out of the neighborhood?"

When the mob caught up with Cedric Sandiford he cried for mercy as they beat him viciously, while Timothy Grimes miraculously escaped injury. Both were luckier than Michael Griffith, who took off on a blind run fueled by desperate fear for his life and ran out onto the busy Belt Parkway. He was struck and killed by an automobile traveling more than 55 miles an hour.

Sandiford, who finally escaped the mob, sought help from police officers who, adding insult to injury, treated him like a criminal suspect rather than a crime victim, ordering him against the side of their cruiser and searching him.

Partially motivated by the treatment he received at the hands of police in the wake of Griffith's death, Cedric Sandiford retained attorney Alton Maddox to represent him.

The black Brooklyn lawyer was a native of Georgia, where he learned early and painful lessons about the place of blacks in a white-dominated society. During the civil rights movement he participated in lunch-counter sit-ins, during some of which Maddox and fellow demonstrators were victims of violence perpetrated by whites. In 1967, while still an undergraduate at Howard University, Maddox himself was beaten by a white police officer during a visit to his home town. After graduating from Boston University Law School the young lawyer opened a private practice in New York City after working on several community legal projects.

Maddox made no secret of his distrust of whites and particularly of white police officers. In 1984 he made headlines as a representative for the family of Michael Stewart, a black graffiti artist choked to death after New York City Transit Police Department officers arrested him in a subway station. The officers were acquitted of criminal charges, but Maddox was successful in subsequent civil litigation.

He also successfully represented the brother of Edmund Perry, a black prep-school student slain by a police officer. Police said Perry was killed in an attempted robbery committed with his brother Robert, who was tried for that crime. Maddox and the family said Perry was the victim of a racial murder perpetrated by the police officer.

At the outset the Queens County District Attorney's office and the New York City Police Department conducted an investigation that might have led to no murder charges at all if sudden pressure from black activists had not caused higher authorities to intervene.

The Howard Beach case posed several problems for investigators and prosecutors. The most difficult to overcome was the fact that Griffith was not killed by the mob of young white men through a direct action perpetrated by them. The driver of the car that struck Griffith was not part of the posse; he was merely passing through when the victim ran out onto the highway. Had death been caused by the sticks or bats the white youths wielded, murder would have been easy to prove. But most investigators and assistants to District

Attorney John Santucci felt that the best they could hope for were assault convictions.

Maddox and other activists knew that crimes against blacks committed by whites were rarely prosecuted to the fullest extent possible under the law. Surveys by the New York State Human Rights Commission had pointed out that even in cases where there was successful prosecution, judges were more lenient with sentences, especially if the offenders were young. Maddox believed without any doubt that the death of Michael Griffith was nothing less than murder, and a way had to be found to force authorities to push the case to the fullest. The means to accomplish that end were manifested in the person of a fiery Pentecostal preacher and community activist named Alfred C. Sharpton, Jr.

Sharpton, born in Brooklyn in 1954, had already amassed a considerable amount of air time on local television news shows. Ordained at the age of five and billed the "Wonder Boy Preacher," Sharpton became involved with the youth arm of the Southern Christian Leadership Conference (SCLC) in Brooklyn, and in 1969 associated with the Reverend Jesse Jackson, then a young upstart activist who headed Operation Breadbasket.

At sixteen Sharpton incorporated the National Youth Movement, to encourage the employment of minority youth and call attention to inequities that affected them. As he began courting the television cameras in an effort to draw attention to black inner-city community problems, the teenaged minister was launching a new kind of campaign, a media blitz worthy of Madison Avenue.

Firmly believing that he was part of a new civil rights vanguard, Al Sharpton used every showman's trick at his disposal to gain coverage of National Youth Movement events, and pulled out a few more stops to make certain that the videotape aired on the evening news. He was becoming a formidable spokesman, locally at least, for a new voice that boomed from the inner city into the microphones of outlets like WLIB, New York's black-owned radio station.

In the early 1980s crack was not yet a household word, but crack houses were well known in places like Bedford-Stuyvesant and Harlem. Sharpton gathered NYM supporters and brought them to the neighborhoods in rented schoolbuses, where they marched and chanted while painting red Xs on the doors of suspected drug dens.

He became a master at turning phrases into ten-second sound bites tailor-made for newscasts. Sharpton was a clown with a social conscience, and his trademark girth and James Brown hair style made him difficult to forget.

"I was advised once to change my haircut and get rid of the pounds," Sharpton says. "But then James Brown himself said to me that if I did that, nobody would remember who I was or what I stood for. I'd be just another face in the crowd."

The rotund rabble-rouser got favorable press in those years, and his antidrug marches even won the praise of New York's junior senator, Alphonse D'Amato.

"The world needs more Al Sharptons," D'Amato said at a Washington dinner. "We need more movers and shakers, more people to rock the system."

The collaboration of Maddox and Sharpton resulted in massive protests in Howard Beach decrying the murder and the failure of authorities to act decisively. It was Maddox's involvement in the case that drew Sharpton, who was then spending a lot of time with the attorney. After being introduced to Sharpton, the Sandifords and the Griffiths agreed that his suggestion of public protest would help them obtain justice.

Carrying placards and chanting "Howard Beach have you heard, this is not Johannesburg," the marchers forced their message into the homes of millions of television viewers who perceived the activism as containing implied threats of violence. While Sharpton kept the pressure up on the streets Maddox told prosecutors he would withdraw Sandiford's cooperation, which would be crucial to any prosecution. The Queens County District Attorney's office, the activists claimed, was incapable of mounting an effective case against those responsible for Griffith's death. A special prosecutor would have to be appointed if murder indictments were to be obtained, they said. And Sandiford, an eyewitness to the attack and a victim of the mob, would continue the policy of noncooperation unless such an appointment was made.

In most criminal prosecutions lack of assistance from a complaining witness would only mean the loss of a case to overcrowded court dockets, and the loss would ultimately be that of the reluctant witness. But the combined one-two punch of noncooperation and protests created a pressure situation for officials who would have to play by Maddox's rules.

The idea of a special prosecutor was not pleasing to Mario Cuomo, New York State's governor. A Queens Democrat whose name is often mentioned as a possible presidential contender, Cuomo has a strong belief that whenever possible the prosecutors elected by the people should be the ones to take cases to court, although special prosecutor appointments are within his gubernatorial powers. Nevertheless, District Attorney Santucci agreed to step aside and Charles J. Hynes, a criminal justice system veteran who headed special prosecutions of nursing homes in the state, was tapped for the job.

A respected and able trial lawyer, Hynes rolled up his sleeves and jumped headlong into the controversial case. He and his hand-picked staff obtained manslaughter indictments against Jason Ladone, Michael Pirone, Jon Lester, and Scott Kern, young Howard Beach men considered ringleaders of the attack that led to Griffith's death.

The indictments drew fire from families and supporters of the defendants. They believed the young men were being unfairly singled out for harsh prosecution because authorities were caving in to the demands of blacks.

Defense lawyers representing the accused youths attempted to defend their clients by suggesting that blame for the attack rested on the shoulders of the victims themselves. Through direct statements and through nuance during cross-examinations the victims themselves were placed on trial. The most abrasive practitioner of the victim-blaming tactic was Stephen Murphy, a short, silver-haired bundle of kinetic energy. Loud, dramatic, and sneering, Murphy succeeded in riling witness/victim Timothy Grimes enough to cause him to storm off of the stand following a blistering cross-examination that included intimations that the black men had come to Howard Beach to commit a crime and pressed leading questions about a knife Grimes admitted having in his possession. The tactics employed by the

Screamer of Queens Boulevard, as Hynes referred to Murphy, and his staunch insistence that the attack on the black men was not racial, caused the lawyer to be branded a racist by some blacks and lauded as a hero by working-class whites.

Murphy scoffed at the charges, noting that a large number of the clients he regularly defended in his practice are black defendants. "I don't go up there and work any harder for the white guy than I do for these black guys, and they swear by me," Murphy said. His client in the Howard Beach case, Michael Pirone, was the only defendant to be acquitted.

Hynes won three convictions (other defendants in a later trial faced lesser charges) through inventive and aggressive employment of the long-standing legal theory of causation, which imputes criminal liability when an unlawful act by one person paves the way for the unintentional act of another to cause death.

Bitter reactions by blacks to the crime, the white community's apparent acceptance of the defense tactics, and white displeasure with the convictions won by prosecutors fed strong negative emotions that were already running like electricity through the streets of New York.

As resentments continued to percolate, Al Sharpton, his image bolstered nationally by the Howard Beach case, emerged seemingly triumphant. He believed Howard Beach proved that only by placing immense pressure on the system can blacks hope to achieve the measure of justice that was won in the Howard Beach trial. But while the jury deliberated in the Queens courtroom, Sharpton was already involving himself in another scenario that would almost irreparably tarnish his new coat of armor.

In November 1987, Tawana Brawley, a sixteen-year-old from the small upstate New York town of Wappingers Falls, was discovered in a garbage bag covered with excrement and with *KKK* scrawled on her body. Brawley claimed she had been attacked by white police officers and an assistant district attorney who raped and humiliated her.

The case was already generating publicity when Sharpton was contacted by the Brawley family, and along with Maddox and another activist attorney, C. Vernon Mason, he became their adviser.

Sharpton and the attorneys decided not to cooperate until, they said, they could be sure the case would be thoroughly and fairly prosecuted. State Attorney General Robert Abrams, appointed as a special prosecutor, convened a grand jury to investigate the allegations, but without Brawley's testimony the probe was worthless. Both Abrams and Governor Cuomo became grist for a rapidly revolving Sharpton–Maddox–Mason mill of accusations, rumors, and near character assassination. Among these were assertions by Maddox, made on a New York radio station, that Abrams masturbated while viewing nude hospital pictures of Tawana.

WCBS television reporter Mike Taibi ran stories that cast more doubt on Brawley's claims, and a thorough investigation by a team of New York *Times* reporters failed to substantiate a story that had more than a few loose ends.

However, Sharpton continued to stand by Tawana and her tale, and when asked if he truly believed in the accusations had a question of his own: "If you were me and given all you know about me, and you had a choice between believing this little black girl and Robert Abrams, who would you believe?"

Eventually, the Brawley story sank into a murky cesspool of doubt and half-truths, destroying Sharpton's credibility with the media—and even with many middle-class blacks, who saw his tactics as counterproductive and were embarrassed by the turn of events in the Brawley fiasco.

Throughout the late 1980s Howard Beach and Tawana Brawley defined race relations for much of the nation's large cities and New York in particular. Resentment in the working-class white enclaves over the Howard Beach convictions was bolstered by the seemingly fraudulent nature of the "Brawley hoax."

Each side had its own bad guys for the opposing groups to point fingers at, and the color gap grew wider with each passing incident of violence.

Blacks in New York roundly criticized three-term mayor Edward I. Koch, whom they accused of being an apologist for police-perpetrated violence against blacks and whose acid rhetoric was dubbed inflammatory and racist. Koch had also lost some supporters among whites who felt that he rushed to judgment when he made inflammatory statements about the defendants in the early days of the Howard Beach case and later suggested long prison terms for them. Blacks were not impressed by the remarks, which they felt were too little given too late.

Sharpton, on the other hand, was seen as a loud-mouthed buffoon who befriended liars and criminals, representing the worst that New York's black community had to offer.

Racial attacks continued; some generated sporadic publicity while others melted away into the back pages. In 1988 a seventeen-year-old Staten Island youth was struck and killed by an auto after being chased through the streets in what is believed by clergymen and community activists to have been a racial attack. The death of Derick Tyrus resulted in no indictments.

Any lessons to be learned from the Howard Beach case seemed lost on large segments of New York's blue-collar population. There was still strong evidence that blacks could not walk through white neighborhoods without fear for their safety, and a belief by both whites and blacks that racial crimes were judged by a different standard, although each group thought so for different reasons. Whites thought that standard too harsh; blacks believed it was less stringent than the one used in black-on-white crimes.

With each incident of violence, whether publicized or not, segments of the black community began to feel that justice was theirs only in situations where they took to the streets and demanded it, like in Howard Beach. The sentiment was even expressed in some circles that the law was useless to protect black people. They might have to take it into their own hands.

POWDER KEG

I F it appeared that whites were being singled out for prosecution in highly charged cases that involved race, the perception would change in the spring of 1989.

Late on an April night a young white woman, referred to here as the jogger, was running down a deserted path on the northern end of New York's Central Park.

Ambushed by a large group of young men, she was dragged into a wooded area. As she screamed and struggled, she was mercilessly beaten with fists and a pipe. Her assailants then raped and sexually abused her before leaving her for dead in a muddy ditch, where she lay for several hours until she was finally found bleeding and unconscious.

The suspects charged with the attack were black and Latino teenagers. Police said they were part of a larger group, numbering as many as thirty, who had gone on a robbery and assault rampage in the park earlier that night, victimizing as many as a half-dozen people.

The newspapers said the youths had gone on a "wilding" spree, stating that the word was uttered by the youths themselves, according to police. The terminology was new to inner-city kids interviewed after the attack, and some published reports, most notably a *Village Voice* article by journalist Andrew Cooper, suggested that what the youths had actually said that they were doing "Da Wild Ding" [*sic*]. Black activists believed the use of the *wilding* term to be racist, since words with feral connotations like "wolfpack" and "animals," especially prevalent in the city's tabloids, are not used to describe group violence by whites, only by blacks.

POWDER KEG

In response to the Central Park crime, financier Donald Trump took out a full-page newspaper ad calling for reinstatement of the death penalty in New York State, countered by an ad taken out later in the week by black clergymen protesting what was seen as a racist response to the defendants. Sentiments of outrage, the ministers said, seemed more animated when the crime was crossracial and perpetrated against whites by blacks.

The rape of a black Brooklyn woman who was bound and then thrown off a rooftop during the same week as the Central Park attack was at least as heinous, but would barely have made it to the papers if the jogger case had not already been grabbing headlines.

Supporters of the defendants likened the Central Park arrests to Alabama's infamous Scottsboro case of a half-century before, when a group of black men were convicted of rape, and some executed, because of false allegations by a white woman.

The Central Park incident signaled a serious turn for the worse for race relations in New York, and there was tension in other areas of the nation as well. In Chicago, two white police officers allegedly harassed a pair of black teenagers with threats and racial remarks while driving them around in a patrol car, then dropped them off in a working-class white neighborhood, where they were chased and beaten by a gang of whites. A threatened mass demonstration by blacks was called off only after a Cook County grand jury indicted the officers.

Also in Chicago, there were reports of arson and looting after a black robbery suspect was shot in the head by a police officer while he allegedly had his hands raised in surrender.

In Virginia Beach, Virginia, there was violence when members of a black college fraternity from all over the country clashed with police after a "misunderstanding." There were similar incidents in resort areas of southern New Jersey.

In the Liberty City section of Miami, officials kept close watch and community leaders worked to keep peace as a police officer went on trial for the murder of a black man. The shooting incident from which the charges stemmed had resulted in days of violence.

The tensions that simmered in many black neighborhoods both

29

in New York and elsewhere were attributable to many factors, and activists said that distortions of truth in the media were a large part of the problem.

The broadcast media in particular, the primary information source for many Americans, are highly selective in their approach to crime coverage, particularly homicide. The majority of homicide victims are black, and it is the unusual homicides, usually those where the victim is white, that generate the greatest amount of press coverage.

An assignment editor at a New York news organization vividly recalls an August morning in 1986 when the body of a young woman was discovered in Central Park. When another newsperson informed him that "the chick in the park is white" he sent a camera crew, something he admits he probably would not have done if she had been black. The Central Park homicide of Jennifer Levin, the so-called Preppy Murder case, became page-one material.

When Lisa Steinberg, a little girl who was the adopted daughter of New York attorney Joel Steinberg, was killed by her father, the story received nationwide attention as symbolic of the suffering little children endure at the hands of abusive parents. The commotion over little Lisa was difficult to understand in the inner-city black communities, where child abuse deaths and neglect seem to be more expected and therefore less newsworthy than when they occur in more affluent neighborhoods.

The same week Lisa was buried, three-year-old Lamar Horris suffered the insult of thirty-three bullet holes inflicted by a machine gun as he slept in his mother's Brooklyn housing-project apartment. An alleged crackhead who was a companion of the mother was arrested for the crime. The story made the news the first day or two but the media never tracked the case through the criminal justice system, and there was little editorial outcry.

The resulting perception in black communities is that black life is worth comparatively less than white life when a crime is committed. Relations between the police and New York's black community, separate and apart from racial violence perpetrated by civilians, led to increasing mistrust of authorities that some observers feared could make the summer of 1989 long and hot indeed.

Relations between Ed Koch's police department and the black community deteriorated steadily throughout his tenure, even though the department's commissioner, a capable and respected administrator named Benjamin Ward, was himself African-American. There were other questionable cases of use of NYPD force against minorities, some of them well publicized.

One infamous incident involved Eleanor Bumpers, a mentally disturbed black woman, who was shotgunned to death by a member of the Police Department's elite Emergency Service Unit. Officer Steven Sullivan was found not guilty of criminal charges, but New York City eventually settled a civil suit out of court for $200,000. Other incidents were known about only in the communities where they took place. All were seen by some community leaders as part of a continuing pattern of abuse.

Police shootings are almost always carefully scrutinized, and the law tends to side with the officers in most of these situations. Big-city police have a tough, serious job to do that often involves life-and-death decisions. An increase in the number of emotionally disturbed individuals, often irrational due to ingestion of crack or other drugs, meant an increase in situations where police officers, even though dealing with an unarmed person, were still at grave risk.

Less defensible, however, are those instances when the person, usually black or Hispanic, died while in handcuffs or when the cause of death was somehow related to police restraint.

Cocaine-related heart failure is often cited as the cause of death in such cases, although suspicion usually continues when that explanation is offered. It had been used in the past when later evidence tended to show that the police officers' activities immediately prior to the decedent's last breath included a nightstick choke hold.

Allegations of excessive force when death was not involved poured in to the offices of lawyers and the city's civilian complaint review board. In the Bedford-Stuyvesant section of Brooklyn police took to calling the local volunteer ambulance when a prisoner "fell."

"I don't know what happened," an officer said to attendants who responded to the station house late one night, seeming surprised and shocked. "He just fell down!"

As the weather grew warmer temperatures grew hotter in already tense neighborhoods. Several police stations came under attack from rock- and bottle-throwing residents who claimed to have witnessed neighbors being beaten with portable radios and other objects after being handcuffed. Few of the incidents were publicized.

In July 1989, therefore, the findings of the Medical Examiner in relation to the death of thirty-one-year-old Kevin Thorpe, a mentally retarded Brooklyn man, was seen as particularly alarming.

Thorpe lived with his mother in the Gowanus Housing Project; on July 10 he became aggressive and struck her, becoming so unmanageable that she called police for assistance.

The NYPD's elite Emergency Service Unit is specially trained in the use of constraint equipment for such situations, and a patrol sergeant is supposed to call for ESU assistance in these cases.

Thorpe's mother said she told a 911 operator of her son's illness. Police denied the claim but refused to release the 911 tapes that would back up their side of the story, citing procedural regulations for cases involving litigation.

When police responded to the Thorpe apartment they confronted Kevin and, according to the family, threw him to the floor, hit him with nightsticks, and sat on him while he was bound hand and foot. He was declared dead on arrival at a local hospital.

On August 4 the New York City Medical Examiner's office released its findings: "Toxicological testing disclosed therapeutic concentrations of medications (i.e. Maellaril [sic] and Benadryl) prescribed by Mr. Thorpe's physicians. He was not under the influence of alcohol, cocaine, narcotics or other illicit drugs.

"It is our conclusion that Kevin Thorpe was asphyxiated as the result of chest compression by overlaying during restraint by police officers. It is our further opinion that natural disease neither caused nor contributed to his death."

A New York *Times* editorial decried the killing of Kevin Thorpe: "Is this one more incident that suggests the police respond more brutally when the suspect is black?"

Attorney Colin Moore and the Thorpe family's adviser, the Reverend Herbert Daughtry of the House of the Lord Pentecostal Church in Brooklyn, believed that to be the case. A sharply worded letter to Governor Mario Cuomo signed by the minister, the lawyer, and David Walker, Chief Investigator for the Center for Law and Social Justice at Medgar Evers College, asked that a special prosecutor be assigned to investigate not only the Thorpe case but other questionable police custody and shooting deaths of minorities as well.

"It is incredible to us that when loved ones call the police for assistance, they end up not with competent, courteous, compassionate service, but with a corpse . . . why should it be that Black and Latino persons die so frequently in the custody of police, and so often when the original appeal was for police assistance."

A Brooklyn grand jury refused to indict the police officers involved with the Thorpe killing, meaning that a public trial at which the facts of the case could be aired was never held.

Racial attacks continued. In another Brooklyn incident a young man named Paul Trotman had been beaten into a coma, allegedly by a white youth named John Creamer, as the result of a dispute between them.

The Trotman case was determined not to be bias-related by authorities, but that assessment was disputed by a number of community activists. The Reverend Daughtry believed race to be a prime motivating factor in the bludgeoning of Trotman, who later succumbed to severe head injuries, dying without ever regaining consciousness.

As troubled as New York's black communities were in the summer of 1989, there was also cause for hope. From churches in Harlem and Brooklyn to housing projects in the Bronx, election fever was in the air and voter registration increased as blacks went all-out to support Manhattan Borough President David Dinkins in his bid to become New York's first African-American mayor.

Dinkins had risen from New Jersey shoeshine boy to member of New York's power elite, building a strong political base in the Democratic clubhouses of Harlem. The Koch administration, rocked by scandal through the years and increasingly blamed for the city's racial tensions, was vulnerable to Dinkins' low-key, avuncular charm. His words, while occasionally lofty, seemed a healing balm to the more forgotten segments of New York.

The road to City Hall would be difficult, however. Even if Dinkins could beat Koch in the September Democratic primary he would still face opposition in the general election from the Republican candidate. Former federal prosecutor Rudolph Giuliani was locked in a tight race for the GOP nomination with cosmetics heir Ronald Lauder, and there was no telling what the future might hold for Dinkins in a campaign against either of the two.

While Dinkins preferred that race not be an issue in the campaign, it was a top consideration for many New Yorkers—especially blacks who believed that a Dinkins administration would at least mean fair play and an equal voice in government affairs.

Filmmaker Spike Lee was one prominent black New Yorker who felt that Koch's confrontational style set an unhealthy climate in which attacks on blacks could continue to occur. "Black and Puerto Rican life here is very cheap," Lee said in a UPI interview. "It's sad, and it's no mistake that all the incidents like this have occurred under Ed Koch. Ed Koch has set the climate."

The specter of a black man in City Hall was unsettling for some whites, however. In the white working-class neighborhoods of Bensonhurst and Canarsie in Brooklyn, Ridgewood and Howard Beach in Queens, and the blue-collar Irish provinces of the north Bronx, there were concerns that a Dinkins mayoralty would mean that the blacks had "taken over."

"They're running wild now on the streets. Look at what they did in Central Park. If they have their own mayor they'll think they can get away with anything," said one white woman on a radio talk show. Similar remarks and beliefs were heard in barrooms and at dinner tables.

While less exciting and more predictable than the mayoral primary, other offices were up for grabs as well, and although Charles Hynes listed many accomplishments during his career of public service besides the Howard Beach convictions, it was that case which made his name a household word in Brooklyn, where he was running for District Attorney. It was a particularly sensitive post in light of all the race-related crimes that had occurred in the borough, from police-custody incidents to bias attacks. Based on the former special prosecutor's Howard Beach success, there was a feeling among minorities that Hynes was capable of responding to their concerns.

Elizabeth Holtzman, a forty-eight-year-old native Brooklynite, had served as DA for eight years and was giving up the job to seek the position of New York City Comptroller. A Harvard Law School graduate who had previously served in Congress, Holtzman made a number of changes when she took over the DA's office, including appointment of women and other minorities to key positions.

She first gained national attention while serving on the House committee that investigated the role of President Richard Nixon in the Watergate cover-up, and while in Congress worked to pass laws that made it easier to bring Nazi war criminals to justice. But her tenure as district attorney was not without controversy.

Appeals-court decisions had pointed to a number of procedural gaffes in Holtzman's administration, including prosecutorial errors that prevented a city marshal and seven other defendants from being prosecuted on bribery charges. And a blunder by a Holtzman assistant also led to the 1989 release of a hardened Brooklyn criminal who later shot and killed a uniformed police officer.

Members of the Brooklyn bar who were Holtzman's adversaries in court had little good to say about her, although many of their negative comments, including liberal use of the word *bitch* to describe the DA, seemed as much rooted in resentment of Holtzman's gender as they were critical of her administrative style. The Brooklyn bar is part of a well-established old-boy network, and Holtzman was neither old nor a boy. Most Brooklyn attorneys agreed, however, that even if she possessed adequate administrative capabilities she was not a trial lawyer and, in their estimation, never had been.

Holtzman's critics were anxiously awaiting the expected election of Hynes to the post. He was seen as fair and willing to compromise, qualities not attributed to Holtzman, who did not encourage her assistants to work closely with adversaries to make settlements when possible, especially in high-profile cases.

Neither Holtzman nor Hynes had serious opposition to the offices they sought, and it was expected that in January 1990, after the September primary and the November general election, Charles "Joe" Hynes would be the new boss on Joralemon Street.

But no matter who ran the Brooklyn District Attorney's office, two things appeared absolutely certain. Like the old DA, the new one would be faced with court dockets filled to overflowing with every crime people are capable of inflicting upon each other and, given the city's volatile climate, in at least some of those incidents race would be a factor.

Activists were speaking of the potential of a "long hot summer," echoing the civil disturbances in Detroit, Los Angeles, Newark, and New York during the 1960s. Herbert Daughtry summed up the situation at a press briefing on the Thorpe case when he said, "New York is a powder keg right now, and it will take just a tiny spark to set it off."

Law enforcement authorities and politicians knew too well that the heat generated by the city's intensifying racial friction could provide such a spark. The question was becoming not whether the powder keg would ignite, but when.

I WANT TO DRIVE THE TRAIN

O N Brooklyn's Fulton Street across from the Brevoort Houses project young men glare at strangers as they conduct their drug deals on a corner telephone while marked police cars pass by seeming not to notice. The gold around their necks and on their teeth glimmers in contempt of the law-abiding residents, who shake their heads with the realization that their streets are held hostage by the new junior gangsters, their syncopated rap and reggae beats blasting from the heavy-bass rear speakers of the Jeep Wranglers and small imports that cruise the block.

Arabs and Pakistanis now own most of the tobacco stores open here. In some of the shops coke spoons and crack vials are sold from underneath counters that display gum, candy, and cigarettes. An endless procession of gypsy cabs cruises up and down Fulton, Chevrolets and Fords with yellow CAR SERVICE signs on the visors. Many are not licensed by the City's Taxi and Limousine Commission, but the yellow sign *is* a hack license as far as the people who come out of the subway stations and fear the walk home are concerned.

But while Bedford-Stuyvesant may seem like a fearful place to some, it is simply home to others who own small frame houses, live in once-magnificent century-old brownstones, and try to do the best they can for themselves and their children, who frolic in fire-hydrant spray on hot summer days, giving free car washes to the passing cars. The homeowners of Bedford-Stuyvesant take great pride in their neighborhood, as do most of the people who rent in its apartment houses and projects like the Brevoort Houses. Many are working hard to wrestle it back from some of the more unsavory elements that have also made a home here.

It was in this environment that Diane Hawkins, a pleasant-faced, mild-mannered woman, raised her three sons with the help of their father, Moses Stewart.

For most of their sons' lives Moses and Diane had lived in the Brevoort Houses, where they kept a tight rein on the boys to protect them from the perils of the streets.

Freddy, the eldest and more street-smart of the Hawkins brothers, had learned early to fear the wrath of his parents and avoided hanging out with neighborhood crowds. Yusuf and Amir followed suit, and the brothers developed a close circle of friends who shared their values and interests.

The brothers did not spend much time at the housing project. On weekends during the school year (sometimes during the week as well) and more often during the summer they lived with their grandparents, who owned a house on Hegeman Avenue in nearby East New York. In many ways the little house with the big green awning was more like a home than their legal address, and although the tree-lined street had its problems of drugs, crime, and violence, the environment was still preferable to the volatile surroundings of the project. "It was someplace where we could be outside," recalled the youngest brother, Amir.

Yusuf, the middle brother, benefited in particular from a strong relationship with his grandfather, Henry Hawkins. The elder Hawkins shared his wisdom and experience with the receptive young man, and Yusuf helped his blind grandfather. The two were a common sight as they walked arm in arm along Hegeman Avenue and the surrounding streets. "He was my eyes," the family patriarch said. The quiet, gentlemanly demeanor that teachers and relatives admired so much in Yusuf was a direct result of his grandfather's influence.

Volumes have been written about the difficulties in store for young men in rough neighborhoods who try to avoid running with the pack, and peer pressure at Stephen Decatur Junior High School, from which Yusuf graduated in June 1989, was something to be contended with.

Fights were not uncommon at the school, located in the heart of Bedford-Stuyvesant. Students who didn't want to participate in the occasional free-for-alls that broke out in the hallways would instead often serve as lookouts, keeping an eye open for teachers or security guards while the others settled their problems. But not Yusuf, according to teachers.

"If there was a problem the last person you would see anywhere near it was Yusuf Hawkins," Mary Paul, his journalism teacher, remembered.

Yusuf, described by his friends and brothers alike as quiet and soft-spoken, only had to fight back once, when he was chided for not joining in gangs.

"It doesn't matter if they talk about you," Yusuf would tell Amir. "But if they get in your face you have to fight back, if they hit you or something." The incident was enough to earn him the respect of the school toughs.

The Hawkins boys' lack of desire for the street life that sucked so many others into the evils that lurked around every corner of the inner city was of some comfort to their beleaguered father. Although Moses, like many others of his circumstances, had many chances to use alternative and illegal ways of supporting the family, he refused to take the easy way. Rumors of outstanding felony warrants against Moses were groundless and amounted to nothing more than an old, unresolved misdemeanor case in North Carolina of unauthorized use of a motor vehicle.

His example also made an impression on the boys, who understood that while the easy way might be okay for some people in the neighborhood it was not acceptable for them.

A former serviceman who tried to support his family through a variety of jobs including truck driver, security guard, machine-shop operator and boxer, Moses tried to be a good father. He felt cheated by the economic difficulties that stood in the way of a normal life for him and his sons. His concern about social conditions, particularly the ways in which they affected the African-American community, led Moses to the teachings of Minister Louis Farrakhan, the controversial leader of the Nation of Islam.

The separatist leader preached nonacceptance of the white power structure and rejected the European-American system altogether as being, in his assessment, racist and genocidal toward blacks. The words of the separatist leader made more sense to Stewart than what he learned in traditional churches. He changed his name from Frederick to Moses, and when his two younger sons were born they were given Muslim names.

Moses Stewart often said he wanted more than anything else to be someplace open and green where he could play ball with his sons in the fresh air.

"How can a kid grow up in this place? He gets born, he begins to grow up, he's got no place to play but the concrete, and then all of a sudden he looks around and he's grown up and where did all the time go?" The statement seemed as much autobiographical as it was a description of the problems faced by the younger men in the family.

Articulate, even charming, Moses can also be bitter and resentful. Perhaps that side of him is in part responsible for the sometimes tempestuous nature of his relationship with Diane. The heavier drinking and sporadically violent tendencies caused a desperate Diane to turn to authorities for help, and Moses was arrested by police at the project apartment more than once. Still, Moses looked more toward externals, blaming social conditions more than his own internal difficulties when he tried to understand his station in life. He perceived lack of opportunity due to the social status of blacks as the force that kept him down and threatened to do the same to his sons.

Although conscious of his heritage to some degree, Yusuf did not share his father's concerns about the plight of African-Americans, nor could he understand how someone could be judged by the color of his skin.

While this might seem unusual coming from a young man growing up in an inner-city neighborhood, the fact is that Yusuf, like many other young men and women in similar circumstances, had little contact with white New York—or, for that matter, white America. Living in an all-black community, not traveling far from its confines, and not watching much television except *The Honeymooners* (Yusuf's favorite show as well as Amir's), Yusuf Hawkins had not had the opportunity to experience the individual, one-on-one racism that makes headlines when tragedy occurs. And the institutional racism that creates lack of opportunity and underprivileged neighborhoods is barely understood or even recognized by Americans, white or black, whose education and experience far exceeded his own.

When he heard about the killing of Michael Griffith in Howard Beach (Griffith was related to one of his friends in East New York, Luther Sylvester), he went to his father with questions about the incident.

Moses Stewart knew all too well the cold realities of racial differences, and he tried to discuss these issues with his sons. "There are some people who won't like you because of the color of your skin," Moses would say, explaining that this was a fact of life and that there was not much that could be done to change it.

"Yusuf would just look at me and ask why. He couldn't understand it," Moses recalled. "I didn't know what else to tell him, or how to begin to explain it more clearly."

One reason Moses was not able to get through to his son may have been that it was not a part of Yusuf's nature to dislike anyone because of who or what he or she was, and some of the teachers who worked so hard with him at Decatur and showed genuine interest in his development were Caucasian.

Mary Paul, his journalism teacher in the last year of junior high, was particularly impressed by the quiet solitude Yusuf displayed in and out of class.

"*Nice* is a word that is overused," she said. "It loses its meaning. But more than anything, that's what Yusuf was. A nice kid who knew where he was going and what he wanted."

Yusuf's reputation as a loner was supplemented by another perception schoolmates had of him, that of a nerd, earned more through avid class participation—when he attended school—than through consistently high grades. In an apparent effort to make up for numerous absences, believed to be due in part to the extensive distance he had to travel when he stayed in East New York and in part to family problems, Yusuf often volunteered to answer questions in class. This made the other students think that he was an academic whiz, even though his grades were actually on the average side. In fact, Yusuf tied with another student for the designation "Most Likely to Succeed."

Although Yusuf seldom smiled and always appeared extremely serious, during class discussions his face blossomed into a reserved, self-satisfied smile that seemed to say "See, I know this stuff!"

Mary Paul recalls: "When he answered questions in class, especially if he had been absent, that's when the smile would be coming across. You could read it as it began in his eyes and then his mouth would turn up, and sometimes I would actually have to say 'Yusuf, put your hand down and give somebody else a chance!' " The smile would then become even broader.

Yusuf had been left back for one term in elementary school and he was almost a year older than the other boys and girls at Decatur. His maturity made him intriguing and attractive to the girls in the class. Teachers recalled that Yusuf had such classically good looks that one girl whispered to her teacher that she wanted to be seated next to him in class.

The fast and often short life of drugs and gold chains that sealed the fate of other young men who occupied classroom seats at Decatur before him held no attraction for Yusuf Hawkins.

"That's not for me," he told one teacher who had rhetorically suggested that there were alternative means for people to achieve success. He was not, however, critical of those who opted for nonconventional, even criminal paths to success or mere survival. "People have to do what they have to do, but I don't want that" was his nonjudgmental assessment.

Not that the pain of doing without was not a harsh reality for him. His manner of dress at school was more functional than stylish; he did not wear fashionable clothing and the popular brands of sneakers that so many others sported at Decatur. During the colder months he wore a simple parka and often dressed in sweats. He also did not go on field trips as often as he might have wished. The price of a lunch at McDonald's and the other expenses involved were a luxury that he simply could not afford.

There were few jobs available for young people who could not depend on their parents for money, and Yusuf wanted more than anything else to find the financial security that was unavailable to him as a teenager. He also knew, almost instinctively, that if he was going to break out of the dead-end existence in the crime-plagued neighborhoods he would have to do more than just complain about problems. That was why he applied to Brooklyn's Transit School of Technology.

A diploma from the highly specialized trade school, which takes in a limited enrollment, would earn Yusuf the security and stability of employment with the New York City Transit Authority. He wasn't a hundred percent sure what he would do for the agency but hoped to make it as a subway motorman. The train that rumbled underneath Fulton Street and took people to mysterious places would also be his ticket out of the Brooklyn ghetto.

"I want to work there. I think I want to drive the train," Amir remembers Yusuf saying, smiling with as much excitement as he had ever seen his older brother show. In the spring of 1989, when he found he had been accepted and could begin classes in the fall, his future seemed assured.

WORKING-CLASS HEROES

FARTHER along Flatbush Avenue, roughly eight miles and a world away from the neighborhood where Yusuf Hawkins lived, is the Bensonhurst section of Brooklyn.

Bensonhurst got its name from a farmer named Benson who once grazed his cattle on the grassy hills of New Utrecht, one of the original Dutch settlements in Brooklyn. There were plans during the early part of the twentieth century for development of the area as a beach resort called Bensonhurst-by-the-Sea to compete with nearby Coney Island. But the project never fulfilled the expectations of its promoters and was eventually abandoned.

The population and desirability of the area as a place to raise families increased dramatically after World War II, and as the neighborhood grew so did the number of neat brick two-family houses along the tree-lined streets and avenues. Bensonhurst was particularly attractive to Italian-Americans, who moved there in droves, and to this day the mark of the Italians is all over the neighborhood, although many of its current residents are from a variety of ethnic backgrounds.

Located within commuting distance of Manhattan, Bensonhurst was also home to those who did not work nine-to-five jobs and sought an easier way of making a living. The influence of organized crime's presence in the area is felt in many ways, the most damaging being in supplying the neighborhood youth with less than desirable role models.

The wiseguys, as the Mafiosi are called, drive fancy cars, eat in the best restaurants, and wear tailor-cut suits. Their reputation for ruthless violence is well known and respected; on the few occasions

44

gunshots ring out in the Bensonhurst night they are the result of some internecine mob dispute. There are no witnesses to these shootings, and nobody in the neighborhood knows anything about them when the police come to knock on doors. Like the dockworkers in *On the Waterfront*, everyone is D and D—deaf and dumb.

The raw, violent power of the wiseguys is admired by some of the young men in the neighborhood, whose families tacitly approve of the reputation Bensonhurst has as a Mafia haven. The mob is everyone's big brother who can be called if a dispute gets out of hand. More than one argument in Bensonhurst and neighborhoods like it has escalated to the point where one participant will threaten, "Hey, all I gotta do is make one phone call." The speaker who actually goes to a telephone and picks up the receiver may only be calling Directory Assistance, since people who are really connected have neither the desire nor the need to rattle that particular saber.

One woman working in a bakery echoed the views of other residents when she spoke of why the neighborhood is considered so safe:

"Nobody comes over here and messes around. Those guys don't fool around over here, they don't hurt us, and if anybody was going to try anything here they'd have trouble."

The candy stores and other small shops in the area are, for the most part, legitimate businesses. Others are fronts for gambling and drug operations, and they attract young men who would like to take a shot at what the underworld has to offer.

Eighteenth Avenue is a brightly lit commercial strip in the heart of Bensonhurst and home to some of the most violent and notorious of the area's loosely organized youth gangs. The signs on the pastry shops, salumerias, and restaurants glimmer with lights and are brightly colored with stripes of red, white, and green that give the appearance of a never-ending carnival. Lincolns and Cadillacs double- and triple-park with impunity on the broad avenue, where young men maneuver around them carefully as they cruise, honking at pretty girls and waving at friends.

The openness with which mob capos come and go and card games that go unchecked in the rear of some of the stores may account for the brashness of the Eighteenth Avenue gangs. Signs on the shops are written in English and also in Italian—the language spoken by groups of men who sit around small tables late at night and talk about things they do not wish strangers to hear.

While people who live on the quiet side streets complain about how crack-crazed blacks are ruining the city of New York, the guys in the suits map new strategies for smuggling drugs and guns into the five boroughs and how they will invest the profits into legitimate businesses.

For all of the apparent differences between Bensonhurst and the city's black neighborhoods, there are striking similarities in the attitudes, appearance, and even tastes of the young people from each. Young men with large gold chains around their necks sport initials shaved onto the backs of their close-cropped heads, wear brightly colored muscle shirts, and hang around on streetcorners where rap music relentlessly pounds from the speakers of oversized boom boxes. The music conflicts with the traditional Italian melodies that drift onto the street from the eateries.

Posturing and posing under the pink-orange streetlamps, baseball caps turned around with the bills facing backward, the cugeens emulate the swagger of the wiseguy. Most but not all of the corner boys are Italian-American, and those who are not try to act as if they were. *Cugeen*, from Italian dialect slang for "buddy" or, more appropriately, "cousin," is not considered offensive, so long as it issues from the lips of a cugeen.

Some make a few extra dollars that permit them to buy fashionable high-top sneakers and other luxuries through petty drug deals and not-so-petty larcenies. Others, lacking the fortitude or connections necessary to engage in criminal activity, try to act the part nonetheless in an effort to appear hip.

They are fiercely protective of their turf and will fight for their tiny fiefdoms with fists, feet, bats, knives, and even guns. The play-actors who aren't really certifiable criminals are sometimes the most dangerous in turf-war situations, because their sense of social insecurity makes them feel they have more to prove than the others, so they'll go the extra distance.

But the similarities between these white kids of the Bensonhurst streetcorners and their counterparts in Bed-Stuy and East New York do not end with rap music and the need to affirm a fragile sense of manhood through the use of force.

Substance abuse, shrinking career and employment opportunities, and an extremely high dropout rate trouble the young people in Bensonhurst as well as other working-class communities.

Although there are still enough blue-collar jobs for some to earn traditional livings, at least for now, some researchers and educators say it will only be a matter of time before these kids and their expected progeny end up on the welfare rolls.

Second- and third-generation Italian-Americans who hope that their heritage will serve as credentials hang around the places where the wiseguys go, hoping for an opportunity to be of service, to be recognized, to be employed. Like small-time hams waiting in the wings of old vaudeville houses, they vie for the chance to show their stuff.

"A lot of these guys really believe they have career opportunities with the mob," one Bensonhurst resident says. "They swagger around and try to dress and look the part, and they don't realize that even if they got associated they'd probably never be made [inducted into the Mafia] and they're just going to be somebody's errand boy. And probably be expendable if there's trouble."

Fortunately for many of the disappointed dunskies, as the wiseguys call them, the chance rarely materializes. The neighborhood wannabes, like many other Americans who seek more mainstream employment, are also victims of the immigration boom. Much of the mob's muscle work these days goes to the zips, recently arrived Sicilian immigrants who seek sustenance rather than luxury and prestige. They have the advantage of being easily returned to their native land if need be, coupled with a reputation for being both deadly and dependable.

Like Howard Beach, Bensonhurst borders low-income areas populated by African-Americans. The Marlboro Houses, a project near the destitute Coney Island boardwalk that is every bit as violent as the Brevoort Houses, is within walking distance of the tough Italian enclaves.

Friction between the two groups is old news in this area where racial violence was a problem long before the phrase *bias incident* was introduced.

In almost all neighborhoods, in New York and elsewhere, people of many races and backgrounds share fond, and sometimes not so fond, memories of things that happen in schoolyards.

As hated as the confining links of the schoolyard fence may be during childhood, they are magnetic to teenagers, especially after dark. Like swallows returning to nest, young men and women in some neighborhoods find themselves in the schoolyards where they once played as children long after they are too big for the swings and slides.

Schoolyards are the places they suffer their first broken hearts. It is often in the schoolyard first cigarettes and joints are smoked, first condoms are distributed by knowing friends, and first tales of real or imagined sexual conquests are shared.

Public School 205 on Twentieth Avenue, between Sixty-seventh and Sixty-eighth streets in Bensonhurst, is one of those schoolyards. The school building itself is a formidable red cinderblock structure that dominates the surrounding area in an eerie, institutional way, equal in height to the tallest apartment building on the adjoining blocks.

Twentieth Avenue seems dingier than Eighteenth Avenue. The small stores near the schoolyard serve the immediate vicinity only and most close early. At night the school building looks dark and forbidding, almost abandoned. On the main thoroughfare itself are the businesses, like Joe Fuda's Hair Techniques and a small delicatessen. Some of the businesses are wholesale or to-the-trade-only fabric and materials outlets.

A few years ago the big schoolyard was a hotbed of serious delinquent activity, but the kids got older and moved from the schoolyard to apartments with their wives and children.

The current generation of young men who play ball, make promises to girls they might someday marry, drink and sometimes rumble with other neighborhood cliques in the yard is a relatively peaceful group, according to longtime area residents.

They say that the "schoolyard boys" of Twentieth Avenue may be loud and sometimes even violent, but they are not as bad as kids who hang around on other blocks in Bensonhurst. That doesn't mean that they were not known to resort to violence in turf disputes. The use of force in such situations is accepted as a part of growing up, especially in a community where the tough "wiseguy" image is so revered.

In one incident, someone from another section of Bensonhurst was blowing up M-80s, powerful firecrackers, in the schoolyard, much to the annoyance of the local crew. It's okay to blow off M-80s in your own schoolyard, but you can't just walk into somebody else's and do it.

When the trespasser refused to stop threats were made that were serious enough to prompt him to leave. He returned a half-hour later with some friends from a few blocks away, and a fight promptly ensued between them and the defenders of the schoolyard, resulting in a few bloody noses and black eyes. The next day relations were back to normal, as they were when the fighting was between friends from within the schoolyard. The warfare is accepted good-naturedly as part of being "in the neighborhood."

"We're tight, all of us," one schoolyard boy says. "Sure, I might beat the shit out of you if you make me mad, but it's over with when it's over and nobody holds grudges. You might kick the shit out of me the next day for something else. But we're still friends, and that can't be changed just because of that."

Rose McNamara, a school-crossing guard, has lived on the same block as the schoolyard for over twelve years. "These are good kids," she says. "They never made any trouble for me, and they kind of made me feel comfortable that they were out there."

McNamara and other residents of the block say there are marked differences between the schoolyard boys and the tougher kids from Eighteenth Avenue, where the use of drugs, particularly hard substances like cocaine, is common. The Twentieth Avenue schoolyard regulars frown on the use of coke and other substances more powerful than marijuana.

"One kid was bragging one night that he did some coke," a neighborhood youth said, asking not to be identified. "We smacked him around good. Waddya wanna do that shit for, we said to him!"

What is ironic about the pervasive violence and the reliance upon it for solving problems is that the real tough guys, the ones with the suits and the Lincolns, try to resolve their own disagreements peacefully whenever possible, a lesson lost on the young men of Bensonhurst, who may have learned more about the mob from the movies than from firsthand observation.

Although Italian-American culture has long been the dominant force in Bensonhurst, populations shifted over the years, new groups have moved in, and the neighborhood as a whole has taken on more of a multiethnic flavor than ever before. The changes have not come without growing pains.

When Asians began moving into the neighborhood en masse the community's reaction was not always cordial. In the mid-1980s anti-Asian flyers were circulated, and threats were made to Korean and Vietnamese businesspeople.

There is also a growing Latino population, along with second-, third-, and fourth-generation Irish and Jewish families. The few blacks living in Bensonhurst numbered only a few percentage points in the most recent census.

Whites in Bensonhurst who express disdain for blacks as a group still have African-American friends. Some are young men who have grown up with them, side by side, and they bristle at suggestions that they are disloyal to their own race and heritage.

Joseph Gibbons, also known as Russell, is a twenty-year-old former construction worker who now does data-processing work. He was as accepted in the neighborhood as any of his white friends, and his attitudes are those of his peers.

"They call me an oreo cookie because I don't talk black," Russell says of some other African-Americans. "Well, I've got my job and I'm not going on the streets dealing drugs. I'm not going to get shot up in some street fight, and I don't just sit around and listen to rap music all day long. I've got a future and I know where I'm going."

Russell's mother describes herself as a "light-skinned black" and has nothing but praise for the boys Russell grew up with.

His best friend, a young man with straight dark hair and the build and height of a pro baseball player, is Charlie Stressler. Stressler lives with his mother, a police department civilian employee. He attended Catholic schools and hoped someday to be a mechanic. The two grew up side by side, sleeping over at each other's houses.

"We were babies together," Russell says of Charlie.

Both belonged to a baseball team at a local tavern and often played basketball and football in the PS 205 schoolyard. They were part of the schoolyard's core group—which during the summer of 1989 included eighteen-year-old Pasquale "Pat" Raucci, a diminutive kid with a wisp of a mustache who played disc jockey at parties and particularly enjoyed spinning rap records; eighteen-year-old Steven Curreri, a quiet teenager who only occasionally spent time in the yard and sometimes spun records at parties with Raucci; and James Patino, a tall, thin twenty-one-year-old who attended classes at Kingsborough Community College.

The most popular of the group was a young man of Italian and Jewish parentage with a tendency toward practical jokes and a bit of braggadoccio. Keith Mondello was nineteen years old that summer, and lived diagonally across from the schoolyard with his parents and three younger brothers.

"He always made me laugh," says Carmen Mercado, a thirty-four-year-old woman who lived down the street. "He had a sense of humor, Keith did, and he was always joking around."

Because he showed academic promise as a youngster at PS 226 Mondello originally attended Mark Twain Junior High School in Coney Island, which offered advanced programs. But the eighth-grade curriculum had become too difficult for young Keith, and he transferred to New Utrecht High, where he settled comfortably at a less-than-spectacular but respectable level.

Social activities began to take precedence over books, and his grade percentiles began to slip from their former place in the high nineties.

His extracurricular activities included hockey and football, but what he seemed to enjoy more than anything else was basketball, according to his mother, who was proud of his budding artistic talents and abilities as a swimmer. He won school awards in both categories.

Keith had never spent a summer in Brooklyn until 1989. The Mondello family had always vacationed in the Catskill region, where in his early teens Keith did some part-time work at the stables of the Nevele Country Club in return for free rides. Bob Klipper, the stable manager, recalled him as a nice kid who enjoyed helping with the horses.

By his junior year at New Utrecht, school took a back seat altogether to other interests, and Keith terminated his classes, finding full-time work at a neighborhood fabric finisher's shop. Periodically he did construction work with his younger brother, Phillip.

Another interest that occupied a lot of Mondello's time was a young lady named Sarina Scavone. Sarina was fourteen when she met Keith, who was a year older, through mutual friends.

The raven-haired beauty and the lean, athletic youth from Twentieth Avenue soon became close, and by 1987 they were officially "going out" together.

By the time summer rolled around in 1989, Keith began thinking seriously about the future and how he might possibly earn a living and support a family. Although both he and Sarina were too young to get married, it was a topic they discussed. "It seemed like it was far away but we did talk about it," Sarina remembers. "Keith and I always talked about what we wanted to do."

Sarina was already treated like an in-law at the Mondello home, where she visited often. The floor-through apartment is furnished simply but comfortably, and its many rooms are adorned with religious statues. Susan Mondello had converted to Catholicism when she married Michael, and took great pride in her adopted faith.

The courtship of Keith and Sarina was a decidedly old-fashioned one. The two often double-dated with a friend of Keith's, Cosmo Camia, and his girlfriend. They liked to go bowling, to an occasional movie, and trips for pizza or Chinese food, and on weekends would sometimes go to local discos, where Keith loved to dance.

"He just wasn't afraid to get out on the dance floor and make those moves," Sarina says fondly.

"He was witty. That's the most special thing about Keith, and he was never moody or anything. We used to shoot pool a lot, and he never beat me, but he always made jokes about it."

Although Keith was aware of current events, Sarina and his mother recall that he always read the daily papers "from the back forward," meaning he started with the sports section. He was an avid New York Knicks fan and favored the Yankees over the Mets.

If Keith Mondello had any overt racial prejudices, Sarina wasn't aware of them. When she was attending Harcum Junior College in a Philadelphia suburb, her roommate at Harcum was a young black woman whose friends were predominantly African-American. Her friends were Sarina's friends, and when Keith visited they would all go out as a group to a nearby bowling alley, or visit the King of Prussia Mall in Bryn Mawr.

The general picture that emerges of Keith through interviews with family and friends as well as people less closely attached is one of a young man full of life, with few problems. But there were whispers in the neighborhood of a different Keith who occasionally was involved in small-time drug deals with another neighborhood youth, John Vento.

John Vento, a stocky youth, lived near the school and drove a late-model Mercury automobile, one of two cars that belonged to him. He was more mature and streetwise than many of the schoolyard boys. Mondello's parents say that Vento lent Mondello one of his cars one or two days a week, but investigators, attorneys, and other sources say that the car was given to Mondello and used for business purposes—a drug business shared by Mondello and Vento. Longtime neighborhood residents have said that Vento spent a lot of time at Snacks and Candies, a small store on Sixty-eighth Street across from the schoolyard and managed by a man in his thirties, Sal Mannino, known in the area as Sal the Squid. Neighbors described Sal as "a kid who never grew up." He got along well with the schoolyard clique, who often bought sodas at his store. Sal had business partners who never came to the store at all, according to sources who say that one was a youth from the Eighteenth Avenue area named Frank D'Angelo, believed by some in the neighborhood to be an associate of the Gambino crime family.

A small gambling operation was reportedly run out of the store, and shortly after it opened there was a small but steady trade in drugs. The same sources could not confirm, however, whether Vento's and Mondello's reputed drug involvements were actually connected to any operations at Snacks and Candies, although Vento spent so much time there that some people thought he was one of the partners in the store.

Carmen Mercado, who has lived on the block for more than twelve years, often heard rumors of drugs at the store but says she did not believe them to be true.

"There's no drugs in the store," Carmen said. "They wouldn't sell drugs out of there. They had middle-aged women from the neighborhood, mothers who worked at the store," she said.

One of the strongest arguments to be made against the stories of drug sales at the store, or by Mondello and Vento, was that a habitual drug user and admitted crack addict who lived upstairs, Gina Feliciano, bought her crack and powdered cocaine in Coney Island and on Newkirk Avenue in Flatbush. The Brooklyn District Attorney's office was provided with information that she purchased some of her marijuana supply from Keith Mondello, but those claims were never publicly confirmed.

Gina lived with her mother, Phyllis D'Agata, and according to neighbors there were constant, bitter fights between the two. Much of the trouble centered around Gina's drug use and her general conduct. Police had to be called to the residence on several occasions in 1988 and 1989.

Gina was a troubled young woman who made no secret of her fondness for Keith Mondello. Keith would be seen speaking to her from time to time, but his friends and family deny that he had anything to do with her. Gina's practice of bringing black and Hispanic friends to the block was not looked upon kindly by many.

"Gina believed that Keith was her boyfriend, or at least she wanted him to be," Carmen Mercado recalled in statements that were substantiated by other neighbors. "But he didn't want to have anything to do with her. He would joke with her sometimes, you know, play around. Keith had a girlfriend. He didn't need Gina."

Sarina was aware of Keith's problems with Gina. "We would walk together and sometimes she'd just give a cold, hard stare. But I ignored it. If I was going to worry about Keith it wasn't going to be with Gina, that was for sure. Anybody but Gina."

The tension between Gina and Keith continued to grow, made worse by Keith's disapproval of some of Gina's friends, a fast crowd of drug users who were mostly black and Latino.

Gina had problems with other people in the neighborhood as well. Elizabeth Galarza, a heavy-set woman in her thirties, raised her young children in an apartment near the school and often spent time with the neighbors. Everyone knew everyone else's business in the close-knit neighborhood, and during the summer of 1989 one of the chief topics of discussion was Gina. The troubled girl would threaten the women and speak harshly to them because she knew they were talking about her and didn't like it at all. When the women discussed Gina they talked about more than her provocative manner of dress. Feliciano's relationship with one of the women's husbands, a man named Nick Nipitello, had become a scandal. The man's wife, Linda, said she was just as glad that he had taken up with Gina, because she was tired of his sometimes violent behavior: "I was just as glad that he was with her. I didn't want him."

But Nick would sometimes visit Linda so that he could see their seven-year-old daughter, Crystal. The visits made Gina Feliciano furious, and she was convinced that Linda was trying to win Nick back, although Linda maintains that nothing could be further from the truth. During the early summer Gina threatened Linda, telling her she'd better stay away from Nick "or else."

"I can have you taken care of just like that," Gina would say, waving her arm in a wide arc and snapping her fingers to punctuate the *that*. Linda took the threats seriously, because Gina had a reputation for getting whatever she wanted done.

A neighborhood man who dated Linda after Nick had been asked by Gina to pick up some marijuana in front of a candy store on Twentieth Avenue and Sixty-fifth Street earlier in the year. But he was turning over a new leaf, he confided later, and decided against the mission. Gina got someone else to go for her, and while standing near the Twentieth Avenue subway kiosk the substitute was shot and wounded.

Nobody in the neighborhood knows who the real target was—the man who was shot, Harold, or even Gina herself. If they do they are not talking.

The threats against Linda escalated, with Gina pointing her index finger like a pistol and telling the frightened mother "Be careful."

During one confrontation on the street in July, Linda and Gina had words over the situation. "Take him, go ahead and keep him. I don't want that no-good drug dealer in my house," Linda said.

The relationship between Gina and Nick continued, but even Linda's blessing did not make Gina happy. Every time Nick would visit his daughter Gina would fly into a jealous rage, convinced that Linda was going to take him back. One day following a visit, Gina ran into Linda on Twentieth Avenue and laced into her:

"You listen to me, you cunt. Try to get him back, you just try, and I'll blow your fucking head off!"

Not long after that Linda and Elizabeth Galarza were walking with little Crystal on Twentieth Avenue. A pleasant breeze wafted across Seventy-first Street as they passed Tony's Pizza Store and talked about the threats Gina had made.

Suddenly their conversation was interrupted by the sound of a single gunshot very close by, and the two women hit the pavement.

Elizabeth pulled Crystal under a parked car and held onto Linda's hand as they tried not to breathe or move. Crystal began to cry, and Linda held her hand firmly over the child's mouth as Elizabeth carefully watched the sidewalk from between the parked car's tires. A man rapidly crossed the street, past the car. Both women remember him as being tall, with long blond hair and a mustache.

After he crossed Twentieth Avenue he began firing shots into a window on Seventy-first Street and seemed not to be interested in looking for them.

"Let's get the hell out of here," Elizabeth said, and the two held hands as they ran with Crystal toward Elizabeth's apartment. The two women were terrified and didn't speak a word as they raced with the child down Twentieth Avenue. Elizabeth felt as if she were going to throw up.

The police were called, and while they were still en route Elizabeth heard more gunshots coming from the direction of the pizza store, where she and Linda had ducked for cover. Other people reported the gunshots as well, and in a few seconds Twentieth Avenue was filled with police cars and the sounds of their radios.

Once she was sure that police were on the scene, Linda came out of her apartment with Elizabeth and they walked up to some officers. They related their story, including the threats made by Gina.

"So what did this guy look like?" one cop asked Elizabeth. She and Linda both recited their descriptions. But when the police also interviewed the man whose windows had been shot out he seemed strangely calm to Elizabeth, and then became upset only when the women excitedly described the gunman.

"She's crazy," he said. "She's talking about a neighbor of mine. She doesn't know what she's talking about." Suddenly doubtful of the story the women had told, the officers put them in separate cars and took them on a search of the area. The gunman did not turn up and the police became more skeptical.

"I'm telling you the truth," Elizabeth said. "I know what I saw."

Linda repeated her story again to the police officers in the car she was in, but when she tried to explain the convoluted triangle between Gina, her husband, and herself, the officers seemed to lose interest.

It is possible that the window-shooting and the round fired in the direction of Elizabeth and Linda had nothing to do with the Gina dispute. But if Elizabeth Galarza was not involved before, she was now.

She began to receive disturbing telephone calls.

"If you know what's good for you, you'll mind your business," one male voice said.

Other voices during other phone calls made her uneasy as well, and although she called police about them several times she was treated like a flake. She continued her assertions that the man with the blond hair had fired the shots and began to believe that she was a marked woman. She seemed to have stumbled into something well over her head. On several occasions she looked out her window and saw the man with the blond hair standing on the corner of Bay Ridge Avenue. She tried to ignore his presence.

After the night the shots were fired problems between Gina and Linda seemed to subside, but Gina had turned her attention to other people she had problems with. Her black and Hispanic friends were still coming around and Gina was still smoking crack in the neighborhood. Sal the Squid, in particular, seemed concerned about the people hanging out near his store. He wanted nothing to do with them and talked with Gina about the situation several times. Linda's new boyfriend, a Hispanic who occasionally used drugs, said neither he nor other Latinos bought their drugs at Squid's because blacks and Hispanics were not welcome there.

Sal, Keith Mondello, and others from the neighborhood would not let up on Gina, and by Monday, August 21, her friends, mostly Hispanics, were outside Sal's store at the entrance to her apartment building, playing a radio and, some people in the neighborhood said, smoking crack. Keith and some of his friends argued with Gina and the strangers, telling them to leave and warning Gina that this had to stop.

"Stop bringing those niggers and spics around here or there's going to be trouble," Keith told her, and his sentiments were echoed by other neighborhood boys.

On Tuesday, August 22, Gina Feliciano was a woman possessed. She paced up and down Twentieth Avenue, stopping into a candy store every so often to make telephone calls. She accosted Rose McNamara, the school crossing guard, early in the day.

"I'm gonna show these white bastards, these little motherfuckers, who they're messing around with," Gina said, shaking her head back and forth. Rose suggested that she calm down, but tranquillity was the furthest thing from Gina's mind.

"Gina, I thought you were going to go to school. Stop worrying about all this and go to school to be a secretary like you said you were going to do."

Ever since Gina had dropped out of New Utrecht High she had talked about going back to school, although she never acted on her plans.

"Fuck that, I'm pissed," she said.

At one store on the block the pay phone is also connected to a private telephone extension. Gina had been ranting and raving on the phone about "bringing people down" and "kicking some white ass" when someone in the store picked up the private extension to make a call. Gina's voice came through loud, clear, and grating. But there was no one on the other end of the phone. When night came Gina's wrath had not subsided, and every time she saw Keith on the street there were words once again.

Gina would be celebrating her eighteenth birthday the following day, Wednesday, August 23. She had already told several people that she was planning to have a party, but that the surprise would be on the neighborhood.

"None of these white motherfuckers are going to come, either," she said.

What she did tell everyone, including Keith Mondello and Sal the Squid, was that her Hispanic friends were coming and that they were bringing a platoon of their black friends to "beat the shit out of all of yez." '

"They want to say they don't want niggers and spics coming to the block; I'm gonna show them. My friends are coming down and they're going to kick their pussy little white asses," she said, adding that Sal's store would not be spared damage in the bloodbath.

She also told Sal of her plans directly, and he wasted no time relaying her messages to the neighborhood boys. "Gina's bringing twenty of her nigger and spic friends to the neighborhood to kick our asses" was the general line that buzzed from block to block, but specifically the threat repeated over and over again was that the chief target of the invasion was Keith Mondello.

Keith felt that if Gina was going to sic her friends on him, he would have serious problems. He had seen some of these guys, and they were big. There was only one thing he felt he could do.

Mondello started gathering together what he would later tell police was "a small group of friends."

John Vento helped spread the word, and Squid continued to do so as well. The threats against the store were something he took seriously, since his partners would not be pleased if anything happened to it. Nor if the situation became so serious that the police would decide to do something about the items besides potato chips that he was selling.

Even if the encounter just ended in a staring match, which was doubtful, it was important to get together as many people as possible to give the woman's friends the message that nobody on Twentieth Avenue was afraid and that if the intruders returned they were going to be injured. Keith had heard stories about Gina's vengeance on other people she got mad at, and he wanted to be ready.

Wednesday was hot and hazy. There weren't many people in the schoolyard during the morning and early afternoon. Most were at work or had other things to do. But as the day progressed so did the tension.

Vento and Sal made telephone calls to people who made other telephone calls, and Vento made rounds throughout Bensonhurst in his Lincoln seeking recruits. Before long the news had spread all over the neighborhood and into adjoining areas as well. The details may have changed from person to person, like a game of telephone, but a common thread ran through all versions of the story. Niggers and spics were coming to Bensonhurst and there was going to be trouble, which in Bensonhurst translates loosely into a simple "Break out the baseball bats."

The opportunity to break some heads was a welcome diversion for some of the people who said they would come to help. Eighteenth

Avenue was only two long city blocks away, but it might as well have been in Queens. Usually people from Eighteenth Avenue kept to Eighteenth Avenue and people from Twentieth Avenue kept to Twentieth Avenue. But with the element of race added to the equation, young men from Eighteenth Avenue expressed gleeful willingness to come down the street and help "teach the niggers a lesson." Word even reached a few scattered members of a notorious gang from another neighborhood called The Kings Highway Boys.

Some of the neighborhood women who heard about Gina's threats tried to tell boys they knew to relax.

"She just wants attention, that's all she ever wanted," one women remembers telling them. But the threat was too serious to let pass without a show of force, even if it was just idle chatter from a disturbed girl.

The local people who knew and despised Gina Feliciano were gleeful at the prospect of showing her up by beating and chasing away her friends, and the fact that they were said to be black and Hispanic made the possibilities all the more inviting.

The scorn directed toward Gina and her outcast status shed some light on the attitudes of the neighborhood. Although Keith Mondello, for example, vigorously denies ever having had any association with Gina, there is little doubt that at some point in time they had some sort of relationship, if only briefly. Several men in the neighborhood have claimed to have firsthand knowledge that "Gina will do it for a bag of pot," but even if that were true no one disapproved of the men who might have sought her favors in such a manner. Feliciano, who continuously fought with her mother over why she couldn't be more like her sister (a respectable and well-mannered woman named Dawn who no longer lived at home), may well have felt resentment and outrage any time she saw Keith and Sarina parade around the neighborhood like a prince and princess.

For all the talk about how Gina was destroying the neighborhood with the friends she was bringing around, no one had ever done anything about it before. But to the young men of Twentieth Avenue the line had been drawn on the pavement by Gina Feliciano and there was no time like the present.

The problem was not just that Gina had black friends and not just that she did drugs with them. It was the combination of the two that provided all that was needed to downgrade Gina's status from laughable, annoying outcast to outlaw. Bensonhurst was by no means a drug-free neighborhood; besides the coke that young wannabes snorted in clubs or at houseparties, there were the times when certain business establishments around Twentieth Avenue took in shipments of something that looked like large sandbags as police officers drove by unconcerned. And if drug sales in the area somehow related to the bad feelings between Gina and Keith, no hard evidence of that particular connection has been confirmed and the sources of such information provide little more than speculation, as opposed to the issue of Mondello's and Vento's business arrangements, which are more commonly spoken of in the neighborhood and even among law enforcement and prosecutorial sources.

The idea among any of the participants who answered the call to arms on Sixty-eighth Street that they may have been doing something wrong probably never occurred to most of them. Rumbles between groups from different blocks was certainly acceptable, even mandatory behavior, and if anyone had second thoughts, tremendous real or imagined peer pressure might have much to do with a decision to go ahead and come.

By late Wednesday afternoon Twentieth Avenue was ready to rumble, and young men began to gather in the schoolyard. Gina Feliciano looked out her window above Snacks and Candies and sneered at her neighbors. She'd show them. In just a little while her friends would be coming. They didn't mess around.

Downstairs, inside the candy store, business was good. It was a tiny store, with most of its space taken up by a glass-doored soda cooler. The air conditioning was going full blast, and so was somebody's boom box in the schoolyard across the street. Carmen Mercado, the woman who lived above the store, came home from school and stopped into the deli around the corner for a loaf of bread. She saw Phyllis D'Agata, Gina's mother, and exchanged greetings with her. They had an on-again, off-again friendship that lately had been going fairly well. She had eaten ziti and sausages at Phyllis' house just a few nights before. Phyllis bought what another woman in the store remembers was "a very small cake," some birthday candles, and a few odds and ends.

Carmen did not notice anything particularly unusual about the young men gathered in the schoolyard on Sixty-eighth Street.

BLUE PONTIAC

W HILE the young guardians of Twentieth Avenue gathered to wait for Gina's friends in one schoolyard a different scene occurred in another schoolyard eight miles away. Not far from his grandmother's house on Hegeman Avenue, Yusuf Hawkins and some of his friends took turns dribbling a basketball as rap music blared from a large portable stereo.

Pretty frame houses stood next to junk-infested lots all around Alabama Avenue, where the boys were playing. The intense heat of the afternoon sun continued to beat down on the court and the players, causing their enthusiasm for the game to wane, so that by four-thirty they decided to quit.

A winded Yusuf Hawkins, wiping perspiration from his forehead, walked around the corner to Hegeman Avenue with his friend Luther Sylvester, a seventeen-year-old Trinidadian who lived across the street from Yusuf's grandparents. Luther was to begin his last year at Automotive High School in September, after which he hoped to get a good paying job. They spent some time on the wide porch of the Hegeman Avenue house, passing the time of day with Yusuf's brother Amir, and then all three walked to the home of another friend, Christopher Wood, to watch videos. As they sat in the welcome coolness of the air conditioning, they quietly watched *Mississippi Burning*, a film about the murders of three civil rights workers during the 1960s. After the film's release black activists and intellectuals criticized portions, saying the movie did not give credit to blacks for actively fighting themselves for the changes that took place during that period.

64

Such analyses were not a concern of the viewers on Hegeman Avenue, who found the film a little less than interesting.

Shortly before six o'clock the doorbell rang and Claude Stanford, another friend, walked into the living room excitedly waving a piece of paper.

"What's up?" Yusuf asked.

"I found it, I found a car!" Claude said, a broad grin on his face. "And you're all coming with me to go look at it."

Claude had worked all summer at a hardware store, saving his earnings to buy a car. It represented a big step for him. In suburban neighborhoods, and even in the city, a first automobile is almost required as a rite of passage for young men and women. In inner-city neighborhoods like East New York many people can't afford cars or the insurance that must be purchased with them.

The car Claude was so excited about was a 1983 Pontiac G2000. The sporty blue coupé had a little over sixty thousand miles on it and belonged to a Greek immigrant named Nick Hadzimas.

"Where's it at?" Yusuf asked.

"In Bensonhurst," Claude replied. None of them had ever heard of it. "This guy, I called him, and he gave me the directions to get there. It's somewhere in Brooklyn. Come on, we got to go if we're going." Claude was bursting with anticipation.

"I don't know," Yusuf shook his head. "It's really late, and I don't think I should—maybe we can go tomorrow."

Claude was adamant.

"I'm goin' tonight, man. I waited too long for this. You want me going out there by myself?" he asked.

Just then Yusuf and Amir's brother Freddy showed up with Troy Banner, another friend. Claude had to explain all over again about the car and the need to go to Bensonhurst that night. They all agreed to go together, after Amir, Freddy, and Christopher returned *Mississippi Burning* to the video store.

By seven o'clock Yusuf, Claude, Troy, and Luther continued to wait for Freddy and Amir. Claude paced nervously and noticed the time.

"Come on, man, it's late. We can't wait no more."

In a few minutes they were on an IRT subway train in East New York. They traveled a few stops and then transferred to an N train that would take them to this place called Bensonhurst. Yusuf didn't talk much, and Luther and Claude chattered about the start of school. Troy Banner also remained quiet during much of the trip.

The New York City subway system represents many things to many different people. To people who must wait for the train every day in stations that reek of urine and are crowded with other workers, mothers with strollers, and an endless procession of panhandlers, the city's subway is a torture beyond endurance. To others, it is a convenient form of transportation; any above-ground transportation takes considerably longer and a cab is far more expensive. But to Yusuf, Troy, Claude, and Luther, the N train was like a magic carpet. They seldom left their neighborhood, and the ride was an exciting adventure. The train continued to wind its way through the maze of underground tunnels, bumping and jerking every so often.

"Listen," Claude said above the rumble of the train. "You all came with me to see this car, and I'm grateful. So when I get the car, I'll take you anywhere you want to go. We can go to the beach maybe, even this year still."

As the train progressed under the Brooklyn pavements, the ridership began to change visibly. Yusuf, Claude, Troy, and Luther were the only people in the subway car with dark complexions. A white woman sitting across from them gave them suspicious glances and then changed her seat.

Young people venturing out of their tight enclaves often travel in groups, whether to shopping areas or, as in the case of Yusuf and his friends, for other reasons that may take them to strange turf. Safety in numbers is a rule well remembered, although it can just as often backfire. Large groups of young black men are often open to suspicion by police and shopkeepers, and disputes in stores have sometimes erupted from young men wrongly accused of stealing or some other petty crime simply because they were in a group to begin with.

In the Flatbush section the train emerged into the open air, no longer underground, but level with the sidewalks and streets.

The four travelers got off at the Twentieth Avenue and Sixty-fifth

Street stop. They were light-hearted as they left the station, walking into the brightness of fluorescent lights outside the entranceway. At a newsstand and candy store at the subway entrance the four stopped to ask for directions.

Claude showed the store clerk the slip of paper with the address of where the man with the car lived.

"Can you tell me where this is?" he asked the clerk.

"You walk this way," the clerk said, pointing east toward the higher numbers. "Then you make a right at Sixty-ninth Street."

Claude thanked the man and joined his friends as they looked around the store. The clerk eyed them suspiciously. After a few minutes Claude and Troy bought a roll of film and some batteries. Yusuf picked up a Snickers bar and paid for it. The clerk continued to eye them as they left the store and made a left.

Twentieth Avenue is not nearly as busy as Eighteenth Avenue, with its late-night restaurants and espresso shops. Across from the train station there is a small delicatessen, the only business open besides the newsstand for several blocks. The travelers glanced at the street numbers as they walked past the closed stores and saw that they were headed in the right direction.

At Sixty-sixth Street they stopped and looked in a store window. It was a shop where people buy birdbaths, large plaster religious statues, and other lawn sculptures. The unmoving figures behind the plate glass looked eerie, and they continued their walk. Claude was slightly detached, thinking only of the car that was now just a few blocks away and that might become his.

Shortly after they left the statue place they stopped a woman on the street and checked directions with her. She assured them that they were headed the right way and added that in this neighborhood Sixty-ninth Street is called Bay Ridge Avenue. They thanked her and continued.

The woman, who was interviewed by New York *Newsday* several days later, was quoted as saying "They didn't look like they were armed."

The tall brick facade of PS 205 loomed above them as they crossed Sixty-seventh Street. A woman named Cindy Hamburger stood with a small child. Yusuf looked at the child and waved. They noticed a group of white kids standing around on the next corner and were going to stop and ask directions, but thought better of it. They even considered crossing to the other side of Twentieth Avenue. As they approached Bay Ridge Avenue they heard the light sounds of sneak-ered feet behind them, and then a group of the white kids ran past. Amir Hawkins remembers that Claude Stanford later said he won-dered who they were chasing.

They were only a block away from Claude's dream car. As its owner watched television as he waited, the Pontiac sat parked in the driveway on Bay Ridge Avenue, its windshield slightly misting in the heat.

GUNSHOTS

THE Twentieth Avenue schoolyard had been a busy place all Wednesday evening. The only black person who had been seen anywhere near the school that evening was Russell Gibbons, who stopped there with Charlie Stressler after finishing their day's work as carpenter's assistants.

They saw many new faces, people they didn't recognize. All had answered the battle call spread by Sal the Squid, Keith Mondello, and John Vento.

"Are you guys in? Are you coming?" Vento asked.

The pair looked blankly at him.

"Gina's having her friends, those crackheads, come down here to kick Keith's ass, so we're gonna wait for them. Are you comin'?"

"Sure, we'll be there," Russell said. Charlie concurred, although he wasn't the bat-swinging type except on a baseball field. He and Russell had plans to play softball that evening at a local field called the Dustbowl, but the game wasn't scheduled until after nine o'clock, when their team would be permitted on the field.

Upstairs, in the apartment over Sal the Squid's store, Phyllis D'Agata placed candles on the small birthday cake she had bought for Gina. As the crowd grew and no visitors came to the schoolyard, the men and boys grew restless, and a few who knew Gina called up toward the windows.

"Happy birthday, Gina!" they chanted.

"Hey, where are your nigger friends?" somebody called up. "We're waiting!"

Gina stuck her head out the window and called down to them.

69

"All you fucking guys are just pissed off because the black guys are getting all the white meat, and you're not man enough!" she said.

Outside the candy store Keith Mondello listened to the shouting match. Based on what some of his friends later said he felt proud for a moment; only a stand-up guy could muster a crowd like this. But there was also a gnawing nervous feeling, the idea that maybe all of this was getting out of hand as well. In a way he hoped that Gina's friends would chicken out and not show up at all. The momentary lack of bravado, however, was over quickly.

"Wait'll those niggers get over here!" Keith was heard to say. "We're gonna show her but good."

The gathering crowd postured and posed, swinging baseball bats and golf clubs in the early-evening sun. Among them was Joseph Serrano, a bearlike kid whose heft and size made him look older than his nineteen years. His round, chubby face earned him the nickname Babe.

Phyllis D'Agata later claimed that while the troops were assembling in the schoolyard and carrying on their repartee through the window with Gina, she saw several guns. Keith Mondello had one, she thought, and she was positive that Serrano had one as well. Serrano, who worked at an auto body shop, knew D'Agata. He had only recently danced with her at a wedding they both attended. D'Agata also said she saw a gun in the possession of James Patino, a tall, thin twenty-four-year-old who was close with several of the younger men from the schoolyard.

Pasquale "Pat" Raucci, the disc jockey, was off that night from his job at a video store and was there too. Raucci was a short kid, only five-foot-four, and was always considered a follower, striving to keep up with his larger schoolmates in games and sports. He was another schoolyard boy considered a "nice kid" by everyone who knew him.

Franklin Tighe was also in the schoolyard. Frankie, as he was called, had a history of manic depression and was also a hanger-on, someone whose disability was known by most of the schoolyard crew and who fought desperately to overcome the stigma by doing whatever he could to fit in.

Stressler and Gibbons saw more cars pull up on the block; men with bats and golf clubs got out of them. After downing a few beers with the others, Stressler and Gibbons left and went back to Charlie's house. The schoolyard gathering was getting boring, and they later said they believed that Gina's friends weren't going to show. They returned, however, and they were carrying a box containing at least six baseball bats, possibly more.

Stressler carried one end of the box and Gibbons the other.

A cheer of approval went up from the crowd, which was still milling around near the store and in the schoolyard. The bats were laid out in front of Squid's store, which was disturbing to its manager. The candy store would be further endangered if there were bats out front, making it look like the headquarters of the posse.

"Come on, are you guys crazy? Get those fucking things away from here!" Squid said, and the crew grudgingly complied. Most of the group filtered into the schoolyard, joking, cursing, talking about what they would do to Gina's friends, and drinking more beers and sodas. The evening sun was fading by eight o'clock, but there was still light. The boys were getting restless and began to think that Gina's threats had indeed been nothing but another attempt to get attention.

As Gina looked out the window at the mob she had begun to rethink her plans. She called her friends and suggested that they cancel.

Neither Gina nor anyone else on the block thought to notify police of the assembly in the schoolyard, and certainly to do so would have made no sense to Gina since the intended victims of the mob, her friends, were canceling their engagement anyway. Others on the block later said they saw nothing particularly ominous about what was going on in the schoolyard. Rose McNamara left her young daughter sitting on the stoop of her home on Sixty-eighth Street. Carmen Mercado went to the delicatessen around the corner again and back upstairs to her apartment without noticing anything unusual.

Along with the bats, Russell Gibbons brought a large portable radio, and he and Charlie threw a football around as the music played.

Then another friend, Steven Curreri, joined the group. Steven was a quiet, likable college student. His father, Joseph, worked as a tour guide at the Empire State Building, where Steven had a part-time position in the maintenance department.

"What's going on?" he asked one kid.

"There's people coming down here, they're gonna kick our butts. Niggers are coming. So we're getting ready for them if they come!"

Steven looked around and saw many people he knew, like Russell and Charlie.

"Wow," he said. "Are they really coming?"

He picked up a baseball bat, felt the heft of it in his hands, and decided to hang out for a while. Bookish and reserved, Curreri wanted to be accepted by his friends in the neighborhood but eschewed the violence that occasionally erupted in the schoolyard. If there was trouble he could always fade away somewhere, but it wouldn't be a good idea to do so until absolutely necessary.

It was well after nine o'clock and darkness had fallen on the schoolyard. The party was becoming a bore. As the assemblage waited impatiently, it appeared that Gina's friends had definitely chickened out. A few started drifting away, although the bulk still remained.

It was about then, according to police, that Joey Fama, a short young man wearing white pants and a white sweatshirt, arrived at the schoolyard.

Joseph Fama, nineteen, had worked at his construction job during the day and then returned home and showered at about six o'clock. A near-compulsive handwasher, Fama was fastidiously clean and would take many showers a day, according to friends. He attended a wake for a brief while that night, for an older man in the neighborhood whom he knew, and remained at the funeral parlor until about seven-thirty. Short and thin with close-cropped dark hair and a prominent nose, Fama had difficulty fitting in with the crowd as much as he wanted to, and in an effort to do so often tried to act tough.

Joseph, who had two older sisters, was the only son of Rocco and Josephine Fama, both of whom had come to the United States in hopes of a better way of life and had met in Manhattan's Little Italy, where they both lived with their families. Rocco found that way of life in the construction business, and worked with concrete with his brother Joseph, after whom his son was named. The backbreaking labor and long hours were difficult for Rocco, who wanted to spend more time with his family, but he knew that if there was any gold in the streets of America a great deal of effort would be needed to wrench it out.

There was an easier way of life available for Rocco, but it was a world that was not in keeping with his work ethic. The Fama name was feared and well known in Bensonhurst, not because of the hardworking Rocco but because relatives with the same name, described by the family as distant, were deeply involved in the heroin and illegal gun trade. Properties they owned were raided by federal agents in 1986, and a cousin of Rocco's named Joseph Fama along with other associates and family members drew long prison sentences.

Rocco's son Joseph, however, may have yearned for some part of that fast life. He liked snappy imported suits, which he wore at weekend outings to discos in the Bensonhurst area. If local kids like Keith Mondello and the others thought Joey Fama had strong connections to the mob, he wasn't about to burst their bubble or his. But Joe always had a simplistic way of looking at such things, or anything else, due in part to brain damage he suffered as the result of a car accident in 1974, when he was three years old. Doctors predicted that he would never achieve his full intellectual potential. The effects of the accident were compounded when, just a year later, Joseph fell off of a tricycle and once again damaged his skull.

Doctors later said that Joseph Fama would never be able totally to care for himself or work as a result of permanent disabilities caused by the accident, and a medical brief prepared by the State University of New York Health Science Center Department of Neurology, based on examinations conducted as late as 1987, showed that Fama had an IQ of 72: "Joseph has depressed intelligence, memory and cognitive flexibility consistent with early brain injury." Scholastic achievement tests administered in 1987, when he was sixteen, placed him somewhere between second and fifth grade levels.

Joseph was a discipline problem at the schools he attended, from PS 205 through New Utrecht High, and he had a reputation in the neighborhood for bullying other children as he grew up. But Joseph's medical history could have contributed to low-self-esteem problems that made him a prime candidate for becoming a "disappointed dunskie." Babied by his mother and sisters because of his childhood injuries and possibly unfit to make a career for himself in the construction work his father did, Fama may have had illusions of making something of himself in the more exciting world of his more notorious relatives, according to neighborhood sources who knew him.

But people in the neighborhood also said that Fama had a profound dislike of blacks, intensified when his sister was mugged by a black man, something his family vigorously denies. "He had nothing against black people," his uncle Joseph said. "He worked with black people on the job, with me and his father, and he got along with them. There were no problems with black people. He was not prejudiced."

People in Bensonhurst do not like talking about Joseph Fama, and some deny knowing him at all. Those who admit to knowing him say they are afraid to talk because, they say, of fears that his family's connections could result in problems for them. Many who spoke about him would do so only on strict conditions of anonymity. According to some of those acquaintances, Fama carried a gun regularly and once, when they were all going to a beach party, Fama insisted on wrapping his gun in a beach towel and taking it on the trip. He reportedly said it was "in case some niggers give us trouble."

Phyllis D'Agata and Frankie Tighe later recalled words between Joseph Serrano and Joey Fama about a weapon.

"Please, I gotta have it. Come on, gimme the gun," Fama is reported to have said.

*   *   *

74

Every neighborhood has a caste system based on age. Younger men, in their teens, are anxious to break out of the restraints of their "baby" status and look for every opportunity to prove themselves worthy of higher social rank. The gang gathered at the schoolyard, mostly in their late teens and twenties, was like this, eager to win the approval of older men in the neighborhood with families and wives and children. Below them were the younger ones, in their mid-teens.

A golden opportunity arose for one of the younger ones, a sixteen-year-old named Chris Lomuto, shortly before nine-thirty. This teenager, who hung on the periphery of the crowd in the schoolyard that night, saw four black men walking up Twentieth Avenue, just past the entrance to PS 205.

Yusuf, Troy, Claude, and Luther had just passed the front of the school building and were looking at the street signs again when they were spotted by Lomuto, who sprinted to the schoolyard at breakneck speed like a teenage Paul Revere.

"They're here!" Lomuto called out to the others. "They're here! Black kids are here!"

There was a rush to investigate as the four figures walked past the school building and crossed over Sixty-eighth Street past Hair Techniques and a stoop where a few women sat talking.

One of the women, a young mother named Irene Deserio, was near the stoop with her little girl. One of the black youths smiled at the child.

A troop of young men with bats, golf clubs, and bare hands began to walk toward the avenue in the direction the blacks had gone. Charlie Stressler and Keith Mondello were first, walking swiftly, in a stiff-kneed, no-nonsense stride, around the corner of Sixty-eighth Street and on to Twentieth Avenue. As word spread through the schoolyard others followed, some walking and the ones all the way in the rear at a dead run. Many had bats and golf clubs in their hands.

The four black youths kept walking, turning onto Bay Ridge Avenue. The Twentieth Avenue end of the block is dominated by a simple two-story house with a red-brick facade, number 2007. There are hedges along the curbside, and up the block the streetlamps shone through the leaves.

Stressler and Mondello walked ahead toward them, past the entrance to 2007. Both had bats, and some witnesses have said they were brandishing them as if to strike.

The four black youths heard footsteps approaching. Luther turned and saw a group of white men—he would later figure twenty or thirty—coming toward them from further down the street. "We thought they were running past us so we went to get out of the way," he would later tell Amir.

But the mob surrounded the four blacks instead of passing by. There were shouts of "Is this them?"

"What are you niggers doing here?" somebody hollered. Yusuf, Luther, and Troy were half-herded and half-self-propelled around the nearest corner, at Bay Ridge Avenue. Yusuf, clutching his half-eaten Snickers bar, pressed his back against the brick wall.

"We're looking for an address," Troy said, offering the crumbled piece of the Buy-Lines.

Keith looked at Stressler and shook his head. "I ain't gonna hit them. These are babies," he said. "They're kids. These aren't them."

"I ain't gonna hit them either," Stressler said, and turned to leave as an excited John Vento ran up and the larger crowd pressed closer.

"Is this them? Is this them?" Vento asked, and drew back his arm, preparing to hit Hawkins.

A short figure dressed all in white, later identified by witnesses as Joseph Fama, stepped forward. In his right hand was a .32-caliber chrome-plated revolver.

"To hell with beating them up. I'm gonna shoot the nigger!" he reportedly said.

James Patino hollered "No!" But it was too late.

Yusuf's jaw dropped as he saw the pistol pointed directly at him. He stammered and managed to get out a stifled "Oh, shit!"

Four quick pops sounded in rapid succession, and Yusuf Hawkins screamed as he reeled and staggered for about twelve feet, clutching his chest. He crumpled to the pavement, still clutching the Snickers bar.

PANDEMONIUM

HERE was a stampede of running feet and Claude ran around wildly, his whole body gripped by fear, looking for a telephone. He wasn't sure of what he had just seen, and he thought for a moment that he himself had been shot. Troy and Luther disappeared when the shots were fired, and he couldn't see them. There were shouts and screams as blood spilled out of the holes in Yusuf Hawkins' body. Irene Deserio ran to the fallen teenager's aid, and her little girl patted his head while she tried to help.

Keith Mondello and Charlie Stressler were panicked. Neither could believe what he had seen. When the shots rang out Mondello dropped his bat and held both hands tightly against his face in horror.

"Jesus Christ, what'd he do that for?" somebody hollered. Mondello then picked up the bat and ran toward Twenty-first Avenue with Stressler, who still had his as well.

It was every man for himself.

Lights flared on in windows, and several people called police. For a split second there was absolute quiet, and then the night was one big police siren.

Elizabeth Galarza watched the drama take place from a neighbor's window directly above a Korean grocery.

Mondello and Stressler continued to run toward Bay Parkway, throwing the bats in a yard. Galarza recognized some of the people, including someone dressed in white extending his arm and then, after the shots, running toward the higher numbers on Twentieth Avenue. She would later identify him as Joseph Fama.

She left her children with the neighbor and sprinted down the stairs, crossing the street and reaching the shooting scene as revolving lights began to swirl against the haze in the distance. Trained in CPR because of her little boy's congenital heart ailment, Galarza held Yusuf's hand tightly and could see that he was still alive.

"Baby, hang on, just hang on," she said. The crowd around her grew larger.

"Blink once for yes, twice for no," she told the fallen youth, still squeezing his limp hand.

"Are you in pain?" Yusuf blinked once.

"Do you know who shot you?" he blinked twice.

"Do you know why you were shot?" The eyes blinked twice again. No, he didn't know, Galarza remembered thinking, and neither did she.

By the time the first ambulance arrived, Gina Feliciano and Phyllis D'Agata were on the corner, watching along with the other spectators. As Claude Stanford described what happened to the police, Maimonedes Paramedic Unit Thirty-Two Young arrived and joined the EMTs who were already trying to stem the rapid draining of life from the teenager's body.

Steven Curreri was almost to the corner of Bay Ridge Avenue, far to the rear of the main wave of the pack, when he saw everyone ahead turn and run in the opposite direction. Like panicked horses fleeing a burning barn, the last wave of the schoolyard boys, those who had not made it around the corner, stampeded back toward the schoolyard. They didn't know why they were running, but they knew something was wrong. Snippets of phrases and words were heard from the truly frightened, those nearest the bloodshed—"niggers . . . shot"—causing some to think that Gina's friends were shooting at them or had shot someone.

Some cut through an alley on the Twenty-first Avenue end of Bay Ridge Avenue and scrambled a backyard fence. Two baseball bats were thrown on a lawn near a religious statue, and other bats were left at the scene.

PANDEMONIUM

Russell Gibbons, who says he stayed behind in the schoolyard because he couldn't find anyone to babysit his radio, reached the box from wherever he had been, grabbed it, and ran as others were coming around the corner. He heard Frankie Tighe holler, "Somebody just shot a black kid!"

On Sixty-eighth Street Sal the Squid, who helped John Vento spread the alarm on part of Tuesday and all day Wednesday, while egging Gina on and commiserating with her tales of woe, looked at the retreating troops and realized something horribly wrong must have happened. Some of the boys with the bats were already running toward the store, and a few threw their bats under the corrugated metal gate as Squid began to close it down, anxious to leave before the cops started asking him questions. He didn't need this kind of trouble.

Carmen Mercado saw police cars pulling up near the curb downstairs from her apartment and wondered what the commotion was all about. There was a loud pounding on her door and when she opened it up a young man in a sweatshirt, baseball bat in his hand, stumbled into her living room, panting and breathless. Mercado would not identify the visitor and she never spoke of the incident to police. Mercado asked the young man what had happened and he told her he really didn't know, just that someone had been shot. He told her the police might be looking to ask him questions, and Mercado lent him another sweatshirt and led him out of the building. He was only one of many participants that night who would never be publicly identified as taking part in the attack.

On a nearby stoop Mondello, Raucci, and others met and discussed what they should do. Trying to be nonchalant and cool while their hearts still banged against their chests, they quietly made their way to Chris Lomuto's house, where they half-heartedly watched a movie; no one remembers what. Others split off from the group and went to Nathan's Restaurant on Bay Parkway.

Mondello, in a daze, hardly spoke.

Chris Lomuto piped up, "The cops are probably gonna want to talk to us, huh? I don't know either, but I sure wouldn't want to have to be a rat. Keith, who shot him, who did it?"

79

Mondello just shook his head back and forth.

"I heard those shots, I just saw everybody running and I turned around; I ran too," Curreri said.

"Man, whoever shot that kid is in some deep shit," someone else said. "Hey, Keith, you think the cops got him already?"

"You think the cops are coming here?" Lomuto asked nobody in particular. There was no answer, and the gathering began to break up. Steven Curreri left to go home, and a few others followed.

The 62nd Precinct Detective Squad was notified of the incident and responded quickly to the scene. Detectives immediately fanned out in the vicinity and tried to get information, knowing that with any shooting information must be obtained quickly. Witnesses must be located before they melt back into closed apartments or houses, and recollections must be obtained while they are fresh and untainted by local gossip or media reports.

They struck pay dirt when they interviewed Gina Feliciano and Phyllis D'Agata. Interviewed, questioned, and reinterviewed, Gina told her tale of how the boys in the schoolyard constantly harassed her for having black and Hispanic friends and how Keith Mondello and others said they were going to "take care of her for bringing niggers into the neighborhood." Phyllis D'Agata told of a gun passed between Joseph Serrano and Joey Fama, and when the questioning first started Gina said there may have been as many as six firearms on her block.

Detectives also tried to get what they could out of Claude Stanford, who went to a pay telephone immediately after the shooting and, still shaking, called his aunt.

"Yusuf is hurt," he said.

There was silence at the other end of the line.

"Somebody shot Yusuf," he said flatly.

There was more silence on the other end of the line.

"Are you all right? What's this all about? Where are you?" the woman asked.

Claude tried to explain but he wasn't quite sure himself what happened, except that Yusuf had been taken in an ambulance to a hospital.

In East New York, Claude's aunt went down the street to see his mother, who did not have a telephone, and told her what she had learned. The woman was incredulous and went around the corner to the Hawkins residence on Hegeman Avenue with the shocking and frightening news.

Stanford, Banner, and Sylvester told detectives about their subway ride and about the car they had come to look at.

Nick Hadzimas had lain down on his couch just after dark that night and fallen asleep with the television on while waiting for the man who had called to ask about the Pontiac he was selling. There was a knock on his door sometime after ten o'clock and he thought it was the prospective buyer. To his surprise, two police officers stood on the doorstep and asked to come in.

"Yes," he said, trying to communicate as best as he could with his limited English, confirming that he had been waiting for someone to look at the car. The police took a statement from him and said that they might be back for more information. When the police explained to Hadzimas that one of the people who had come to see the Pontiac had been shot only a block away, he got a sick feeling in his stomach.

"I didn't even know it was a black person," he would later tell reporters.

The stories told by Gina and the young black men painted an ugly picture for the detectives. The initial assessment evoked vivid images of a crazed urban lynch mob, armed with the most primal of weapons, chasing four young blacks down a city street that they had every right to walk on, reserving the modern weaponry for the coup de grâce, a bullet in the chest.

In accordance with the procedures in the New York City Police Department Patrol Guide, a supervisor at the scene called in to ask that a duty captain respond to Sixty-ninth Street and Twentieth Avenue.

It was the first step that would have to be made before notifying the Bias Unit, which the sergeant was almost certain had to be done.

In accordance with regulations the crime scene was preserved, the telltale yellow tape placed around the area where Yusuf Hawkins had fallen. Police officers who were getting the first nuggets of information already felt that they were working on an unusual case, that this was not a routine shooting. Routine procedures, such as the gathering of the victim's clothing and preservation of the crime scene, were being performed under the direction of high-ranking supervisors. Two officers were dispatched to Maimonedes to recover the victim's shirt, which somebody said was missing. It was never found.

Elizabeth Galarza spoke with police and told them originally that she had not seen anything and just run down the stairs after she heard gunshots.

"If you had your kids, how come you went there if you knew there was trouble?" one investigator asked.

"Because I know CPR and I thought I could help," she said.

The police began to discount Galarza's story, which changed several times. She seemed to want to tell them something but was either holding back or lying all the way around.

Based on initial accounts from Gina Feliciano, her mother, and other witnesses, police investigators believed that they were dealing with a jealous lover, Keith Mondello, who was angry because his girlfriend Gina Feliciano was seeing a black man, who may or may not have been the homicide victim. If, as investigation had already confirmed, the four young black men had come to see Nick Hadzimas' car, then it was possible that the shooting was a case of mistaken identity.

The full story of what happened was not easy to unravel as the neighborhood's code of silence took hold. Some residents who were questioned had already heard that a black kid had been shot, and word had already spread around the quiet blocks of Bensonhurst that police thought the shooting was racial. Gina and her mother, as well as other witnesses who were brought to the station house almost as soon as they began talking to police, gave a picture of the events that tended to confirm that somehow the shooting was racially motivated. But others who were questioned were quick to point out the presence of Russell Gibbons in the schoolyard. Detectives, already aware of Gibbons' peripheral involvement and not yet cognizant of the fact that Gibbons had brought some of the bats, were more interested in other parties and, most important, who the shooter might have been.

Nobody was home when detectives went to the Mondello residence on Twentieth Avenue, diagonally across from the schoolyard and upstairs from an optical supply house. Keith did not go to the apartment that night at all, and although he later admitted being at Chris Lomuto's house and it is known that he ended up spending the night at his girlfriend's sister's house, there has never been an official account of where Mondello was between roughly eleven o'clock and midnight. But according to police sources, some of whose information was later published in newspapers and confidential accounts given by young neighborhood men and their attorneys on condition of anonymity, a frightened Keith Mondello was not far from the shooting scene. The sources say that Mondello, with Vento and another unnamed participant in the events of August 23, had gone to see a feared and respected neighbor, alleged to be third in command of the Gambino crime family under the most powerful crime lord in the United States, John Gotti.

If Keith Mondello and John Vento were dealing cocaine in Bensonhurst, then Sammy "The Bull" Gravano was one of the reputed neighborhood crime chieftains who would have had to possess some passing knowledge of the operation as a matter of protocol, if nothing else. At the impromptu meeting the advice sought was what to do about police questions, since they were sure to come eventually. The advice given at the meeting was that if Joseph Fama was stupid enough to have taken out a gun and shot someone, then there was no reason for him to be protected. But there was one person whose name, the boys learned, should never be mentioned in connection with the incident. Frank D'Angelo, reported to have been Squid's silent partner at Snacks and Candies, had been instrumental in getting a number of people from Eighteenth Avenue to the scene, including Joseph Fama himself. It is not known how much D'Angelo figured in the actual attack that led to the shooting, or whether he had a weapon. But Keith Mondello later said that someone named Frank had put something in his car prior to the attack, something he thought was a gun. Neither defense lawyers nor police investigators have identified "Frank."

D'Angelo and his entire family had already suffered as a result of the neighborhood's violent organized-crime intrigue. Four years before the Hawkins shooting, to the very day, D'Angelo's father had been gunned down inside Tally's Bar on Eighteenth Avenue in what police believed was a mob hit, on August 23, 1985. The owner of Tally's Bar was Sammy "The Bull" Gravano. No arrests were ever made.

After the meeting on Eighteenth Avenue John Vento left Bensonhurst and stayed with relatives in upstate New York. He had another reason for leaving town, however, besides his involvement in the shooting. According to police sources Vento was neck-deep in debt and owed local mobsters close to fifty thousand dollars for gambling and cocaine obligations.

On the block where the shooting took place detectives and Emergency Service officers combed the sewers and gutters looking for the gun that had been used to shoot Yusuf Hawkins. A car parked on the street was roped off by police after they were told it might have been the place where a gun was hidden. A search of the car later turned up nothing. The murder weapon was never recovered.

Inspector Paul Sanderson, the commanding officer of the NYPD Bias Incident Investigation Unit, asleep in his Queens home, was startled by the urgent ringing of the telephone. The digital clock next to his bed told him it was a little before two o'clock in the morning.

"There's been a shooting in the Six-two . . . ," the voice in the receiver began, relating the few details police already had to Sanderson, who snapped upright in his bed and awakened instantly.

It is rare for a full inspector to be notified of a crime at that hour, and the mere fact that subordinates had chosen to call so late told Sanderson that this homicide had to be mighty important. He told Captain Robert Collins to brief him as needed, and closed his eyes once more after gently replacing the receiver.

Sanderson tried not to think about the possibilities that existed if there was anything to this case. In a multiracial, multiethnic city such as New York there are bound to be clashes between members of various ethnic, racial, and religious groups, but the number of bias-related incidents in the city was increasing dangerously.

Crime reporters, cops, and other people whose occupations bring them in daily contact with the tragedies that occur with such regularity in New York think of the city in terms of a giant precinct map. For any person well versed with how the police department has sectioned out the five boroughs, the digits denoting what precinct covers a particular area bring immediate identifications to mind. Fifth precinct, Chinatown; Thirty-fourth, Washington Heights; Four-one, South Bronx; and so on. The precinct numbers speak volumes to the initiated about their respective neighborhoods and the people who live and work in them.

When Sanderson was told that a black teenager had been shot in the Six-two, he immediately knew that the Bensonhurst area the precinct encompassed was heavily Italian-American, very blue-collar, and the absolute worst place in the city to have a racial killing.

Additionally, the neighborhood had a reputation for having ''deaf and dumb'' witnesses to crimes. Bensonhurst has been the locale for more than a few gangland rubouts, and people get the habit of being bashful about discussing such matters.

Shortly before five o'clock, Sanderson's telephone rang again. The murder had been confirmed as a bias-related incident, and a task force that included the Bias Unit was setting up at the 60th Precinct station house in Coney Island.

It was still dark when Sanderson turned the ignition key on his car's steering column and headed for Brooklyn. The last thing New York City needed was a case like this, he thought. He stepped a little harder on the accelerator, seeing a wide, empty highway before him. The car was equipped with a siren and flashing red bubble light that could be thrown on the roof for use in emergencies, but the Kojak routine had never fit the low-key, no-nonsense style that got him appointed to this job in the first place.

He drove as quickly as he could without making use of the accoutrements, praying that this case, whatever it was all about, wouldn't be the spark people talked about. A serious escalation of racial tensions in New York, Sanderson knew, could also have an effect on other United States urban centers, where much of the resentment, anger, and fear went undetected or unreported by a reluctant news media and few of the events leading to specific negative feelings were of proportions great enough to warrant serious national attention.

The NYPD Bias Unit investigators who still combed Bensonhurst for leads in the early morning hours uncovered patterns consistent with other racial attacks in New York and elsewhere. The causes and circumstances of these crimes have been the subject of close study in recent years, and differences have been found between these, based on turf disputes and territorial considerations, and those committed in the past.

In a report published for the National Institutes of Justice, *Bias Crime and the Criminal Justice Response* (1989), bias crimes and hate groups are described as very much on the rise. The study found an increased frequency of incidents committed by loosely knit neighborhood groups, usually made up of young white males. The report uses the definition of bias crime developed by RERC, the California Racial, Ethnic, and Religious Crimes Project:

"Any act to cause physical injury, emotional suffering or property damage, which appears to be motivated, all or in part, by race, ethnicity, religion or sexual orientation."

On the federal level there are rarely enforced civil rights statutes that call for criminal prosecution of persons guilty of some of the above, but locally there are few laws. New York State has a discrimination statute that can mean extra jail time, but outside that there is little in the way of punishment to differentiate the treatment of the bias offender.

"These types of offenses pose greater challenges for the criminal justice system than do comparable crimes that do not involve prejudice because they are intended to intimidate other people who belong to the same group. The fear they generate can therefore victimize a whole class of people."

It was a definition and a crime pattern Sanderson was only too well acquainted with.

PANDEMONIUM

*   *   *

The office of the Police Department's Deputy Commissioner of Public Information had already sent out fax slips to the media not long after Inspector Sanderson was first awakened, informing them of a "U/M/B Homicide—Shot 2x, Bias Incident." *U/M/B* stood for "Unidentified male black." The Police Department still notes such information on crime victims in its media notifications, even in cases where race is not a factor. It is a helpful way for news organizations to know how newsworthy a story is, since a black person found shot in the head in Harlem is routine and barely worthy of a telephone call for information to some assignment-desk people. A white person found in the same neighborhood, however, would be strange enough to merit further checking. The Police Department's practice of thus pedigreeing victims has never been challenged for its subliminal complicity with racism in the media.

In midtown Manhattan, not far from the United Nations complex, the news day was just beginning at WLIB, the city's often-controversial black radio station. Mark Lucas, a morning reporter, was in early and examined the new fax, then called the cops for additional information. A bias homicide is news for any radio station. For WLIB it was especially big. Comment from someone identifiable as a spokesman within the black community would be needed for a comment on the incident, but there were few such people who could be reached in the predawn hours. Lucas thought for a moment, took a sip of coffee, then dialed a number in Brooklyn. The phone rang several times, and then a gravelly voice answered.

"Hello."

"Good morning, this is Mark Lucas from WLIB."

"Hey." The voice on the other end of the line said, and Lucas asked the Reverend Al Sharpton for comment on the murder of a black sixteen-year-old in Bensonhurst.

"What murder?" Sharpton asked, and Lucas related the brief details he had garnered. Sharpton, who had been speaking before a United African Movement rally at the Slave Theater when the fatal shots were fired, made a statement decrying the murder while keeping the bulk of his comments to racial killings in general, since he still lacked necessary information to comment on the specifics. Lucas thanked him and began to put his story together, while in the second-floor bedroom of a small carriage house in the Prospect Heights section of Brooklyn, Sharpton hung up his telephone, rubbed his eyes, and decided to get a few more hours' sleep.

But Sharpton couldn't sleep, and as the sun began to rise he was already making calls to find out more about the case. He told Anthony Charles, a trusted assistant, to try to arrange contact with the victim's family later in the day to see if anything could be done for them. But there was no need for Sharpton to reach out for the Hawkins clan.

On Hegeman Avenue in East New York the Hawkins family had already learned of the tragedy that had struck them. Moses Stewart, unable to sleep, wracked by anger and his own personal regrets, tried to decide what the family should do to see that whoever murdered his son would be caught and jailed forever. He needed some advice, and decided that the best person for him to reach out for was Al Sharpton.

The sky over the ocean was pink with the dawn as Inspector Sanderson pulled into the parking lot behind the 60th Precinct station house. As he walked through the side door of the station house there was no need for him to flash his gold badge at the security officer. Sanderson had high-ranking cop—in other words *Boss*—written all over him.

He was not the only big shot to have walked through the doors that morning. Already the upstairs conference room that Sanderson was directed toward was bursting with brass, including the Chief of Patrol, the Chief of Detectives, several assistant district attorneys from prosecutor Elizabeth Holtzman's office, and the Police Commissioner, Benjamin Ward.

A deputy assistant from the DA's office, whose regular job was to be on night call in the event that a serious crime suspect had to be questioned, was notified to respond to the station house shortly after two o'clock Thursday morning. But it became obvious that this case was too complicated and far too sensitive to be left to an assistant with minimal experience. Night-call duty is an unpleasant task, usually left to newer attorneys. Dale Campbell, chief of the DA's homicide bureau, was soon notified and responded to the precinct.

When Sanderson arrived Steven Curreri was already being questioned. Detectives knocked on the Curreris' door some time before three o'clock, telling Steven's father that they "just wanted to talk to him."

Accompanied by his father, Steven went voluntarily to the station house and told detectives what he knew about the incident. But he had not seen the shooting, never having made it around the corner.

Joseph Curreri, not used to dealing with policemen and certain his son could not have committed any crime, became nervous. "Does Steven need a lawyer?" he asked one of the detectives.

"No, no, don't do that. That would just complicate things and take more time. We don't want him for anything, and there would just be delays with a lawyer," one of them replied.

The detectives kept rotating, taking turns talking to Steven. Many of them asked the same questions over and over. "Who was in the schoolyard before the shooting? Who had baseball bats? Who called to tell everybody to come?" A lot of them concerned Steven directly, what he did and didn't do as well as what he had seen or heard of. Certain that he was not guilty of any crime, Steven Curreri told the detectives that when he came around the corner he had a bat in his hands.

As the sun climbed higher into the sky uniformed cops starting the day shift drifted into the station house muster room where roll call would be held. The smell of freshly perked coffee permeated the large room along with a buzz of excitement that ran through the cops waiting for roll call, generated by the knowledge that the biggest bosses in the department were in the station house. Teams of investigators from the borough detective command, the Bias Unit, and the District Attorney's office calmly walked down the stairs, ready to canvass the neighborhood thoroughly. Based on statements made by Steven Curreri as well as the story given by Gina Feliciano, her mother, and the young black men, police were certain that Keith

Mondello was the ringleader of the baseball-bat attack that led to the shooting of Yusuf Hawkins.

The homicide of Yusuf K. Hawkins was designated 62nd Precinct Complaint Number 10633 and became the three-hundred-fourteenth case to be investigated by the NYPD Bias Unit in 1989. The murder of a sixteen-year-old who wanted nothing out of life except to be a subway motorman and never comprehended the concepts of racism and bigotry would become the most serious case of racial killing in New York City since the murder of Michael Griffith in Howard Beach three years earlier.

RUDE AWAKENINGS

As word spread via the morning television news shows that there had been a racial murder in Bensonhurst apprehension grew among city officials. The story as told through the initial press accounts was that a group of as many as thirty young white men, many armed with bats and clubs, had pursued four black teenagers through the white, working-class neighborhood in a case of mistaken identity—they wanted to beat up some black kids, but these had been the wrong ones. Police Department Community Affairs officers were especially concerned, given the volatile climate of the city, that hordes of angry blacks might descend upon the neighborhood bent on vengeance.

For Edward Koch, mayor of an already troubled city and running in a primary against a black candidate, the case was a nightmare, not only for the potentially disastrous political ramifications but also because Koch, once active in the civil rights movement and sensitive to injustice in spite of his sometimes insensitive rhetorical exercises, was genuinely horrified at the realization that such a vicious crime could be perpetrated in his city.

Readying for the worst, police community relations specialists were already in place before sunup, as were squads of police officers dressed in riot gear, giving the area around Twentieth Avenue the look of a community under siege.

Sarina Scavone, who had spent the night with Keith Mondello at her sister's apartment, had taken a walk around the neighborhood in the morning while her boyfriend slept, and was shocked when she saw the many police vehicles, including large communications vans, and cops with riot batons and Plexiglas shields.

The blue-and-white vans, trucks, and cars of the New York City Police Department were all over Twentieth Avenue and detectives talked to people on streetcorners.

Sal the Squid's candy store was open, the gate was up, detectives were there, and something was missing: a huge collage that had hung in Sal's store window of pictures of all of the neighborhood kids, from a party they had gone to, including Joseph Serrano, Joey Fama, and of course Keith. Sarina saw a detective emerge from the candy store with the collage rolled up under his arm. She walked past them to Mike's Candy Store on Twentieth Avenue and called her job to say that she was not coming in. When she heard that the police were at her job looking for her she double-timed back to her sister's apartment.

Keith was awake, sitting at the kitchen table in the gray sweatshorts he had fallen asleep in the night before.

"You're not going to believe this," she said, excitedly telling him what she had seen on the street and what they told her at work.

He lit a Marlboro and watched as the smoke circled around his head. The bravado and tough-guy talk were gone from Keith Mondello, who didn't believe he had done wrong. All he had done was get everybody together to protect himself.

Mondello went back to the foldout and fell into a troubled sleep as investigators moved up the block below the brick building, questioning anyone they saw about what they might have seen or heard. Another team of detectives had Sarina's sister's address, obtained at her job, and at eleven o'clock the doorbell rang.

Sarina buzzed the door and heard footsteps in the downstairs hallway.

"Is Sarina there?" a voice called up the stairs.

"Yes," she said "I'm Sarina."

There was shuffling and scuffling of feet, and then two detectives stood near the open doorway. Sarina remembered that they looked awfully large.

"Is Keith here?" one of the detectives asked.

"Yes, he's here," Sarina said.

"We want to talk with him," the other said.

"Wait here," Sarina told them, and turned to get Keith. The detectives followed. Toward the back of the apartment the sound of a shower could be heard. It was Sarina's sister.

"I asked you to please wait here," Sarina said, but the investigators continued to follow her.

As Sarina approached the room where Keith lay under a blanket, still sleeping, the detectives walked around her.

"Keith, there's somebody here, these men want to talk to you," Sarina said.

The form under the blanket stirred, and when Keith opened his eyes the first thing he saw was a .38 police special pointed in the general direction of his head.

One detective, the one without the gun, pulled off the cover and then pulled Keith's arm, raising him up.

"Over there," the detective said, pointing toward the living room. "Over there, let's go."

"Hey!" Keith began to protest. "I didn't do anything, I didn't do—"

"Shut up" was the reply, and now Sarina became nervous—and angry.

There wasn't much to search when they propped Keith against the wall; all he had on were the gray shorts. Satisfied that he had no weapon, they handcuffed the spread-eagled suspect. Sarina's sister came out of the shower dressed in a robe.

"What the hell is going on in here?" she demanded.

Keith, now handcuffed, was wiggling to ease the strain on his wrists.

"I told you, I didn't do anything. I didn't do anything at all. Why are you doing this?" he asked.

One of the detectives, Robert Regina, told Keith to calm down.

"Just take it easy," he said.

"Take it easy? How am I supposed to take it easy like this? I didn't do anything," Keith said.

"How could you?" demanded Sarina. "I told you I'd get him, he's not going anywhere. Do you have a warrant for his arrest? Do you have a warrant? Why are you arresting him?''

"Do you want the cuffs off?" a detective asked Keith.

"Yeah, I want the cuffs off," Keith said.

"If you come in willingly for questioning I'll take the cuffs off," Detective Robert Regina said. "Do you want to come in willingly for questioning?"

"I'll come in willingly for questioning," Keith said.

"Can I come?" Sarina asked.

The detectives thought for a moment.

"Okay," Regina said. "You can come."

Keith was uncuffed.

The trip to the police station was uneventful. Sarina and Keith sat together in the back of the unmarked car, and after twenty minutes or so they were at the 60th Precinct station house.

Mondello had every reason to believe that he was being treated well. Sarina was permitted to stay, and sat on Keith's lap during most of the questioning. At one point she went out and came back with sandwiches. Mondello had access to cigarettes and was not handcuffed.

Neither Keith nor Sarina knew that Steven Curreri was already there and had been questioned for many hours. Nor were they privy to the knowledge that some of the highest-ranking police officers in New York City were there also, monitoring every step of the questioning Keith was submitted to.

The seemingly cordial relations between Keith and the investigators degenerated when Sarina was not in the room. At one point there was shouting, and Sarina heard Keith screaming.

"She's out there! Why don't you go out there and ask her if you don't believe me?"

Detective Regina approached Sarina.

"Can I ask you a few questions?" he asked, and she agreed.

Sarina told Regina what she knew about Gina Feliciano's threats, about conversations she had with Keith after the incident up until the time of his "voluntary" submission to police custody, and anything else she knew that related to the questions.

94

The detective returned to his questioning of Keith, taking turns with another detective, Darcy Callahan.

"What about Fama?" Regina asked him.

"I don't know Fama," Mondello replied.

"Come on, was Fama there?" Regina asked. Keith thought about it. "That was Joseph Fama, wasn't it, the guy in white?"

"I think so," he said.

"All right, that's better," Detective Callahan said. "One more time, what happened?"

Sarina got up and left the room for a moment. When she came back she heard another heated exchange between Keith and Regina.

"Look, you saw Fama. You said he was there. Did he have the gun?" Regina asked.

"I don't know if I saw the gun. Somebody had a gun. Somebody, I think it was this guy Frank, he put something in my car—" Keith began.

"You mean Vento's car," Regina corrected him. "Fama had the gun?"

"I think, I don't know, I don't remember so good and it all happened so fast and, uh, I saw the blue flash, the blue flash at the black and the black fell—"

Regina cut him off.

"Listen, asshole, you do know. And you're gonna be here today, tomorrow, next week, and I'll be out there fucking your girlfriend!" Regina said.

Sarina heard the last part of the conversation and she was horrified. How could they be treating him like this? She was still under the impression that Keith had nothing to worry about because they had not read him his rights, like on television. So they couldn't do anything to him. Then she remembered Regina's remark and shivered. Or could they . . .

With the "girlfriend" statement from Regina Keith's blood boiled. This had been enough, and he wanted to go. The collage had been brought in, the one from the candy store with everybody's picture on it. He recognized Joe Fama's picture.

"If you weren't a cop—"

Sarina, pretending she hadn't heard the encounter, came back into the room.

"Keith, what did he say to you? What did he say, Keith?"

She began to cry and Keith held her.

Another detective came into the room and threw a disgusted look at Keith, leaving the young couple alone. When he returned a few moments later, Sarina was still wracked with sobs.

"All right," a detective said. "What did you see?"

Keith slumped back in the chair.

He began to tell his story again.

"And they came around the corner, so we all went over there. And somebody said, 'Is this them, is this them?' And then I saw the blue flash, the blue flashed at the black, and I saw the black fall," Keith said.

"Who did it? Who fired the gun?"

Keith was hesitant.

"Come on, who fired the gun?"

Keith broke down.

"Fama, Joey Fama. The guy in that picture there."

A detective looked at Sarina.

"We're leaving, honey. We have to take him somewhere else," he said.

Keith was being charged in connection with the murder of Yusuf Hawkins. He hugged Sarina, who walked downstairs in tears. They were going to take Keith to another precinct.

Sarina left and called Mondello's parents, who decided that, since word was already all over the neighborhood that the shooting around the corner from their home was "another Howard Beach," there was only one person they could even think of calling for representation. While Keith sat in a holding cell after being processed at Brooklyn Central Booking, they arranged for him to be defended by the lawyer they thought of as the hero of Howard Beach, Steven Murphy.

*   *   *

While Keith Mondello went through the formal charging process Steven Curreri was still in the same station house, answering a battery of questions.

Steven was holding up well during the questioning, repeating his story time and again. It was almost nine o'clock and he was beginning to feel tired, but he continued to answer the questions as investigators looked for inconsistencies or information that might contradict or corroborate statements being taken from other young men as well as Gina Feliciano.

Gina offered the most cohesive story to investigators of any one individual they had spoken to. She had told them that Keith Mondello was upset because she had black friends, as were others in the neighborhood. She had been abused by them because of this, and the schoolyard gang had threatened her when she said her black and Hispanic friends were coming to her birthday party. She had called the whole thing off, she said, when she realized that the boys downstairs from her apartment were going to hurt somebody. No, she didn't know a Yusuf Hawkins, nor had she ever heard of the other victims of the attack. It was strictly a case of mistaken identity.

Detectives and the District Attorney's office realized early that Gina would be far from a model witness and that she would be subject to impeachment on the stand if she ever testified against anyone. Gina's opinion of the neighborhood boys was obviously uncomplimentary, but few people that police spoke with in the neighborhood had much nice to say about Gina either.

When detectives from the Bias Unit interviewed Carmen Mercado, the woman who lived in the same building as Gina, she told them that Gina was a "troubled girl." Other neighbors said things that were even less charitable, and some asked detectives why they hadn't arrested her.

"She's nothing but trouble. She caused the whole thing and riled everybody up. It's her fault," was what one woman told investigators, but the statement could have come from any of hundreds of people who were spoken with. The investigators learned that Gina had a drug habit, that she was not above selling her body to support it, according to some residents, and then there were the local precinct cops who also knew about her and had been called to her home more than once.

The Bias Unit detectives especially, experienced in the nuances present in racist neighborhoods where anyone but the people who committed the crime would be subject to blame, tried their best to discount the Gina stories.

"We know all about Gina," they told Carmen Mercado. "But Gina isn't who we're looking for. She didn't shoot anybody. She didn't kill anybody. We need to know who did."

Sal the Squid spoke with police but was not of much help. Eventually he told them he would only speak through an attorney.

Elizabeth Galarza had plenty to say, about people in the neighborhood and Gina especially. Just as they had done after the shots were fired at her and Linda Nipitello, however, the police discounted any version of what she told them. She was not considered a credible witness.

Police never gave a specific reason for Galarza's undesirability as a witness. When United Press International was deciding whether to run a story that Galarza said she witnessed the shooting, a police captain said, "If you use her you're going to get egg on your face," but would not elaborate.

Glen Goldberg, a spokesman for Elizabeth Holtzman at the time, said that there were so many difficulties with so many witnesses that one more shaky person on the stand could hurt matters more than help them.

The only official explanation ever given was that Galarza was "inconsistent" and "gave several different versions of the events she claimed to have seen." Police also said that Galarza was a "busybody" who had involved herself in a "neighborhood domestic dispute." The dispute in question was the one between Linda Nipitello and Gina Feliciano. Galarza said the inconsistencies were only due to her fear of telling the truth.

Meanwhile, investigators were facing another problem. They believed Joseph Fama was their gunman, but he was nowhere to be found. Rumors began to circulate that he might have fled to Italy.

RUDE AWAKENINGS

The newspapers published brief accounts of the shooting the follow-
ing morning, although there was little hard information to be had.
Mary Paul saw Yusuf's name in print while having breakfast in her
Astoria, Queens, home.

"I was reading *Newsday*," she remembered. "I saw this story about
a racial murder in Bensonhurst and it didn't register with me, the
name or anything. And then something hit me, I don't remember
what."

"Oh my God!" she said, out loud. "That's my Yusuf!"

"Anybody, anybody but him," she remembered thinking, and was
bitter at the irony of the fact that his murder was racially motivated.

"Yusuf . . . he wasn't a black kid, he wasn't a white kid; you just
didn't think of him in those terms. He was everybody's child, was
all."

Mary Paul had taught in the New York City school system for two
decades and grown to love the children she taught in the tough
Brooklyn neighborhood. She knew that the impression the public
sometimes received of young blacks, even when they were victims
of vicious crimes, could be less than favorable.

She immediately determined that she would do what she could to
see that no aspersions were cast on "her Yusuf."

She got in her car and immediately set out for Decatur. Classes
were still out for the summer, but the school building was open for
a community children's breakfast program. Word of the shooting had
already begun filtering through the skeleton crew of teachers and
administrators working that morning, and some of the employees
who remembered Yusuf Hawkins fondly were beside themselves.
When Mary Paul walked into the school building she spoke with a
female security guard who had watched Yusuf come and go through
the big doors during his years at Decatur.

The women fell into each other's arms, in tears. Then the teacher
went to her classroom and frantically began digging through files
until she found what she was looking for. It was an article that
Yusuf had written about the problems that teenagers face finding

employment, which he saw not in terms of race or class but as a universal. If difficulty in finding a job that would also permit continued schooling was a problem for him, Yusuf reasoned, then it must be true for other people his age all over New York and elsewhere. She sat at her desk and quickly wrote a letter to former *Newsday* columnist Dennis Hamill.

"I liked the way he wrote about things," she said, explaining her choice. "He had a special sensitivity and I thought that he would see that my letter got published."

Although the letter itself was not printed, the information supplied by Mary Paul got into the newspapers, and soon the entire city knew that Yusuf was indeed a good kid who had never been in any kind of trouble.

Even before such background appeared in the papers, however, there appeared to be differences between this case and Howard Beach. Unlike the suspicions cast on the Howard Beach victims and questions of why they were really in the white neighborhood, the story of the blue Pontiac was verified by police and prosecutors. The shooting was considered even more tragic and vicious, and the media were drawn to the Hawkins home on Hegeman Avenue, trying to find out more about who Yusuf Hawkins was and what his family was like.

Moses Stewart was taken aback at first. The family had other things to worry about besides reporters and was still reeling from the shock. Diane was devastated and having trouble coping. But even though the Hawkins family rallied around her for strength and support, Moses felt they would need something more in order to deal with the growing pool of press people outside the house, and the system that was ostensibly to provide the family with its share of justice.

He picked up the phone to call the Reverend Al Sharpton.

BOY PREACHER FROM BROOKLYN

HE Slave Theater on Fulton Street used to be just another Bedford-Stuyvesant movie house, but now it serves as headquarters for the Reverend Al Sharpton's United African Movement. The red-carpeted lounge area's walls are decorated with giant full-color murals depicting slaves rising up against their masters. Another mural asks "Who Is the Nigger?" and answers its own question in small print below which says that "The Nigger" is the black man who would sell his brother into slavery or poison his brothers with the deadly charms of the white man, alcohol and drugs.

Sharpton holds UAM rallies at the Slave on Wednesday nights and Saturday afternoons. Between two and three hundred followers come to hear vitriolic diatribes against those he calls "the crackers," the white establishment.

The son of Alfred and Ada Sharpton, Al began preaching at the age of four and was well known at the Washington Temple Church of God in Christ and other Brooklyn churches by the time he was five.

"He was a fat, chubby little thing," recalls one woman who is still a member of the congregation.

Mahalia Jackson was one of several gospel luminaries who came to the church to visit Ernestine Washington, wife of Bishop Frederick Douglas Washington, founder of the church and little Al Sharpton's mentor. Mrs. Washington was recognized as a powerhouse gospel singer herself, and celebrities would often drop by to pay their respects to her. Jackson saw young Sharpton preach, and was favorably impressed.

"That boy is cute," she said, according to Sharpton, who says she then decided she wanted to take him on the road with her.

Shortly thereafter Al Sharpton, dressed in a black-and-gold robe with black trim and wearing his hair in a short "natural," was touring the East Coast of the United States with the Queen of Gospel.

"It was a tremendous opportunity," Sharpton says of the experience. "Mahalia Jackson was bigger than life at the time."

Black churches were the bedrock of the civil rights movement, and Sharpton became aware of the movement and its importance during his elementary-school years, when freedom riders came to speak at Washington Temple.

Alfred, Sr. and Ada separated when Sharpton was five and the bitterness between them increased over the years. When Sharpton was nine his parents were engaged in angry court proceedings over their separation, and Alfred Sr. sought to stop the boy's preaching. At issue was the money the elder Sharpton agreed to pay to his wife and children as part of the agreement, and he did not think it proper that the boy should be earning money as a preacher while he had to dig deep into his pockets for child support. A Brooklyn family court judge issued a verbal order that prohibited the boy preacher from engaging in his church activities. But Sharpton continued to preach, maintaining that his evangelizing, while encouraged by Ada, was something he himself felt he had been called to do. When word reached the judge that his order had been violated, Sharpton says, he called the boy into his chambers.

"Didn't I tell you not to preach?" the judge asked.

"Yes, sir," Sharpton said.

"Didn't you understand me, then?" the judge asked.

"Yes, sir," Sharpton said.

"Well then, why did you continue preaching?"

"Because God told me to."

Skeptical but not unconvinced, the judge said, "If you disobey a judge's order you can go to jail." Sharpton said that yes, he was aware of that, and that he was still preaching because it was what he believed.

The judge rescinded the order, and the following Sunday Al Sharpton was back at Washington Temple. The father's bid to curtail his son's preaching drove a wedge between the two that lasted for decades.

Sharpton's closeness to Bishop Washington grew, and the cleric continued to guide the boy, ordaining him when he was ten years old and taking him on a preaching tour of the Caribbean. Drawn to books in large part because of his admiration for the bishop ("He was always reading something," Sharpton says), it was a book that would crystallize the boy's interest in yet another mentor.

While attending classes at New York's PS 134 a teacher Sharpton remembers as "Mrs. Greenburg" helped him read a book that held special interest for him.

"It had a picture of Adam Clayton Powell, Jr., on the cover. I had gotten it at a black bookstore in Queens," Sharpton says. The Harlem congressman and minister was held in high regard by many in the black community, and Sharpton was impressed that this man, a minister just like him, was actually on the cover of a book and had even been on television.

"What attracted me was the idea of a preacher with this power and profile," Sharpton says. He convinced his mother to let his sister Cheryl take him on the train to Harlem but Powell was not at the Abyssinian Baptist Church that day. Undaunted, they returned the following Sunday and young Alfred watched in awe as his new hero took to the podium.

"He preached a sermon on love," Sharpton remembered. "It was incredible. He was a fantastic preacher."

Powell and Sharpton eventually met and continued the acquaintance. This opened doors for Sharpton, who through Powell met other celebrities including the Godfather of Soul himself, James Brown, who became almost an adoptive father to the teenager. But it was Sharpton's admiration for Powell and the controversial congressman's eventual downfall that caused him to make the leap from boy preacher to teenage activist.

In 1966 Sharpton was crushed to learn that Congress had accused Powell of misappropriating funds and other ethics violations. The twelve-year-old got busy with a picketing and petition drive on behalf of Powell. "I formed a youth committee, and we were active until Powell was excluded and went into semiretirement at Bimini," Sharpton says.

In the years that followed Sharpton kept busy with Jesse Jackson's Operation Breadbasket, the Southern Christian Leadership conference, and his own National Youth Movement. He continued his association with such high-profile figures as fight promoter Don King and James Brown, through whom he met Kathy Jordan, a back-up singer for Brown who eventually became Sharpton's wife and the mother of his two daughters.

Straddling the fast-paced world of entertainment and the traditionally sedate, studied life of the ministry is a difficult juggling act by any standard, and as the activist began to achieve notoriety with his anti-drug marches and other activities he became increasingly open to attack. Associations on the fringes of the New York underworld, which Sharpton claims were unwitting and unintentional, even led to his wearing a wire for the Federal Bureau of Investigation, according to some reports that Sharpton has termed exaggerated and inaccurate.

Television was an important component of the wide public support the civil rights movement had in the 1960s. Gray-and-white images of peaceful black men and women besieged by vicious police dogs, beaten bloody with long batons wielded by mounted sheriff's deputies, and hit with high-pressure streams of water from fire hoses flickered into millions of American living rooms, helping to turn the tide of public sentiment toward the freedom marchers. The television thrust was incidental, however. Marchers would have marched and picketers would have picketed whether or not the cameras were there to record the images. But to Sharpton, television would be the primary tool for change.

As Sharpton's public profile grew, first with the National Youth Movement antidrug marches and then later with the Howard Beach and Tawana Brawley demonstrations and press conferences, it became clear that the rhetoric-spouting firebrand was a new kind of civil rights advocate, different from the old-guard marchers. His contacts in the entertainment industry taught him how to promote, and the product he believed in most, justice for African-Americans, was what he believed he could promote best. His mastery of pithy phrases that worked just right on the evening news shows were a boon for producers and reporters.

Marchers led by Sharpton during the Howard Beach trial and after the Tawana Brawley revelations tied up traffic at airports and brought segments of the New York City subway system to a halt. Sharpton himself was arrested and later jailed for his part in the "Days of Outrage" along with other activists. Some of them, such as the Reverend Herbert Daughtry, accepted plea bargains that precluded jail time. Sharpton refused, saying that an activist must always accept his sentence and never compromise with the system.

His acceptance of jail sentences and other difficulties he has encountered make Sharpton laugh at suggestions that he somehow profits from his activities.

"What do I get in return for this?" he asks. "I've been unjustly indicted, jailed, arrested, all kinds of things. How can they say I'm making a profit off of this?"

The news media have often been criticized for the attention they gave Sharpton during the Howard Beach case and later during the Tawana Brawley controversy. Some critics have even said that he was a creation of the media that covered him. Sharpton disagrees.

"I don't give them credit for creating an Al Sharpton. It is the black community that creates an Al Sharpton," the activist says of such remarks, explaining that the existence of inequality makes the creation of a crusader almost a chemical reaction.

Sharpton calls himself a television activist in a television age whose confrontational, high-profile style is essential to spreading his message.

"They covered me because the things I did were outrageous," Sharpton says.

"My style is just as conducive in the age I'm in as 'In Living Color'. . . . We're not in the age of Julia and Amos and Andy, we're in the age of Arsenio Hall."

Sharpton says there is no difference between his "Day of Outrage" marches during Brawley and Howard Beach and Dr. Martin Luther King, Jr., leading marches designed to land demonstrators in jail as a means of making a point. Sharpton believes that his way of approaching racism, through what he calls "creative confrontation," is not anything new.

"I am more traditional," he says. "Blacks in power (such as David Dinkins) is new. Blacks protesting is not new."

"I don't really think the white community understands how a lot of blacks salute what I do, even blacks in power behind closed doors . . . if it wasn't for there being a very abrasive and confrontational activist out there we wouldn't have made any progress in the past few years."

Among the "creative confrontations" Sharpton led was the bringing of a funeral procession for a black police-shooting victim to New York's City Hall in February 1990 to protest police brutality against blacks and a spate of questionable shooting incidents. Sharpton and other ministers conducted funeral services over the casket through the open hearse's back door as police directed traffic around the cortege on busy lower Broadway, long before national attention was focused on excessive use of police force.

Sharpton walks a delicate line between the media that publicize him and the hard-line United African Movement rank and file, who have no use for the television and print reporters, whom they see as arms of the white power structure.

"The media says I don't care what they say about me and in a sense they're right. It's not about me, it's about this movement," Sharpton says.

Press writeups critical of him personally do not disturb the flamboyant clergyman. He has often pointed to an article or column and said, "They were pretty rough, but look here, they said something positive here." In private, Sharpton can be charming to members of the press he feels have given him—and the movement he is part of—fair play. He has a keen sense of humor, even when the joke is at his own expense, if he is comfortable with the company.

But at public events, particularly when tensions are highest, he maintains a maddening stand-offishness in keeping with his "celebrity" status, and access to him is restricted by sometimes friendly but often unaccommodating aides.

Sharpton has an ego twice the size of his body, a necessary asset for one in his position. He has made constructive use of an inherently manipulative nature, and as an armchair psychologist the buttons he knows how to push are not limited to those that belong to the news media. Associates and confidants are often bullied verbally into delivering what the preacher wants. Those closest to him, a handful of bodyguards and several aides, are slavishly devoted to Sharpton because of their belief in his leadership of what they call "the movement" and devotion to the charismatic man himself.

He is known to run late for appointments and sometimes avoids or forgets about them altogether, part of his belief that he is graced with superstar status. If he doesn't have time for someone or inadvertently snubs them his pat excuse is, "Listen, I've got a movement to run."

The negative publicity caused by the Tawana Brawley case should have washed Sharpton up as any kind of a responsible spokesman for anyone.

"Sharpton was supposed to die with Tawana Brawley," he says. "The fact that they had to cover us even after Tawana Brawley meant that the white media was not able to destroy a black leader when it got ready to. Part of the resentment by the white media is that they resent that I disprove the infallibility of the white media. They pride themselves on being able to destroy people's careers. But the New York *Times* still quotes Al Sharpton," the activist explains, referring to himself in the third person, a practice he is fond of.

It would indeed seem that Al Sharpton's career was Teflon-coated. He survived the Brawley case with his core support group—disenfranchised New York blacks—more supportive than ever. If Al Sharpton would stand behind the Tawana Brawley story even though disavowing his belief would be more expedient, then he was certainly worthy, some people thought, of representing them. One of those people was Moses Stewart.

NIGGERS GO HOME

SHORTLY after ten o'clock on the morning of August 24 the telephone at Sharpton's home rang and Anthony Charles, his assistant, picked it up.

"Who's calling for Reverend Sharpton?" he asked.

"This is Moses Stewart," the caller said.

Anthony placed the call on hold and told Sharpton who it was.

"Who's Moses Stewart?" Sharpton asked, and Anthony repeated the question to Moses.

"My son got killed in Bensonhurst," Moses said, and Anthony handed the phone over to his boss.

Moses introduced himself and explained the reason for his call.

"Reverend Sharpton, the press is already harassing me, it's upsetting my wife, and I don't know what to do over here."

Sharpton calmed the grieving father, took down the address and called Roy Canton, another activist prominent in the United African Movement.

Not much more than an hour later Sharpton, Canton, and Anthony pulled up in front of the house on Hegeman Avenue. Moses was standing on the front porch with his nephew Walter, and Diane, still numb from the shock of losing her son, was inside the house being comforted by relatives. Moses was surprised that the minister had responded so quickly, and the two men embraced as Sharpton and his companions walked up the concrete steps.

"I can't believe it," Moses said to Walter. "It's really Al Sharpton."

Once inside, Moses introduced Diane to their guest, and the family sat down with him to discuss their plans.

Sharpton immediately began dispensing advice.

"You're going to get all the politicians, and you see the press out there already," he began, and mapped out the ways in which he thought the family should deal with the sudden attention.

"How did you call me, anyway?" he asked Moses. Moses told him that Dominic Carter, a black reporter from WLIB, had given him the phone number. "I told Dominic that I'd give him an exclusive interview," Moses said.

Sharpton suggested that the family take a different approach.

"I'll explain it to Dominic," he said. "But I think what you need to do is go on the air live."

Gary Byrd, the popular host of a daytime talk and discussion show dealing with black issues, broadcast live on Thursdays from the Apollo Theater in Harlem on WLIB. Sharpton made a phone call and arrangements were made for the first public interview of Moses Stewart, live with Byrd.

When the assembled media outside the house got word that the father of the victim was being interviewed live on WLIB they were not terribly happy. But Sharpton has always felt that when he is involved in a situation that directly affects the African-American community primary consideration must be given to the black press.

What listeners heard on the WLIB airwaves were the words of an angry but articulate man.

"Should I say that I love everybody right now and that everybody loves me and my family? That would be a big lie. My son was shot twice and killed. . . . I want to see peace, I want to see harmony, but what is it going to take and how many of us are going to have to die?" Moses said.

The show was far from over for the patient reporters on Hegeman Avenue, however, who still wanted their piece of the story. Diane stood by Moses' side as he announced that Sharpton had been chosen by the family to represent and advise them. The news was not received well by a media corps that already had had a bellyful of dealing with the sometimes uncooperative and often manipulative activist during Howard Beach. They also felt betrayed by Sharpton because of the Brawley case and were bitter that he had been responsible for pulling a hoax on them.

The immediate question to many, of course, was why Sharpton needed to be in the picture at all. Nobody had accused this family or their dead son of any wrongdoing. Why was an "adviser" needed?

Moses Stewart had never dealt with the double whammy of politicians and the press, but his interest in current events as they concerned blacks told him that a buffer would be necessary.

The system is not always quick to dispense justice when whites are accused of crimes against black people, and the information he had from the outset was that there had been a huge mob of white boys involved in the attack that led to the death of his son, many of whom might escape justice if pressure were not brought to bear on the system.

There is a sense of powerlessness and rage during times of tragedy, and the delicate political and social situations in New York, Moses felt, most certainly led to the death of his son. The victim of the mob could have been any young black man, just as the recipient of the bullets in Bensonhurst could have been either or both of his two other sons, had they made it back from the video store in time.

The introduction of Al Sharpton into the story was an immediate slap at the system, a disdainful gesture that said the institutions of society and people who were responsible for running them could not be trusted to see that justice was done.

Sharpton, whose questionable and oft-criticized tactics made him the object of scorn and derision, was a perfect choice for the father who said to the listeners that what he was most of all on that hot and humid Thursday was a bitter man.

Members of Diane's family were not especially pleased by the decision to involve Sharpton and were concerned that the death of a beloved and gentle child would be made even more tragic by the ugly specter of racial politics. Moses was well aware of the mayoral primary campaign between Koch and Dinkins, and he feared that his son's memory would become the object of a political tug-of-war. Politics, Moses argued, was specifically what he hoped not to have his son's death become a part of. He was therefore less than pleased

110

when word filtered through the media contingent that David Dinkins was on his way to Hegeman Avenue.

The mayoral hopeful arrived with the Reverend Herbert Daughtry and a press aide.

After expressing his condolences to the family, Dinkins spoke with reporters while Daughtry and Bill Lynch, the campaign's press spokesman, attempted according to the family's recollections to turn the visit into a photo opportunity. A newspaper picture of Dinkins with the grieving family would give the impression that Dinkins had somehow received the family's support. The effort was blocked and Dinkins left after giving a final statement.

"I deplore violence of any sort," Dinkins said. "It is important that the whole city is outraged at this."

After the candidate's departure Moses and Sharpton left the house and walked a few blocks to a diner where they would begin meeting regularly. They discussed the difficulties the family would have in making funeral arrangements. They were not financially prepared for that expense, and Sharpton made a note to contact the Crime Victim's Compensation Board for emergency burial expenses. Moses told Sharpton that Daughtry had offered his church for the services. Later they decided to have the service performed by Diane's cousin, the Reverend Curtis Wells of the Glover Memorial Church, a Baptist congregation.

Sharpton also offered assistance for burial from the UAM treasury, which Moses said he would accept.

"Is there anything else you need?" he asked. Hesitantly, Moses said that he hoped that Minister Louis Farrakhan might be informed of the services and attend. Stewart was no longer actively associated with the Nation of Islam, and when he was part of the movement he had never personally met its controversial leader.

Farrakhan's movement, which had split from the Muslims when founder Elijah Mohammed's son Wallace began preaching a more conservative, less black-separatist line, believes in a separation between the races altogether. Sharpton's movement, although counting many separatists among its supporters, is decidedly prosystem. His marches and other public displays of militancy have been geared

FOR THE COLOR OF HIS SKIN

toward moving the courts and prosecutors' offices that are part of the system already in place.

"In the Yusuf Hawkins trials, we never said we don't want those white boys tried, they should be taken out on the streets and lynched," Sharpton explains. "In the Central Park case, we didn't say cut those young black men loose, don't have a trial. What we said was we wanted them to have a fair trial. If we were antisystem we wouldn't be dealing with trials."

Sharpton went to a pay phone, dialed a number, and handed the telephone receiver to Moses, who was shocked to find Farrakhan on the line. Moses invited him to the funeral and Farrakhan said he would get back to Moses through Sharpton.

"He's going to come," Sharpton said later. "If he wasn't going to come he'd just say no, but he wouldn't commit ever on the telephone for security reasons."

Back at the house on Hegeman Avenue, phone calls were made to the compensation board after Sharpton and Moses returned. An autopsy had been performed on Yusuf, and plans had to be made for the funeral. The remains of Yusuf Hawkins were still at the morgue, awaiting formal identification.

Diane Hawkins, accompanied by several cousins, would tearfully make the claim herself.

As the day wore on, media reports were already airing, with the voices of Bensonhurst residents protesting the growing accusations that their quiet streets were the spawning grounds of bigotry, racism, and ignorance.

"There wasn't anything racial about this. This was just something between a bunch of guys because one guy was jealous over the girl," one man said to a radio reporter.

Another voice was more blunt in her assessment: "How do we know it was racial? How do we know why they had come here?"

It wasn't the first time that view was expressed, nor would it be the last. Sharpton told the family that if the people of Bensonhurst were so adamant that there was no racism in their neighborhood, they should be challenged by one of Sharpton's "creative confrontations." The activist felt that a march through the streets of Bensonhurst should be held as part of a demand that the community itself give up all of the perpetrators of the crime. Moses and Diane should not go, Sharpton said. But Yusuf's brothers, Freddy and Amir, could lead the march with Sharpton and other activists. It would be planned for that Saturday, after a rally at the Slave Theater. Moses agreed.

As Sharpton and the Hawkins family made plans for the Bensonhurst march Steven Curreri was being introduced to his new attorney at the station house where he was still being questioned.

"I'm Matthew Mari, Steven, and your family has called me to represent you," the lawyer said, shaking Curreri's hand.

"Mr. Mari, no offense," Steven—who had been in the police station at this point for over sixteen hours—said. "But you're not going to mess things up, are you?"

"I don't understand what you mean," Mari said. "How?"

Curreri explained that if he had a lawyer, it would mean delays in his getting out of the precinct and getting home. This didn't sit well with the attorney, who immediately tried to find out just what was in store for his client.

A veteran homicide detective who knew Mari from other cases and had a good working relationship with him said the hands of the cops were tied.

"What do you mean?" Mari asked.

The detective motioned with his head toward a staircase, where the council of bosses was monitoring how interrogations were going.

"I think they want him in a line-up, Matt," the detective said.

Mari protested.

"Come on, he's just a stupid kid. He didn't kill anybody; he wasn't even there when the kid was shot. What are they going to put him in a line-up for?" he demanded.

"Look, just put him in the line-up, and then he can go," another detective said.

Above the intense objections of his lawyer, Curreri was viewed by Luther Sylvester, Claude Stanford, and Troy Banner as well as Irene Deserio. None of the witnesses picked Steven out as being part of the mob.

"Okay, that's it," Mari said. "My guy goes home now."

"Not so fast," a detective told him. "We have his videotape and other statements."

Mari furiously stormed through the station house, looking for a familiar face he could trust. Assistant District Attorney Paul Burns was standing next to Dake Campbell, his boss, in a conference room. Mari approached Campbell, who referred him to Burns.

"He's going to be charged," Burns said, keeping his head down.

"What are you talking about?" The veins on Mari's neck started to stand out. "Charge him with *what*? How can you tell me this boy is being charged with a crime like this, for what, for being in a schoolyard with a bat? Come on, let's get real here!"

Before the night was over Curreri, Keith Mondello, and another suspect, Pasquale Raucci, were all charged with assault and lesser crimes in connection with the murder of Yusuf Hawkins. While the suspects began their first hours segregated from other prisoners in the overcrowded and slow-moving Brooklyn criminal justice system, families of young men all over Bensonhurst called lawyers, trying to find out what to do if their sons were questioned by the police—or worse, if the police came and said they wanted them to come down to the station house.

There was anger and there was fear. Anger because many of the people in the immediate vicinity of the shooting knew Gina Feliciano, or at least had heard of her before the incident took place. They knew about her threats and felt the only reason so many young Bensonhurst residents were suddenly being processed through the criminal justice system was that police did not want to hear the real story, because it was politically inconvenient.

"Come on, these kids fight among themselves all the time. Black, white, it doesn't make any difference. One guy had a gun and did something stupid. So everybody has to pay?" Many residents aired such views when the microphones were pressed into their faces, although few would give their names.

"Come on," one woman said to a reporter. "This is Bensonhurst."

It certainly was Bensonhurst, and the fact that the murdered victim was black and his attackers Caucasian made a major difference, particularly with elections around the corner.

Reporters swarmed all over Stephen Murphy when they learned that he would be representing Mondello. If this Bensonhurst murder was seen as similar to the Howard Beach case at first, then the drama would be matched or heightened by the recasting of Murphy in the sequel.

"This was strictly a boyfriend-girlfriend thing," Murphy told reporters. "It wasn't racial, there wasn't anything racial about it," he said.

Police Commissioner Benjamin Ward had expressed similar sentiments while appearing at a joint press conference the day before with Mayor Koch, who characterized the killing of Hawkins as heinous and said the perpetrators must be prosecuted. Ward made no similar comments after that.

Sharpton spent most of Friday on Hegeman Avenue, trying to get the compensation board to release money for the burial and fielding media calls, answering questions with uncharacteristically low-key comments. The New York *Post* had quoted him as saying, "I will keep my head cool and not be reckless," as he had been accused of being in the Brawley case.

The murder and the charging of the suspects was front-page news by Friday, August 25, with reaction sought from and offered by public officials. To lawyers for the defendants and their families, the high-profile case was becoming a media circus and the prosecution, in its infant stages, was becoming nothing more than a political platform for headline-grabbers.

Jesse Jackson called the Hawkins family and offered his condolences. Later in the afternoon Governor Mario Cuomo called and spoke briefly with Moses and Sharpton, accepting an invitation to the funeral services from the family, made through Sharpton.

Cuomo was deeply troubled by the shooting but declined a suggestion by Koch that a special prosecutor be appointed. Approached at a political dinner that he attended with Holtzman, Cuomo said that he had full and absolute faith that the Brooklyn District Attorney could handle the case herself.

Parallels between the death of Yusuf Hawkins and the murder of twelve-year-old Emmett Till in the early 1950s were being drawn publicly. Till had been visiting relatives in Mississippi when he was killed, supposedly for whistling at a white woman and addressing her as "Hey, baby." The men charged with his death were acquitted by the all-white jury.

The public was also drawing similarities between the neighborhoods of Bensonhurst and Howard Beach. Bensonhurst residents rejected the accusations of racism and resented the fact that black marchers were planning to come on Saturday. There were fears that the blacks might get violent and that the march would only make tensions worse instead of better. Storekeepers fearing vandalism said they would close their stores, and statements made by Moses that if Bensonhurst wasn't going to give up the thirty people responsible for his son's murder, then blacks would have to go and take them out of Bensonhurst themselves caused fear and more anger.

On Saturday afternoon the Slave Theater on Fulton Street was packed with angry blacks who had come to march. After hearing Sharpton speak and being introduced to the Hawkins family, the assembled protesters piled into buses that idled outside.

There was a heavy police presence bolstered by mounted units, motorcycle cops, and plainclothes undercover officers who mingled with a crowd of angry whites that began assembling along Twentieth Avenue, waiting for the march to begin.

Preceded by police cars with flashing lights, the marchers, numbering at least four hundred, stepped forward. Sharpton was in the lead, standing between Freddy and Amir, with whom he had locked arms.

NIGGERS GO HOME

There was a look of determination on his face, and as the march began the expressions of the surviving Hawkins brothers transformed several times, from confusion to fear to anger and back to fear again.

The chanting of "Yusuf, Yusuf" began slowly, then like a freight train began to pick up steam and started bearing down Twentieth Avenue in full force. The name of a peaceful and quiet youngster had become a war cry.

On the sidelines hundreds of white hecklers began booing, and there were chants of "Niggers go home" while young men in bright tank tops held up watermelons in front of the television cameras and other residents cursed and spat at the contingent of invading blacks.

The potential for disaster was enormous.

"We were scared," Amir recalled, and Sharpton remembered that the two boys held so tightly to his arms that he thought they would be broken off.

"I was never so scared at any march I've ever been part of in my life," Sharpton (who rejected suggestions that he wear a bulletproof vest) remembered. "I thought this was going to be it."

There were several tense moments, particularly when one deranged individual broke through police lines brandishing what looked like a knife. He was quickly hustled away.

The march continued all the way to the Bath Avenue station house, to the conflicting chants of "No justice, no peace" from inside the lines of demonstrators, who were rapidly becoming incensed at the reaction their presence brought out of the white mobs, and "Niggers go home " from the young whites who continued their heckling in frightening numbers and in full unified voice. It was more than Freddy could take, and at one point he wanted to lunge blindly toward the crowd. The beefy arm of the family's adviser remained locked on his.

At Bath Avenue police and reinforcements who had been called in ringed the demonstrators, desperately trying to keep the two groups separated as the protest wound down.

A few doors away from the police station there was a catering hall where a wedding reception was being held. The entire entourage, even the bride in her long white gown and tuxedoed groom, joined the crowds on the street that jeered the marchers.

The march ended at the station house and the demonstrators reboarded their buses without further incident, returning to Bedford-Stuyvesant under heavy police guard.

If the hatred and ignorance of some people in Bensonhurst and surrounding communities was a secret to the city and the world at large, that all changed with the march. The New York *Post*'s front page featured a single word, SHAME!, accompanied by a picture of some of the young taunters.

The murder now represented more than a deranged act or an exercise in stupidity. For the people who had the most to fear from such actions it was the throwing down of a gauntlet, a challenge to the justice system. If as many as thirty people or even more participated in the attack, would they be prosecuted to the fullest extent of the law? There was debate around the entire city over whether anyone but the shooter should be prosecuted at all, and a tendency to forget that in addition to the murder victim there were three other young men who had been subjected to the fearful conduct of the mob.

A nerve had been touched in the city's black community, and anger that had been kept from reaching its full potential began to surface. Had Bensonhurst not reacted the way it did to the march, perhaps the feelings would not have run so deep. But the reactions, photographed, recorded, and written about in newspapers and magazines, had been duly noted. And, many blacks reasoned, if so many people were unashamed to show this evil side of themselves, then how many whites, people they worked with every day and said hello to, harbored such hatred as well?

The march and the neighborhood's reaction drew mixed reviews from the politicians whose careers stood to be affected by their comments and posture. Edward Koch, who had never been a fan of Al Sharpton's, thought that the march itself was divisive although he roundly criticized the behavior of the counterdemonstrators.

David Dinkins, who had been aggressively courting the support of the city's unions, was reportedly pressed by some advisers to publicly denounce the march, but he refused to do so, stating that the marchers had a right to march wherever they wanted to.

Primary day was a week away in a city that was ever more racially polarized than it had been prior to August 23. Al Sharpton vowed that the marchers would be back, possibly before the elections.

DEADLY CONCERT

B Y Monday, August 28, Keith Mondello was free on $100,000 bail; Pasquale Raucci and Steven Curreri had been freed on $75,000 each. The crime that had occurred on August 23 was a homicide but nobody had yet been charged with the crime of murder.

The District Attorney's office, on the fourth floor of the Brooklyn Municipal Building on Joralemon Street, is a busy place even when there hasn't been a major homicide with national implications. Under normal circumstances the DA is not involved to any great degree in the early stages of a homicide investigation, but even though office staffers said that things were "fairly routine" at the outset, according to other observers that could hardly have been the case.

High-level staffers said that neither Holtzman nor others in the office realized the public impact the case would have, but that appears doubtful if only because some of the highest-level people in Holtzman's office, including Homicide Chief Campbell, were at the station house within twenty-four hours of the murder, while suspects and witnesses were being questioned.

A joint investigation was being conducted by the District Attorney and the Police Department as prosecutors struggled to come up with a theory that would see the maximum number of suspects charged with the least chance that something could go wrong. Critics of Elizabeth Holtzman said that she personally involved herself in the case because of the upcoming primary and that a high public profile in the early stages of the much-publicized investigation would increase her margin of victory in the City Comptroller primary.

The "personal involvement" that made defense lawyers' hackles stand up was her insistence on appearing in court, something she had never done before, as well as the numerous press releases churned out by her office. One reporter, Jerry Capeci of the *Daily News*, even asked Holtzman herself why she had appeared in court, and she replied that she had certainly been in courtrooms before. Defense attorneys made frequent note of this, but it would not be unusual for a D.A. to make such appearances, given the fact that part of the bias crime prosecution formula is the creation of an impression that the authorities most certainly take such cases seriously.

Holtzman's hands-on involvement made her the object of scorn by defense attorneys who had never cared for her much to begin with.

After one early proceeding a defense lawyer speaking in front of reporters referred to the District Attorney as "that no-good bitch up there." An associate caught him and with a smile said, "That was off the record." But the television cameras were taping and the pens were flying and there is little doubt that had the same words been uttered by Alton Maddox, for example, they would have most certainly ended up on the evening news or at least somewhere in print. That double standard aside, the gaffe indicated something more was taking place as the Bensonhurst case shaped up than the usual antagonism that exists between courtroom adversaries.

Neil Ruskin, a Brooklyn defense attorney who originally represented Pasquale Raucci but was later replaced by other counsel, is one of many lawyers who believed that Holtzman's approach from the beginning was skewed by her political ambitions.

"She recognized the significance of this thing. She realized this was going to push her where she wanted to go," Ruskin said. Community leaders in Bensonhurst and other members of the Brooklyn bar agreed.

Holtzman herself has never responded to such comments publicly except to say that "a fair and thorough investigation was being conducted."

The District Attorney decided that a team approach would be best for piecing the case together, and some of the most talented people on her staff worked full-time on the Hawkins case almost from the beginning.

Rhea Kemble Dignam, Holtzman's chief assistant and now Executive Deputy Comptroller for the City of New York, and Harry Dodd, who now teaches at St. John's Law School and John Jay College of Criminal Justice, were the big guns. Both had extensive federal court experience, which figured heavily into the prosecution game plan.

Dignam's office, which looked out onto downtown Brooklyn's busy and dingy Court Street, was established as the command center almost from the first day. It was a small, simple chamber with a large desk, a few chairs, a worn couch, and what Dignam described as a "horrible" orange carpet soiled throughout with coffee stains. Dignam, Dodd, Dale Campbell (chief of the Homicide Bureau), and Bruce MacIntyre (now in private law practice) were among many attorneys who were daily poring through the DD-5s, Police Department follow-up reports, sometimes past eleven o'clock at night, as decisions were made on who should be charged and with what.

Under normal circumstances detectives and their supervisors have a great deal of discretion as to who they will charge and with what crimes, but the sensitive nature of this investigation took those decisions out of their hands. Success or failure of any prosecution would ultimately rest with the District Attorney's office, and the District Attorney's office was calling most of the shots.

The office had staged successful bias-crime prosecutions in the past. The murder of Willie Turks, the Transit worker beaten to death in Gravesend in 1982, was won by Holtzman's staff, with lengthy terms of imprisonment given to the defendants.

Based on hundreds of papers already filed by detectives between the night of the murder and Monday the twenty-eighth, here is the scenario the prosecutors believed occurred.

Keith Mondello, who was having a disagreement with Gina Feliciano because of her black friends coming into the neighborhood, rounded up as many people as he could to "teach her a lesson." They brought bats and golf clubs, and several people—possibly Mondello himself— had a gun. John Vento helped spread the word to everyone that "niggers were coming" to the neighborhood and got some of the heavy hitters from Eighteenth Avenue. These included Joey "Babes" Serrano and Joseph Fama. Serrano had a gun, which he gave to Fama (according to what Phyllis D'Agata told police).

When Yusuf Hawkins and his friends came down the street they were mistaken by the mob, numbering as many as forty, for Gina's friends. They were confronted by the mob and unable to move, penned and hemmed on the corner of Bay Ridge Avenue and Twentieth Avenue with nowhere to run, giving ample opportunity for Joseph Fama to reach out with his pistol and shoot Yusuf Hawkins, causing his death. The ramifications of race were inescapable. At the very least, if Yusuf and his friends had not been black the shots never would have been fired. For that matter, their color was the sole reason they were stopped by the mob to begin with.

Key to the prosecution's theory was the presence of the baseball bats in the hands of the mob and the fact that the prevailing situation in the neighborhood pointed to the eagerness of the young men to beat Gina's friends up because they were black and Latino, no matter how much they later protested that they were merely defending themselves. The answer to that was simple: They could have all stayed home. The favored theory, then, was that all of the players contributed to the death of Yusuf Hawkins, making them culpable for his death.

There were several ways the prosecutors could go. The first was to prosecute Joseph Fama as the gunman, the killer, using statements from any or all of the other people involved willing to talk about his actions. Keith Mondello had already implicated Fama and was an eyewitness. Gina Feliciano had given the background needed for setting up the scene. Phyllis D'Agata said a gun had been passed to Fama.

But there was a hitch. If the sole target of the action was to be Joseph Fama, then all of the people without whose encouragement, involvement, and assistance by way of hemming Hawkins in with the bats and committing crimes against the others by doing the same could be held criminally blameless.

Charles Stressler had also been questioned by police, and the District Attorney's office knew that he had admitted to bringing bats to the schoolyard. Yet he could also be a witness against Fama. Wasn't Stressler, however, criminally liable? If he testified before a grand jury against Fama, he could never be prosecuted for the crimes he committed in connection with the incident. In New York State grand jury witnesses have what is called use immunity. Unless the witness signs a waiver of such immunity, he or she cannot be charged with anything having to do with the crime in question. The same would hold true for Keith Mondello, the ringleader. Certainly he could testify against Fama if he so desired. But didn't he share in the responsibility?

The victim's family had already made its wishes known. Moses Stewart believed that any and all people involved in the attack that night were guilty of murdering his son, and he wanted them held accountable. Didn't he have the right to feel that way, prosecutors reasoned? Also, since the Saturday march and the intense barrage of publicity sparked by it, there was no question that the District Attorney's office was under the gun.

During the 1950s, when New York was besieged with gang rumbles that resulted in murders, prosecutors had been able to put away entire gangs with an application of the law called "acting in concert." That is, each person who engaged in the acts leading up to the death of the homicide victim, assuming they all shared the intent of the actual killer, were responsible for the end result.

According to key Holtzman staffers, the decision was made early that each person who made a sizable contribution to the events of August 23 would be charged with murder. Such a prosecution would serve a dual purpose, they reasoned. In addition to seeing that all those responsible were meted out their fair share of punishment, the case could then be used to make living case law. Appeals of defendants convicted of acting in concert could end up in the state's highest courts, perhaps even the Supreme Court of the United States. If the acting-in-concert theory was upheld all the way up the line, then in addition to ensuring that justice was done in the immediate case the stage would be set for future prosecutions where the established case law could then be pointed to as a guide for prosecutors and judges. This was seen as especially important by some, since bias-related homicides often involved such concerted acts and there were few tested weapons at the disposal of prosecutors to win convictions where multiple parties are involved.

Other obstacles had also to be overcome, however. For one thing, there was a dearth of cooperating witnesses from outside the mob of youths. Detectives were dealing with a phenomenon they referred to as "Bensonhurst amnesia." Word was already out on the street that Joseph Fama's family had mob connections, and potential witnesses were afraid to talk.

One example of the type of cooperation, or lack of it, was the series of visits detectives made to the home of Carmen Mercado, Gina's and Phyllis' neighbor in the apartment upstairs from Squid's candy store.

"I don't want to rat anybody out," she said when questioned about what she might have seen or heard in connection with the shooting. Like other people in the neighborhood, Carmen insisted that Gina started the entire incident, although she did go so far as to tell detectives that Sal the Squid had made phone calls to people telling them to come to the candy store the night of the murder. When detectives questioned Mercado further she insisted that Sal continued to tell people that Yusuf Hawkins was Gina Feliciano's boyfriend, a blatant falsehood some people in the neighborhood continued to believe even though there was ample evidence to the contrary.

Subsequent interviews of Mercado and other potential witnesses shed further light on the fear factor.

Carmen and others said that they had received hang-up calls when word got out that they had been talking to detectives, even though they had not said anything. If any other detectives came to her house, Carmen said, she was going to close the door in their faces.

"You can send me to jail if you want, I'm not going to rat," she said. "I'm not naming names."

The detectives of the elite Bias Unit are in some ways a cut above their colleagues who work the precinct detective squads. Both witnesses and suspects reported that they were treated more gingerly by the Bias Unit investigators, that the precinct approach was more heavy-handed. But it was also the precinct detectives, some of whom were acquainted with families of the suspects, who offered apologies to some after their sons were arrested. "If it were within my power

I would not have arrested your son for this," one detective told Keith Mondello's mother, Susan. Other parents reported similar statements from local detectives.

But a disingenuous approach by local investigators to cases where race is a factor was one reason the Bias Unit was formed to begin with. Although never documented to the point of confirmation, there was speculation that there were disagreements between the Police Department and the District Attorney's office as to how the case should be handled. This may have been why the initial charges against Mondello and others were headed by the crime of assault rather than murder.

One Brooklyn lawyer close to the case later said that law enforcement personnel were "pressured" to make arrests they might not have effected otherwise.

"The police were forced to satisfy the black community. Holtzman did not care about . . . the community's sensitivity and what the case was all about. They were pressured into it just like the politicians were pressured into it and they needlessly arrested people who weren't involved, then they charged them in a conspiracy that never existed. If we accept the fact that Fama did this and nobody else had anything to do with it, with the shooting. And then nobody in the District Attorney's office, which I once had a lot of respect for, had the balls to say this is a lot of crap." The attorney made his comments on condition of anonymity.

But if the Police Department had indeed refused to go along with murder charges, that would change once the case was presented to the grand jury, which was done almost immediately. Grand juries sometimes will refuse to indict, and even indict on lesser charges than those which prosecutors offer. Rarely if ever are the charges a grand jury returns higher than those originally offered by prosecutors.

The District Attorney's office decided that the line of demarcation that would determine who was and was not criminally liable for the death of Yusuf Hawkins would rest on a simple issue. Anyone who admitted or was particularly implicated as being at the scene of the crime with a baseball bat would be charged as a participant in the events of August 23 that resulted in the death of Yusuf Hawkins.

The main thrust of the investigation nevertheless still focused on Joseph Fama, whose whereabouts were unknown. Detectives were able to ascertain that he had gone to his construction job the morning after the murder, picked up his paycheck, cashed it, and then disappeared. A task force that included Interpol, the United States Customs Service, the FBI, and state and local agencies were conducting surveillances in hopes of finding the eighteen-year-old.

Airports were monitored closely in the United States and in Italy. The Fama home on Seventy-first Street was under surveillance, as were the homes of friends and relatives.

Police thought there was a possibility that Fama would turn himself in if enough pressure was brought to bear on ordinarily unmolested organized crime enterprises in Bensonhurst and elsewhere. Card games, small-time gambling operations such as numbers outfits, and drug spots were raided by police who hoped the mob would get the message. Joseph Fama had to be given up. What they didn't know was that word had already gone out, on instructions of Sam Gravano, that Fama was indeed expendable, so that if anyone knew where he was they would not have hesitated to turn him in. Gravano's caveat had merely applied to Frank D'Angelo, whose existence in terms of the Bensonhurst incident was not even known by investigators, or so they said.

Fama had already been advised, perhaps by his own family, just to lay low for a time and then surrender, perhaps after the furor over the case died down. In any event, the manhunt need not have been so extensive had investigators known that Fama never left New York State, and as exotic theories of where he might have fled were bantered around in squad rooms and patrol cars Joseph Fama, hungry and afraid, was sweating in the summer sun with his thumb extended, hitchhiking somewhere north of the New York City line.

He had no way of knowing, nor might he have particularly cared, that the shots fired on Bay Ridge Avenue had within a week's time begun to turn New York City against itself.

In addition to growing fears that additional Bensonhurst protests could escalate into wholesale violence, given the angry emotions on both sides, police and other city officials were seeing a pattern of crimes committed against innocent people, supposedly in retribution for the murder of Yusuf Hawkins. Several assaults, mostly perpetrated by young blacks, were recorded in police blotters. Victims had said that when they were robbed or beaten the criminals would tell them "This is for Bensonhurst" or "This is for Yusuf Hawkins."

Inspector Sanderson of the Bias Unit had become well acquainted with such occurrences during the height of the Howard Beach furor, when he was commanding officer of the 75th Precinct, in a predominantly black area adjacent to Howard Beach:

"It impacted upon us there, when you found that persons involved in crimes like robbery and larceny would say, 'This is for Howard Beach,' but it really had nothing to do with it."

Some of the attacks that occurred in the wake of the Bensonhurst murder were investigated as bias incidents, but most were not, although some received a fair amount of media attention. According to Sanderson, the existence of a high-profile race-related case was a cheap excuse or justification for a crime that would probably have been committed anyway.

But such distinctions are lost on the general population, unsure of the specifics that made a case bias-related to begin with. The mere fact that a crime is cross-racial, for example, does not mean that it is a bias crime. For that reason, many whites felt during the height of the Bensonhurst furor that a double standard was being applied when it came to the actions of whites and blacks.

If the Bensonhurst shooting was a case of mistaken identity, then how was it a bias crime and the Central Park jogger attack not?

Whatever criticism the prosecution would be subject to, Inspector Sanderson said that the men and women under his command did their jobs admirably. But while increased displeasure with how the case was being handled was voiced by whites, the city's tense black communities, convinced that most of the perpetrators of a monstrously unjust crime might yet go unpunished, became even more adamant in their resolve that authorities must arrest and charge all of those who in any way were responsible for the death of Yusuf Hawkins.

REQUIEM

O N Tuesday, August 29, the body of Yusuf Hawkins lay in an open silver casket at the Armwood Funeral Home on Troy Avenue in Bedford-Stuyvesant. Affixed to his jacket lapel was a button that said I LOVE BEING BLACK.

Two more arrests had been made. Charles Stressler, who had brought bats to the schoolyard, and James Patino, who was believed to have been on the corner when the shooting occurred, had both been charged with assault after being questioned. They had surrendered to police at the 62nd Precinct.

On the small block where the funeral home was located, just off of Fulton Street, hundreds of black men, women, and children gathered to pay respects, even though the general public was not permitted inside. Many were initially stunned by the murder, then outraged by the reaction of the counterdemonstrators in Bensonhurst. Most upsetting to many was that in spite of all that had taken place, there were still only five people arrested, none of them charged with murder, and the triggerman was still at large.

"If he shot a cop they would have got him already," was a comment made by more than one of the mourners assembled that day.

Moses and supporters of the family reasoned that if the same crime had been one involving finances, a larceny, or a bank robbery and it was known that thirty people were involved there would have been thirty arrests.

Sharpton was still surprisingly subdued and even said that "this must be a time of examination and re-examination for all of us. We all bear some of the responsibility for this tragedy."

Some reporters wondered if those comments were an admission that the heightened racial climate in the wake of the Tawana Brawley case, for which many held Sharpton responsible, had somehow indirectly led to the August 23 tragedy. But if that was the case no one could know for sure. Sharpton did not elaborate on his remarks.

The press treated Diane Hawkins gingerly. She stood by Moses' side as he did the talking when questions were asked of the family.

"This didn't start in Bensonhurst with my son," Moses angrily said to the scribes. "This started four hundred years ago." Comments like those made Moses Stewart a "bad guy" to frightened whites, who found them inflammatory. Moses publicly insisted that authorities arrest everyone involved in the crime, and the chant "We want thirty" became a staple of protesters. The logic was simple, on its face. Moses' outspoken nature, combined with the fact that he had involved Sharpton in the case and was a one-time follower of Louis Farrakhan, won him few friends among a public who wanted a different kind of grieving father.

As the crowd in front of the funeral parlor grew in the intense morning sun nervous police officers tried to keep order while setting up barricades on the sidewalk to keep the entrance clear.

"Yo, man, we animals you got to pen in or something?" one man called out. The officers, who had been given orders to avoid escalation of tension at all costs, tried to ignore him.

Chief of Patrol David Scott, the highest-ranking black police officer in the department, tried to calm the man down as the mostly white street cops went about their tasks.

The invited guests inside the funeral home were a veritable who's who of prominent African-Americans whose names were associated with the old civil rights guard as well as the new wave of hard-liners. Hazel Dukes, former chairperson of the NAACP, stood side by side with C. Vernon Mason and the Reverend Sharpton.

More conservative members of the black activist community like Dukes had often been at odds with the attorney and the activist, although Mason himself was more a part of the Harlem establishment than his counterpart Alton Maddox. The fact that the Hawkins family in their hour of grief and need turned to Sharpton was something the old guard had to accept, whether they wanted to or not. For better or worse, his presence offered something to Yusuf's family that it felt in need of, and the point was not lost on the conservatives.

Moses was not in a good mood, having been at odds with the funeral director over eating arrangements. Sharpton had sent for sandwiches in the hope of trying to get Diane to eat. When the food arrived, the funeral director told them it was against Health Department regulations to bring food inside. So after a brief discussion Moses and Sharpton went outside, near the mortuary loading dock, and ate in Sharpton's car. Diane would not touch any food. When they returned Diane said she was ready to do what she had been trying to work up the courage to do all morning.

The smell of flowers wafted through the doors of the viewing room as Diane took small, tentative steps toward its entrance. She was glad in some ways that all these people were there in the lobby, with its marble floor that made her high-heeled shoes click loudly. Some were supposed to be pretty important, she was told, but at this moment there was no person more important to her than the son she had lost. The bereaved mother walked toward the open coffin as recorded choir music played in the background, fell to her knees, and began to pray. She was a simple woman, who wanted good things for her sons and, had she ever taken the time to wish them, for herself as well. Now she felt old, and suddenly the responsibilities of motherhood were supplanted by the new role of grieving parent. Diane gazed down at Yusuf and a wave of nausea swept over her. This wasn't her son. This was a doll. This dead thing was a waxen sacrilege, an ugly substitute for the boy who had been Yusuf Hawkins. Suddenly the room was a blur, and she was on her feet screaming.

"That is not my son!" she screamed. "That is not my son in there! Get it out of here: It isn't my son. . ." and she collapsed into the arms of her cousin Felicia, who rushed to her side. It was a blood-curdling shriek that spoke of all the places and times that mothers and wives have lost sons and husbands to war and fighting and stupidity.

"She can't stay here. Get her out of here, she can't take this," Moses said. Another cousin, Walter, led her out of the room and suddenly Yusuf was alone again. The other mourners remained in the hallway.

Diane was led out of the lobby past Dukes, Mason, and the others. They looked down at their shoes, out of respect and helplessness.

The crowd outside grew silent as the shattered woman walked through the doors, her head bowed. Some shook their heads and others prayed. The sight of Diane only intensified the emotions of the crowd and added to the tension in the air.

Shortly after Diane was out of sight, a murmur began at one end of the crowd and worked its way through, developing into a chanted roar of "Jes-se, Jes-se" as the former presidential candidate arrived with three police officers, the Reverend and Mrs. Herbert Daughtry, and some others.

Jackson and Sharpton shook hands in the hallway. Moses eyed the preacher-politician carefully, not entirely sure if he was happy about the visit, and exchanged perfunctory greetings.

"We need to talk privately," Jesse said. "Where's the bathroom?"

Sharpton sent out again for some food, because Diane's cousins still hadn't eaten. When the food arrived the funeral director told Jackson he had a private room where he and the family could sit, talk, and eat. Moses flew into an immediate rage.

"What the fuck is this? I've got to eat in a car like a dog because you tell me we can't eat in here and now that he's here you got a room all of a sudden where we can eat as soon as someone comes that can get you some publicity, and I'm the one that's paying you? What's the story, man? What's the matter with you?"

Sharpton calmed him down and gathered the family, the Daughtrys, Jackson, and the officers in the conference room.

Jackson's words of condolence were compassionate and gentle. He told Moses that his own son, also named Yusuf, could have been the victim of this terrible crime.

"We must look for the good in these things somehow," Jackson said.

"I don't know about any good in this, Reverend Jackson. What I want is justice," Moses said.

"Well," Jackson said, "that is something that I understand, but you see there is some good that can come out of it, that could come out of it. That boy laying in there in that casket could be the reason David Dinkins becomes mayor."

Moses bristled again and jumped to his feet, startling Sharpton. He began to shout.

"Wait a minute! Don't be equating my son with anyone's politics! We got nothing to do with nobody's politics and we don't care who becomes mayor! How can you stand there and—"

The angry father's tirade was interrupted by a policeman.

"Excuse me, we've got to clear the building. There's been a bomb threat," he said.

Sharpton stepped up to Jackson, shocked at the churlish impropriety of Jackson's remarks. He pointed a finger at Jackson's chest.

"You're the bomb that the threat is about, Jesse," he said. "How could you come in here and say that about Dinkins, talking about politics? You stayed away and didn't fight with us—Howard Beach, Tawana—and now you come in here talking politics about David Dinkins. That man don't care about David Dinkins, he lost a son."

Daughtry followed Moses into the hallway as the police repeated their order. The building had to be cleared.

"I ain't leaving," Moses said. "If I'm gonna die I'm gonna die with my son. Just leave us alone."

He went into the viewing room, looking at the casket with his back to Daughtry, who tried to repair the damage caused by Jackson's gaffe.

"Mr. Stewart, please don't blame Reverend Jackson. It's my fault, I didn't brief him about—I didn't explain—" Daughtry said.

A chastened Jackson walked into the viewing room with Sharpton and the cousins.

"I will view the body, and we can all join hands and pray," Jackson said.

They formed a prayer circle as Moses tried visibly to hold back his anger.

"You don't have to explain nothin'. I understand," Moses said to Daughtry as they all held hands, his emphasis on the last syllable.

Jackson then left the building to the excited cheers of the assemblage outside and held a press conference, a move that further angered Stewart.

"Rev, go stop him," Moses said to Sharpton. "How the hell is he out there holding a press conference not even authorized by us, after what he said in here? Please go stop him."

Sharpton told him that making a scene by interrupting the press conference would be a disservice to Yusuf's memory.

"Just let it go," he said.

Suddenly they could hear loud boos from the crowd outside.

"That's got to be Ed Koch," Sharpton said.

Koch looked pale and a bit shaken as his characteristically rumpled frame strode into the funeral parlor. He was flanked by an army of police officers.

In the private room that had seen the firestorm sparked by Jesse Jackson's comments a half-hour before Koch greeted Sharpton by pinching him on the cheek. Sharpton returned the handshake and the pinch.

"Al, how've you been? How's James Brown?" Koch asked.

"He's fine," Sharpton replied. Koch knew that Sharpton spoke to the jailed musician on a regular basis.

The mayor greeted Moses and expressed his regrets and condolences.

"I'd give a million dollars to show people that you and Koch talk civilized in private," Moses said to Sharpton, dumbfounded at the chemistry between the mayor and the firebrand preacher.

Sharpton and Koch had long been at odds on a number of issues, but there was always a mutual respect between them. The activist regarded Koch as someone who was always straightforward, and even when the two had bitter disagreements there was never any question about the mayor's motives. That was the difference between Koch and Mario Cuomo, so far as Sharpton was concerned. Cuomo might say things that he liked to hear, but it always seemed to amount to nothing more than lip service.

Koch and Moses spoke, and Koch offered a five-thousand-dollar donation from an unnamed friend to help cover the funeral expenses.

"If you need anything, come see me. If you need work, I think we can get you a job or something. We can work something out," Koch said, as he and Moses walked to the viewing room where each prayed silent prayers.

It was time for the mayor to leave, and Sharpton and Moses offered to walk him out.

"You don't have to do that," Koch said.

"It's all right," Sharpton replied, as Moses nodded. "If you hadn't come I would have criticized you, so how can I be critical that you came, and let you deal with all those angry people out there?"

Koch, Sharpton, and Moses headed for the back door as the mayor's driver, careful of the many people who were now pushing past the barricades, swung in reverse to the loading-dock area. The crowd began to surge toward the dock as uniformed police, clearly outnumbered, tried to keep up. There was running and shouting, and the frightening sound of breaking glass as the security men half-pushed, half-carried Koch into the back seat. The driver, still in reverse, hit the accelerator hard as a scattered group of about twenty blacks ran toward the Cadillac, pursued by confused police officers and television camera crews, who had broken out of the barricades of their assigned area, followed by more of the crowd.

"No-good racist motherfucker!" somebody yelled, and there were more epithets as an iced-tea bottle glanced off the left front fender, but in a siren blast Ed Koch was gone.

The crowd that had broken off rejoined the main group of mourners in front on Troy Avenue, and all stood vigil. Relatives came and went through the glass doors. One, identifying himself only as Yusuf's uncle and the first name Jim, kept walking back and forth, in and out, talking to anyone who would listen.

"All I want to see is justice," he said, shaking his head. "That boy was clean-cut. He didn't drink, he didn't smoke, no drugs. . . . All I want is justice."

The elderly man paused for a moment and then continued.

"That boy never hurt nobody," he said, talking as if a lump were rising in his throat. "Justice is that that boy that shot him should be tried by a jury and if he's convicted he should go to jail and pay."

The man took out a handkerchief, looked at the sky, and before returning to the funeral home said one more thing.

"I don't believe in an eye for an eye," he said quietly. "That's the old way . . . that's the way to be lost." And then he was gone, through the double glass doors.

The crowd looked menacingly at the only white faces there, which belonged to a few print reporters and the majority of cops. A representative of the funeral home came outside and addressed them.

"The family is very grateful for your support, but the funeral home is closed except for family members. You may all wish to go home and pray, but remember if you stay outside that only family members may come in." But nobody left, and cousin Walter stood outside identifying family for the police officers at the doors.

The television cameras left as daylight began to wane. Throughout the afternoon the humidity had been building steadily, along with the emotions on the avenue, until suddenly the sky violently erupted into a torrent of blood-hot rain that pounded in time to a rising wail from the locked-out mourners, who began to pray out loud.

"It's raining! It's raining for the boy! He never going to see the rain again and it's raining for him! Praise God!" one woman with a West Indian accent shouted. Her voice was joined by a chorus of others, shrieking above the sound of the pounding rain. It was one big outdoor, spontaneous church service that ended with the last of the raindrops.

In full darkness the crowd dissipated, headed for the subway on Utica Avenue and a few parked cars as the rainwater flowed down the curbside into the storm drains. Troy Avenue took on the tentative coolness of a forehead with a fever that has broken.

With the sidewalk almost empty, the family left the funeral home and got into waiting cars.

There were a few orange flyers scattered about on the sidewalk that said, "Justice for Yusef [sic] and for Huey Newton . . . meet at Grand Army Plaza . . . bring a subway token."

It was an invitation for what would be first blood in the Bensonhurst-related protests.

REQUIEM

* * *

The following day close to a thousand mourners gathered at Glover Memorial Church for the funeral. To the chagrin of the church elders, Louis Farrakhan had come as promised, along with the bow-tied and zombielike Fruit of Islam, the young men chosen as his personal guard.

Governor Cuomo was kept waiting outside the church before he could enter, and although some observers said the delay was a deliberate snub engineered by Sharpton, the minister claims that he had nothing to do with it.

"That was because of the security arrangements, and I wasn't involved with any of those. Farrakhan's people handled that," Sharpton said.

Once again the mourners were a who's who of political clout in the city. Besides the governor and the mayor, David Dinkins and a number of other politicians attended and heard Sharpton's invocation:

"We came today to bury one of our children. It would be easy to be bitter. It would be easy to attack. But the first thing we must all do is examine ourselves because there is something that all of us are not doing right. When our children are pitted against each other at a tender age, when young black children are getting buried and young white children keep feeling justified, there's something that we're not doing right. I'm looking at the man in the mirror. It's time for us to change our ways. . . . But this time they are going to pay, they're going to pay, Yusuf."

The overflow crowd outside the church, listening to the services on loudspeakers, broke into applause, as they did when Farrakhan spoke.

"The Jews say never again, and now we, too, say never again!" Farrakhan said.

After the services the funeral cortege, headed by police cars with their lights flashing, made its way to Cemetery of the Evergreens in East New York, not far from the house on Hegeman Avenue.

The mourners were not aware that four miles away, in downtown Brooklyn, a grand jury had already indicted Keith Mondello and Pasquale Raucci. The top charge was murder in the second degree.

137

MY NAME IS JOEY FAMA . . .

O NE of the saddest places in the borough of Brooklyn is the Criminal Court building, located at 110 Schermerhorn Street. The six-story granite courthouse is a massive neoindustrial structure that takes up half a city block on the seamier end of the downtown area. Each morning shortly before nine o'clock the "line-up" starts outside. Regardless of the weather, hundreds of men, women, and children stand outside waiting for court officers to unlock the doors of justice, which are closed at one in the morning and open up eight and one-half hours later. The daily crowd is overwhelmingly black and Hispanic. Some are criminal defendants out on bail or their own recognizance, others are crime victims who have come to speak of the harm others have done to them, while still others are victims of domestic violence who must follow a complex and rigorous procedure of verifying their accusations.

The proceedings and procedures at the City Criminal Court building bear little resemblance to the more dignified administration of justice in the nearby state trial courts or the federal court down the street.

Families awaiting friends or loved ones besiege the first-floor clerk's window with questions, constantly asking when the arrested party will be arraigned. The answer is usually always the same. Maybe today. It depends on when the paperwork comes. Sometimes it takes more than a day or two. Sometimes not.

The families of James Patino and Charles Stressler, however, knew that their sons would be arraigned Wednesday morning. Like Mondello, Raucci, and Curreri, the two had been placed in a protective unit of the tanks while awaiting their turn before the judge, and rather than arraignment in night court they would appear before Judge Seymour Gerschwer on the fourth floor.

Gerschwer is an affable-looking, large fellow with a receding shock of blond hair whose overall appearance, even without his robes, spells *judge* in capital letters. He is liked and respected by the members of the Brooklyn bar who ply their trade before him. A former Borscht-Belt comedian, the judge is known for sometimes acerbic wit. His court calendar, always full to capacity, is run smoothly.

A motion by attorneys for Raucci, Mondello, and Curreri to have their clients remain seated with their families in the courtroom because of the volatile nature of the case had been made and honored. Several rows in the front were reserved for sketch artists and reporters, who came in droves, although there was difficulty seeing past the sea of white-shirted court officers who ringed the well area.

In a corner of the well, to the right of the judge, stood Elizabeth Holtzman. In her eight years as Brooklyn District Attorney she had not been known to appear in a courtroom, to anyone's recollection. Her personal style was low-key and low-profile, and she preferred to leave the drum-beating to a capable corps of press assistants.

A Kings County grand jury had been hearing testimony since Monday, and Stephen Murphy was informed that there might be an indictment against his client, Mondello.

"Your Honor," began Bruce McIntyre of Holtzman's homicide bureau. "There has been action by the grand jury this morning. With respect to the defendant Keith Mondello the grand jury has returned an indictment charging the defendant with two counts of murder in the second degree. . . . With respect to the defendant Pasquale Raucci the grand jury has returned an indictment of two counts of murder in the second degree. . . ."

Susan Mondello, Keith's mother, wanted to stand up and scream, to say something. But she could not. She thought she was going to pass out.

Murphy, who was already standing, seemed to jump when he heard the word *murder*. He fully expected a charge of assault against

139

his client, which was what he was arrested for. But murder was something beyond his comprehension.

"Your Honor," he began, his voice already raised and echoing against the marble walls. "This is nothing more than a political indictment. I'm asking that a special prosecutor be appointed. This is the most absurd indictment that I've ever seen! They know he's not the shooter . . . at the line-up there was one person who identified him as being there who was present at the scene among the three black men, and he said that my client did absolutely nothing. How can they return a murder indictment? It's absurd! They know who the shooter is! They're looking for the shooter supposedly for a week now, and almost everybody has indicated that one person did this." Murphy's carotid artery was bulging; he looked as if he was going to have a stroke.

"After they returned the indictment they bring Ms. Holtzman down here for the big political interview and everything else! That's an absurdity! This is a travesty of justice. They can't try this case, Judge."

Gerschwer listened patiently. It was Bruce McIntyre's turn to speak again: "Your Honor, since the defendants Raucci and Mondello have been indicted we are requesting that they be remanded."

The Mondello and Raucci family members, scattered throughout the courtroom, collectively gasped.

Murphy looked disgusted.

"On behalf of my client, Judge, he has no intention of fleeing any jurisdiction. He is here today, he has received death threats. He has risked his life coming here today," Murphy said.

Several of the defendants and their families had reported seeing carloads of blacks passing by their homes.

"They'd just stop and look and drive on," Matthew Mari, Curreri's attorney, said that day. There were also phone calls.

McIntyre spoke up again.

"The circumstances have obviously changed from when the defendant's bail was originally set. Now he's facing a minimum of fifteen years to life. The people are asking that you remand, especially in light of the fact that one of the people with whom the defendant may have acted in concert may have already fled the jurisdiction. We ask the Court that defendant Mondello be remanded."

Murphy was livid, and as he retorted he looked like an angry child threatening to hold his breath. He did everything but stamp his feet. Murphy pointed toward his client as he shouted, "He's not the one who did the shooting! Gina Feliciano, she's a crackhead! And she caused this whole thing!"

In a calm and collected baritone, Judge Gerschwer said he would not make any recommendation for a special prosecutor.

Neil Ruskin, Pasquale Raucci's attorney, was next.

"I would ask Your Honor to show some courage with regard to this matter," Ruskin said. "I'm going to ask that Your Honor not be intimidated by the fact that the District Attorney is here, and that she has two or three other assistants with her, and that the media is here. Unfortunately, Judge, this case is being tried by the media and in the media. These are not rich people. This is not a Howard Beach. The District Attorney would like you to believe that it is a Howard Beach. The District Attorney's office is using this case for political purposes. Obviously Ms. Holtzman needs as much publicity as possible."

McIntyre reiterated his request that Raucci and Mondello be re-manded, but Judge Gerschwer refused to grant the motion. Bail was continued at a hundred thousand for Mondello and seventy-five thousand for Raucci and Curreri. Patino and Stressler were freed on seventy-five thousand each. And Elizabeth Holtzman held a press conference.

At the press conference the DA introduced some of the bureau chiefs and detectives who had been working on the case, then reiter-ated what was contained in the indictments.

When substantive questions about the investigation were asked, however, she usually said that she could not comment, and answered other questions with a pat, prepared statement: "We are going to see that justice is done in this case, and that it is investigated thoroughly and fairly."

Raucci and Mondello were out of the courthouse in an instant, shielded by their families, who were deeply concerned about the possibility of violence against the defendants. The assembled collection of unfortunates waiting to get into the courthouse smiled, waved, and mugged for the television cameras as the defense attorneys gave statements about what they regarded as an outrageous development.

Other people in the courthouse were not happy that day as well. Legal aid attorneys, who bear the brunt of the labor in the criminal court, were astounded at what they called "preferential treatment" given to the defendants. In a letter to Deputy Chief Administrative Judge Milton Mollen they complained of procedural discrepancies. A total of sixty-nine lawyers signed the letter, the first being legal aid staff attorney Abby Warshowsky.

> We represent thousands of poor men and women who come through the criminal justice system daily, the majority of whom are people of color, who do not receive [these considerations] . . . [these defendants] have not been subjected to the intolerable conditions faced by our clients as they are processed through the system. If this treatment is available for these defendants, it must be made available for all. . . . [These] defendants were permitted to remain seated in the courtroom with their families . . . scattered around the courtroom. The defense counsels merely acknowledged their presence. Our clients are never given this kind of consideration or privilege. . . . As is the custom in Brooklyn when an individual is indicted on murder charges the District Attorney's office requested that Judge Seymour Gerschwer remand them. The judge refused to do so. Any one of our clients facing similar charges would have been remanded by Judge Gerschwer without a second thought—that is the practice in Kings County and he has been known to put people in for less cause. . . . This demonstrated bias is inexcusable.

There were other expressions of unfair treatment that week, from the community of Bensonhurst itself. Leaders of Italian-American organizations in the area and elected representatives such as Assemblyman Steve Barbaro decried the picture that had been painted of the neighborhood as a bastion of reactionary racism.

"These were just stupid kids," many of the community leaders said. "They are not representative of the people of Bensonhurst."

The reaction to the Bensonhurst march and a never-ending stream of stories about the murder kept a spotlight glaring on the once-quiet community. Residents objected to the characterizations of the neighborhood as racist by noting that the killing was purely a case of mistaken identity.

"The fact that this was a mistake does not negate the racial overtones," Police Commissioner Benjamin Ward said at Elizabeth Holtzman's press conference after the indictments were announced.

The big question on reporters' minds was what progress police had made in locating Fama, and whether he was indeed still being sought as the trigger man.

"We just want to talk to him," Ward said.

Police officials have to be careful how they publicly refer to someone they wish to "talk to." An open reference to Fama as the suspected shooter by Ward could jeopardize how authorities may have planned on handling him.

At a Brooklyn station house, meanwhile, detectives were questioning another young man who had been at the schoolyard the night of the shooting. Joseph Serrano, who according to Phyllis D'Agata had passed the murder weapon to Joey Fama, had surrendered to police after securing the services of Al Aronne and James DePietro, Brooklyn lawyers with offices not far from the courthouse. Serrano was charged with assault, and later he, too, was released on seventy-five thousand dollars bail.

It is sometimes difficult for New York City residents to realize that an entirely different world exists away from the noise, bright lights, crime, and pollution they take so much in stride. There are places, with clean sidewalks and main streets called Main Street, where law enforcement does not turn a blind eye to "small" drug-related offenses and where all murders regardless of the race or social status of the victim are front-page news.

Sergeant Joseph Redmond of the Oneonta Police Department

knows only too well what happens in places where unlawful activity is allowed to flourish, and that the distance between Oneonta and his native Brooklyn is in many ways far greater than the hundred eighty miles he travels to visit his Bay Ridge in-laws every Thanksgiving.

Upstate cities like Oneonta get the New York City papers, and Redmond made a mental note of the picture of Joseph Fama that appeared on the front page of the *Daily News* earlier in the week. As a former Brooklynite, Redmond had a passive interest in the Bay Ridge Avenue incident.

Wednesday the thirtieth started out as a routine night for Redmond. Hartwick College and the State University of New York have campuses in Oneonta, which sometimes makes late hours busy for the twenty-eight-officer department, although the crime rate is low compared to other places. Oneonta's first homicide that year had only just occurred in July, when a young girl was struck and killed by an automobile that left the scene.

Shortly after 2:00 A.M. Redmond and his partner, Officer Kenneth Olsen, spotted a young man near a local store and saw in his hand something that looked suspicious. A quick check determined that the young man was carrying a bag of marijuana, and he was arrested. Redmond and Olsen placed the handcuffed suspect in the back of their car and drove to 79 Main Street, a municipal building erected in 1983 that houses the police and fire departments as well as some city offices.

Inside the building, they walked past a wall case filled with trophies won by the fire and police departments and through a hallway to the police department door.

A stranger who looked vaguely familiar to the sergeant was seated in a chair near the booking desk. He had close-cropped dark hair and a prominent nose, wore two-tone black-and-gray jeans with a sweatshirt, was well-groomed, and could easily have been one of the students who attended school in the college town.

While Redmond and Olsen were arresting their drug suspect the young man had walked into the station and announced to the officer on the desk, "My name is Joey Fama and I'm wanted for a murder

Sixteen-year-old Yusuf K. Hawkins, from a family photo. (*New York Daily News*)

Above: Leading the September 2, 1989 march through Bensonhurst to protest the release of the suspects involved in the Hawkins killing were (from right to left) Yusuf's father, Moses Stewart, the Reverend Al Sharpton, Yusuf's younger brother Amir, activist lawyer C. Vernon, and Yusuf's older brother Freddie. (AP/Wide World Photos)

Opposite, top: As black activists marched through Bensonhurst, they were met by crowds of neighborhood youths who shouted "Niggers go home!" and other racial epithets. (AP/Wide World Photos)

Opposite, bottom: White counterprotesters waved watermelons at marchers while others insisted the neighborhood was not racist. (NYT Pictures/Michelle Agins)

Opposite, top: In the middle of a heated mayoral campaign, incumbent New York City mayor Edward Koch came under considerable fire. (David Cantor)

Opposite, bottom: Students and Youth Against Racism protested the death of Yusuf Hawkins in front of Mayor Koch's apartment. (*Newsday*/Richard Lee)

Above: In part because of the influence of a black community galvanized by the slaying of Yusuf Hawkins, David N. Dinkins defeated Ed Koch in the Democratic primary election in September 1989 and went on to become New York City's first black mayor. (Marty Lederhandler)

Above: As the investigation of the killing dragged on, demonstrators continued to march through Bensonhurst, demanding swift justice. As usual, at a March 3, 1990 demonstration, columns of police separated marchers from spectators. (*Newsday/ Donna Dietrich*)

Opposite, top: As Brooklyn District Attorney, Elizabeth Holtzman pursued an acting-in-concert prosecution of the suspects. (*New York Daily News*)

Opposite, bottom: Charles Hynes (right) succeeded Holtzman as Brooklyn District Attorney in January 1990. (*New York Daily News*)

Above: Keith Mondello (center), who was seen as the ringleader of the Bensonhurst gang, with his attorney, Stephen Murphy, during early proceedings in Brooklyn criminal court in May 1990. (*New York Daily News*)

Right: Joseph Fama, from the collage seized by police at Sal the Squid's store to make the first identifications. Fama was accused of firing the fatal shots. (*New York Daily News*)

Gina Feliciano as she arrived to testify on April 24, 1990. (AP/Wide World Photos)

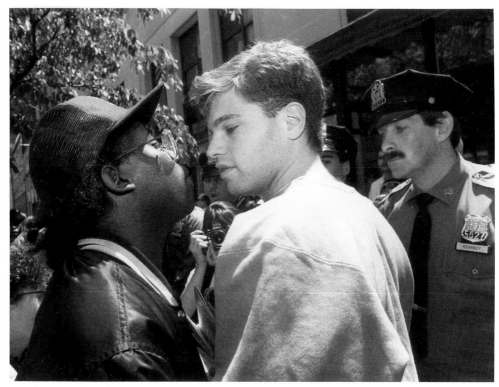

Tensions were high during jury deliberations for the Bensonhurst defendants. On May 15, 1990, outside a restaurant where Stephen Murphy was having lunch, a near riot was quelled by police. (AP/Wide World Photos)

The Hawkins family's jubilation after Joseph Fama's conviction was quickly replaced by shock and dismay after Keith Mondello was acquitted of murder and manslaughter charges on May 18, 1990. Al Sharpton accompanied Yusuf's parents, Moses Stewart and Diane Hawkins, out of the courthouse after hearing the verdict. (AP/Wide World Photos)

With Mondello's acquittal on murder charges, angry protests broke out in front of the courthouse. Demonstrators burned an American flag. (AP/Wide World Photos)

At a march led by Sharpton the day after the Mondello verdict, Bensonhurst spectators show their approval of the verdict. (AP/Wide World Photos)

Charles Stressler as he arrived at the beginning of his trial, which ended in a mistrial. In a second trial he was acquitted of all charges. (*New York Daily News*)

Left: Joseph Serrano (flanked by his mother and his attorney) was convicted of possession of a baseball bat and given probation. (*New York Daily News*)

Below: James Patino leaving Brooklyn Criminal Court under police guard after a pretrial hearing. He was acquitted of all charges. (*New York Daily News*)

After the sentencing of Fama and Mondello on June 11, 1990, Moses Stewart and Al Sharpton left Brooklyn State Supreme Court showing a strong front. (AP/Wide World Photos)

in Brooklyn." Suddenly the *Daily News* picture Redmond had seen took on far greater significance.

Redmond found a number in New York City and called. After several rings a telephone was picked up.

"This is Sergeant Redmond from the Oneonta PD. We've got someone here, a Joseph Fama? He says he's wanted for a murder down there...."

The officer on the other end gave Redmond another number to dial. He called and got a detective at Brooklyn nightwatch. As he again relayed the information the detective asked perfunctory questions and took down the information Redmond gave him.

"Wait a minute. Did you say Fama?" the voice asked.

"Fama, Joseph Fama," Redmond said.

"You're kidding. All right, uh, listen: What's your telephone number there?" the surprised detective asked.

Redmond gave him the number and the detective told him someone would call back, and to please hold on to the suspect. Nearly two hundred miles south of Oneonta it was like a bomb had fallen. There was a flurry of telephone calls and incredulous cries of "Holy shit, I can't believe it!" as supervisors called their supervisors. In Oneonta, Redmond waited for the telephone to ring and had the feeling that it was going to be a long night.

He chose not to question Fama while he waited for the call, and notified his own superiors. He wished as any cop would that this apprehension had been the result of some slick police work, but it had been just dumb luck.

The worst thing he could do would be to question the short young man who sat patiently near the front desk. Fama had told them he had an attorney. The name Dave DePetris was written on a crumpled piece of paper extricated from some deep pocket in his jeans.

Besides, Redmond didn't know much about this murder except what he had read in the papers. No sense sticking your nose into something that didn't belong to you to begin with only to have it backfire and blow somebody else's work.

Fama was polite and quiet in the police station. All he wanted was for the New York police to come get him and get it over with.

145

The phone rang and New York was on the other end. They wanted a picture of the person Oneonta had, so Redmond had an officer snap a picture of him and faxed it to the number he had been given. New York also faxed a photo back to Redmond. There were lots of bosses getting awakened in the middle of the night in New York, and before they called their bosses they wanted to make sure these upstate cops really had their man.

After another hour, it seemed confirmed that they did, and four New York City detectives began the four-hour drive to Oneonta.

Still seated in the station-house chair, Fama expressed no desire to sleep, although he was offered a cell. He did lay his head down on a desk every so often but didn't seem overly tired.

At four o'clock Redmond sent out for food and Joey ate a sandwich with the cops as he reminisced with Redmond about people and places in Brooklyn and expressed his impatience with waiting for his ride.

Since Redmond and Fama had Brooklyn in common, they chatted about incidental things. Fama said he had gone to New Utrecht High School, and Redmond told him that New Utrecht was where he attended his junior high school graduation. Talk shifted to the Mets and Yankees, and then there was a long silence as Redmond went about other duties and Fama waited.

"When are they flying up?" Fama asked.

"They're not flying, they're driving," Redmond said. This was a disappointment to Fama, who did not look forward to the prospect of being cooped up in a car for four hours before being cooped up again for what he knew might be a long, long time.

"If they fly, I'll pay for the gas," Fama said.

During his talks with Redmond Fama offered no explanation of why he chose Oneonta for his surrender, telling the sergeant that he selected the town at random after hitchhiking and survived on candy bars and potato chips, catching what sleep he could in cars along the way.

Shortly before eight o'clock an unmarked car occupied by the New York City detectives and a New York State Police cruiser pulled up to 79 Main Street and picked up Joey Fama.

Police and government officials were pleased to have Fama in custody, although the "massive manhunt" was not what yielded the suspect. The word *apprehension* was repeatedly used, however, in and out of court proceedings that followed. *Surrender* was a word that never came up in public record, although to speak of surrender would have been truthful and accurate.

Politicians and lawmen praised the nonproductive effort of the manhunt and hoped Fama's arrest would ease the festering tensions that only seemed to get worse. In a statement released through her office, Elizabeth Holtzman spoke as if law enforcement had actively cracked the case: "I am pleased that another suspect in the tragic and senseless racially motivated murder of Yusuf Hawkins has been apprehended."

Governor Cuomo's office also released a statement it considered appropriate, since a State Police cruiser had escorted the New York City detectives and their new charge back to Brooklyn:

"I have directed that the full resources of the State of New York be made available to see that justice is done in this case. Today, the New York State police are assisting the New York City police in returning Joseph Fama to New York for questioning . . . yet another example of the effort and commitment to justice in this case by the New York police, the state and the Brooklyn District Attorney's office."

It is no disrespect to New York State troopers to suggest that their services in escorting the detectives were somewhat less than necessary for justice to be served, or at least no more disrespectful than the suggestion in the governor's release that New York City police needed the troopers to help them find the Thruway.

The troopers and detectives pulled up to the 60th Precinct station house in Brooklyn after noon, sparking a day-long wild-goose chase by photographers and camera crews who tried desperately and unsuccessfully to get a picture of Fama as he was moved from station house to station house for reasons of security and to accommodate other needs of law enforcement.

*   *   *

FOR THE COLOR OF HIS SKIN

While Fama was being processed and questioned and detectives tried to arrange line-ups, a small group of demonstrators led by activist Sonny Carson and others gathered at Grand Army Plaza in Brooklyn in preparation for the march that had been touted on the yellow flyers at the wake of Yusuf Hawkins. Police were monitoring the gathering, which did not appear particularly threatening.

The procession began heading down Flatbush Avenue, past many black-owned businesses and on the periphery of the Park Slope section, with its elegant turn-of-the-century brownstones and town houses. At the head of the march was a wooden coffin with the name Yusuf Hawkins and another that bore the name of Huey Newton. The former Minister of Information of the Black Panther Party had been shot to death in California that same month and some black activists thought the killing one more example of police persecution, although no police officers were shown to be involved in the shooting.

The march proceeded with a small contingent of escorting police officers past Prospect Place, then past St. Mark's, down the street from Al Sharpton's house. As it progressed men and women came out of their houses and businesses. Many blacks had been angered that Raucci and Mondello were not jailed while awaiting trial on the murder charges.

Suddenly the class lines that had kept higher-echelon African-Americans off of the march lines disappeared, and many professionals wearing business suits and ties joined the march, swelling the number of participants until there was a huge crowd at the intersection of Flatbush and Atlantic avenues, not far from where the Hawkins family was meeting with Elizabeth Holtzman.

On the fourth floor of the Brooklyn Municipal Building on Joralemon Street Holtzman assured the family, accompanied by Reverend Sharpton, that "justice would be done" in the prosecution of those responsible for killing Yusuf. She disclosed at that time, according to Sharpton, that murder indictments would continue to be sought against those believed responsible, and an agreement was made that no plea bargains would be made or other deals entered into without the knowledge of the family.

148

The meeting was an agreeable one, according to Sharpton, except for a minor disagreement after it was over. As the family was leaving the conference room and heading toward a reception-area door Holtzman walked next to Diane Hawkins, who was still numb and unaware of what the family later termed an attempt at photo opportunity. Photographers were outside the reception area, and their cameras flashed—just after Sharpton and Shawkee Mohammed, Sharpton's bodyguard, maneuvered to get Diane between them. No one spoke about the incident to Holtzman.

Gerry Mullany, the United Press International New York bureau chief, saw activist Sonny Carson leading the assemblage, and remembered having received word that there might be a protest march and deciding to check it out on the way to his Brooklyn home. "At first it was a couple of hundred people," Mullany recalls. "Then it went down through Flatbush and there were people who came out of their offices. It seemed to swell, and Sharpton was leading."

It was when the people converged on Tillary Street, a broad avenue that leads to the Brooklyn Bridge, that trouble began.

Mullany was on the telephone at the corner of Tillary and Cadman Plaza, near the federal courthouse. He already had notes on the march and had begun to phone them in when he was heckled by a black woman. At first she told him that she had the phone first.

"She was calling me a racist white bigot and trying to draw attention to me," Mullany recalls. The bureau chief demurred, insisting that all he wanted to do was use the telephone.

"Then I just got out of there quickly," he says.

There were several hundred police officers at the foot of the Brooklyn Bridge decked out in riot gear when the marchers turned the corner and started to cross. The line of blue was four officers deep, and confused drivers coming over the bridge into Brooklyn had fear etched on their faces as they saw the angry crowd. One of the first cars to come off the ramp was a station wagon driven by a Hassidic Jew, who was visibly shaken as the crowd, now a mindless mob, began to jump over his car and the hoods of others chanting antiwhite slogans.

The crowd was past the thousand mark, and many in the front

lines were young men, angry at being black in New York and gleeful that, perhaps for the first time ever, they had a contingent of New York City police officers in a defensive posture.

A few objects were thrown and soon there was the sound of breaking glass. The coffins became a rallying point for the pressing throng, and either by accident or purposefully—nobody knows for sure—one of them fell and was broken during a scuffle. Gerry Mullany remembers that the crowd became louder and more vocal as they neared the wall of officers:

"I got up there [by the bridge] and the cops were pretty shaky. . . . Sonny Carson was sort of appealing for calm, and by the time everybody got to the bridge some were starting to pick up sticks and bottles and that's when the violence all started. Some started throwing bottles at the cops."

Mullany says that some of the restraining tactics used by police against the demonstrators appeared harsh but also that the police seemed in many instances to be restraining themselves from overt excessive force. The overwhelming majority of police officers at the bridge were white, in contrast to what was described as a "98-percent black crowd." The sight of white officers using force against black marchers infuriated some in the crowd, and the violence escalated. Nightsticks began to wail in the air as the police officers tried to keep the crowd from taking the bridge. One police captain was helped away, covered with blood. It was not clear whether he had been hit by a bottle or received his injury some other way.

Mullany watched as the crowd became louder and more determined. One black woman grabbed his notebook as another chastised her: "You're not going to help your cause that way."

Large numbers of people in the crowd seemed bent on violence, but the leaders continued their call for calm, eventually leading them toward Fulton Street. Mullany and other reporters followed, watching as the angry blacks catcalled white employees of a pizzeria on Fulton Street.

Most of the people inside the shop were black, and the demonstrators called to them not to patronize the white business. "It almost looked like a scene from *Do the Right Thing*," one reporter recalled.

Terrified, the pizza-store employees began to shoo out their customers, trying to be polite as they frantically closed their gates.

"What was interesting was the broad base of the protest," Mullany says. "It was obvious people were extremely angry, and some of the voices you heard were sort of enraged, but the whole case of people criticizing me, calling me a racist, was discouraging. It was a summer day and people seemed really agitated." Mullany added that the behavior appeared reflective of the frustrations born of a racial situation in New York that went back far beyond August 23.

As Mullany covered the protest-turned-riot he paid special attention to the leaders, whom he sees normally characterized as provocative militants who will do anything for violence.

"But that was not necessarily true," he says. "Many people who were bent on violence that night were frustrated people; they wanted to disrupt. But the leaders sort of short-circuited that violence, which was pretty impressive."

United Press International reported that a total of seventy-five hundred people had taken part in the protest. Twenty-three police officers were injured, and there was a total of four arrests.

There are two all-news radio stations in New York, WCBS and WINS. Both reported on the Brooklyn Bridge incident, as did other New York stations. But on the porches and stoops of Canarsie near the station house where Joseph Fama was being questioned by detectives the sound of the newsradio stations dominated. Residents were curious about what was going on in the precinct, certainly, but also fearful of rumors that the angry blacks at the bridge were headed to their quiet neighborhood to lynch Fama.

The rumors were, of course, unfounded, but a ripple of excitement went through the few curiosity-seekers when Al Sharpton showed up at the station house with Shawkee Mohammed. According to Sharpton, he had received a call from Claude Stanford's mother. Her son had been with the police for some time, she said, and she was worried.

The precinct captain invited him to leave and words were exchanged. A livid Sharpton, speechless for one of the few times in his life, stormed out of the station house with Mohammed close behind. They refused to speak to reporters before driving away.

It was already past five o'clock, and the planned line-ups were delayed. Fama's attorney, Dave DePetris, had not shown up yet at the station house, and there were delays in getting ringers—people to stand in the line-up alongside Fama.

Finally, shortly after six o'clock, DePetris arrived with his partner, Stanley Meyer, and they disappeared inside the precinct house. About an hour later they emerged and were besieged by reporters, who asked them what had transpired.

"Nobody picked him out in the line-up," DePetris said. "Joseph Fama was never there."

Still, on the basis of statements by Gina Feliciano, Phyllis D'Agata, Charles Stressler, Keith Mondello, and others, Joseph Fama was formally arrested for the murder of Yusuf Hawkins. By then, a large contingent had gathered outside, enjoying the evening warmth of the last night of August. Just in time for the tail end of the eleven-o'clock news shows Fama, looking very small, walked outside as two policemen held his arms gently.

There were alternating cheers and boos from the crowd, and across Joe Fama's face was the slightest hint of a smirk, as if he were savoring this brief moment of fame. The back door of the Plymouth Fury sedan slammed shut and the car took off while kids in shorts, looking just like the kids of Bensonhurst, mugged for the television cameras.

Suddenly there were bright sparks of light and the sound of an explosion. A police lieutenant tripped over his own foot as he hit the pavement, protecting himself from whatever it was. Some police officers scattered, and then there was relief. There had been no sniper, no terrorist attack on the precinct or an attempt on Joseph Fama's life. A television live truck, its huge antenna pole still extended, had snagged on high-tension wires, and that was what caused the commotion.

In the back of the police car Fama said little to the detectives who escorted him to Brooklyn Central Booking, except to inquire about two of his friends. Referring to Serrano and Patino, Fama said, "Are

152

Jimmy and Joey okay? I hope those guys are okay. They're like brothers to me."

Earlier in the day, while reporters were trying to find out where Fama was being held, a thirteen-year-old boy with a ducktail haircut pulled on a reporter's shirttail at the 62nd Precinct in Bensonhurst.

"Is it true the blacks are coming here to march on the feast?"

The reporter hadn't heard anything about such a thing and said so. As the possibilities rolled over in his mind he shook his head. Even Al Sharpton wouldn't try something that crazy.

OTHER MARCHES, OTHER VOICES

THE high point of the Bensonhurst summer is the Feast of Santa Rosalia, held during the week of Labor Day. Eighteenth Avenue is magically transformed into a carnival midway with the arrival of trailers and erection of booths for games of chance, food stands, and children's rides, including live ponies.

Young men in the booths leer at pretty girls and women who try to shame their boyfriends or husbands into risking a quarter or a dollar on the toss of a ball or aim of a dart, their voices blending in with the cacophony of disco music, spinning roulette wheels, ringing bells, and the hiss of sausages sizzling on hot grills, thick coiled snakes sweating olive oil.

Food is undoubtedly the biggest attraction at the carnival. Osso bucco, hot and sweet sausages with roasted green peppers, spaghetti with sauce made right at the stands, clams on the half shell, wine and beer, and the zeppole that dunk and bob in vats of hot, bubbling fat, are all available in abundance.

For the devout, the focus of the feast is the saint in whose honor it is held. Her statue, brought to Brooklyn from Italy in 1978, is ensconced in a small shrine near the storefront office of the Società de Santa Rosalia at Seventy-second Street. It is the likeness of a young girl in a simple brown robe, a human skull beside her feet. Bills of different denominations are pinned to the saint's dress, which is real cloth, and below her platform is a small wood-and-glass display case holding jewels, keys, pictures of babies.

John Balando, a small, thin man with white hair and eyeglasses,

154

points proudly to the display case. Although born in this country, his speech is laced with the idiosyncrasies of heavy Sicilian dialect. "She got the diamond, the gold, everything there. The people donate, they pray. They believe in miracles. They put the baby's picture and she protect the baby," he says.

On September 2 word had already reached the hawkers and sausage makers at the feast that angry blacks might come marching in the neighborhood, only this time they would be heading for the feast itself.

Al Sharpton was at home early Saturday morning, returning reporters' calls.

Bensonhurst's reaction to the first march had been frightening in many respects, but another march was guaranteed coverage for the movement. A line had been drawn on Twentieth Avenue, in a community that said we don't want you here and don't come back. The marchers vowed to return, and so the stage was set for conflict, which would bring the cameras. If conflict was the only way to draw media attention to racism, that was what they would get.

"We're leaving the Slave at two o'clock," Sharpton told a reporter on the telephone. "We're going to get on the bus and we're going to Twentieth Avenue and Sixty-seventh Street, then we're marching to Eighteenth Avenue."

The reporter's next question was answered before it was asked.

"We're going to the feast," Sharpton said. When asked the purpose of what was certain to be seen by the Bensonhurst community as no less than an invasion, the minister spoke as if he were addressing a small child who had asked an incredibly stupid question.

"The purpose is these defendants are out free on Labor Day to enjoy their Italian feast and Yusuf is dead."

White people are not welcome at the Slave Theater except on special occasions when the press is invited. Even then, however, strict rules are enforced by UAM security personnel, and the white media's presence is tolerated rather than welcomed.

As prayers issued from the mosque across the street on Bedford Avenue that Saturday morning, four yellow schoolbuses idled outside the Slave, along with several police vans and unmarked cars. The word had gone out on WLIB that there would be another march, and there was an appreciable response. An older woman carrying a sign that read WE WILL PICK OUR LEADERS accosted a white reporter in the lobby.

"Why don't you stand outside, over there? You are diluting our African purity with your presence," she said. The reporter moved and the woman began hawking copies of *The City Sun*, one of New York's black weeklies. She looked as if she could be somebody's grandmother.

Not all of the attendees were as hostile as that woman or some of the men who nudged reporters and said, "Get the story straight this time, white boy." Others had come for the first time and had no difficulty sharing their feelings.

A well-built black man in his forties emerged from a Cadillac parked across Fulton Street from the theater. "I'm not one for protest marches," he said, before entering the Slave. "I knew about when King marched, of course, but that was a different time. But first what they did to that boy, and now what they did when the people marched. I guess the cat's out of the bag. In the South, where I'm from, I can remember that there were water fountains with the signs and we had to sit in the back of the bus. But up here the only difference is there aren't any signs, but the message is still the same. It was the law they fought down there, but here"—he pointed to his head—"it's people's minds. No, I never thought I'd be marching somewhere. But times have changed, I guess."

Jimmy, an auto mechanic, owns his own business in Brooklyn. Others who had come to the Slave were marching for the first time as well.

"The problem is, we go to visit our relatives in the South and we tell them how good everything is up here. It's lies, a lot of it. But you don't want the people back home to think you were all stupid for coming up here. But up here it's bad. I guess we didn't know how bad until this happened."

When everyone was seated Joseph Mack, an activist attorney and African historian, spoke briefly and introduced Al Sharpton.

There were cheers and applause as Sharpton, flanked by security people and with Moses and Diane walking behind him, marched up to the stage. The Hawkins family took seats on the stage and Sharpton stood, a stern expression on his face, sizing up the crowd before him. The applause died down and Sharpton raised his fist in the air.

"No justice!" he boomed.

"No peace!" the crowd answered.

"No justice!" again.

"No peace!"

"What do we want?" The voice was at its full volume now, and the answer echoed against the walls:

"Justice!"

"When do we want it?"

"Now!"

"All right!" Sharpton said, and the crowd applauded again.

Diane, Moses, Freddy, and Amir, seated next to Alton Maddox, were expressionless.

"We're gonna *march* today!" Sharpton hollered, gesturing with his hands as the crowd cheered and a few amens floated up from the front row.

"We gonna march today in Bensonhurst! Gonna meet the enemy because we said we were coming back!" He was on a roll, speaking nonstop.

"Thirty of them killed Yusuf, and the ones they arrested are out on bail! See how fast thirty black men get out on bail if they kill some cracker!" There were some guffaws and then more clapping from the crowd. "Thirty crackers kill Yusuf Hawkins, whose grieving parents are here with me, with all of us! Thirty crackers murder a black child, and they are free to celebrate their Italian feast, eating their pizza, while Yusuf is in the ground. We are going to that feast!" More applause, cheers and amens. "Yes, we are going to the feast! And we're gonna tell them we want thirty! We're gonna tell them they're not gonna rest! We're gonna tell them we want justice!"

The theater broke into wild applause.

157

"In a little while you will be boarding the buses, proud African men and women who are going to say, 'You can't turn us around!' Police can't turn us around! Crackers can't turn us around! We're going to march with dignity. We're going to march for Yusuf!"

The white press was asked to leave the theater at that point, and as the reporters filed out there were catcalls. "Murderers!" somebody shouted.

Then the collection baskets were passed. The money helped pay for the buses and was also used for other projects. UAM money collected in those baskets had helped bury Yusuf Hawkins and also helped Sharpton by supplying his leased car and covering other living expenses. This supplemented income from his speaking engagements and the money his wife Kathy brings in working for the United States government. (She is attached to a Fort Hamilton medical unit.)

After the last of the marchers boarded the buses there was an eerie silence; the tension made it feel like 1963 instead of 1989. Especially tense, their faces grim, were those who had never marched before. The sirens of the escort cars from the Police Department Community Relations Division and the vans with uniformed officers began their back-and-forth *whoop-whoop* sounds, as if they were talking to each other. Between twenty-five and thirty private automobiles with their headlights on queued up behind the buses, forming a motorcade that wound down Fulton Street, turning left onto Franklin Avenue.

On the buses the veterans were more at ease. Some people debated how African-Americans should most effectively react to white racism, and there were a number of "ballot or bullet" debates. Some of the newcomers, hearing talk that seemed radical to them and foreign to their reality, had trouble accepting some of the viewpoints expressed until they remembered why they were going to Bensonhurst. Howard Beach had not just been a mistake of circumstance, a deadly hybrid. White people are killing black people out there, and they are charging killers with assault and letting them out on bail.

A heavy-set, gentle woman on the lead bus, a nurse, spoke.

"I was a little girl when they killed Emmett Till," she said. "I was going to school in South Carolina, and it was mostly black. It was like there was a panic. We heard white people have started to kill

Negroes. They shot this boy and dumped him in the river because he whistled at a white woman, and we were scared. We looked at white people differently then. I don't hate anybody, but I remember how I felt then, and this has got to stop. It can't be happening all over again. I don't want my little girl to be scared."

Jimmy, the mechanic, was driving several people in his black Cadillac, a car or two behind the last bus. His horn joined in the symphony of those that had begun blowing as the motorcade turned onto Eastern Parkway. He waved a beefy arm out his window, calling to black people in a car that was going the other way.

"Come on, come with us!" he called.

"Where are you going?" a woman answered back, shouting above the horns.

"Bensonhurst. We're going down to Bensonhurst for that boy they killed. It's for the boy!"

In Montgomery and Selma blacks and whites joined hands and marched together for freedom, for the right of a people to vote and hold office and have jobs, for the right to be able to live anywhere they wanted. There were the old freedom songs like "Keep Your Eyes on the Prize" and "Oh Freedom" and, of course, "We Shall Overcome." But those ghosts were long ago laid to rest and in their place had developed the rap rhythms of the street and songs like "Fuck tha Police" and "Fight the Power." These marchers, if provoked sufficiently, would fight back. They did not seek violence; many had made that clear. But if it came to violence there would be no submission. There would be violence in kind.

It did not matter if the police with helmets who lined the bus route or the people of Bensonhurst felt the response to the Hawkins murder to be an overreaction. It did not matter even if the facts indicated that the murder of Yusuf Hawkins was not a racially motivated crime, but rather a horrible and tragic mistake. The anger and frustration felt by these people was something that was not captured by the television cameras, yet it had stewed and simmered in Bedford-Stuyvesant and East New York long before the shots were fired on Bay Ridge Avenue, during and before the murder of Michael Griffith in Howard Beach. Murders, arrests, possibly but not necessarily justifiable police killings that made it into the newspapers and then disappeared did not disappear in the streets of Brooklyn and Harlem and Jamaica, Queens. What mattered was their perception, and their perception was that something in New York was very wrong.

Security marshals from the UAM youth group began closing the windows on the buses, and the chattering ceased. There was an electric anticipation inside the bus, becoming hot and stuffy in the afternoon sun. The sight through the bus windows of the riot-helmeted cops was frightening, and the apprehension was palpable. Nobody knew what these people were capable of in Bensonhurst.

The bus cabin was silent as the driver made his way up Twentieth Avenue. The storefronts could not be seen through the wall of police officers, but there was nothing for the window-shopper to look at. The metal gates on most had been pulled down.

Sixty-eighth Street was closed between Twentieth and Twenty-First avenues. The buses rolled through the barricades, which were opened up by the army of cops who manned them, followed by the cars. The silence was broken by someone on the bus who said, ''We're here.''

Slowly and quietly the demonstrators got off the buses. The private cars were directed into the schoolyard that just over a week before had seen young men gathered with bats. Sharpton and the UAM had been at odds with police in the past, but now the New York City Police Department was protecting their First Amendment guarantee of freedom of assembly. The right for a people, any people, to peaceably assemble for the redress of grievances was now being honored on the streets of Brooklyn. But there was a hitch. The group's plans to march to or through the feast would have to be altered. A short man in police uniform with a sparkling white shirt placed his cap on his head and strode forward to meet once again with Al Sharpton. They had met in the past, and he hoped the bridges they had built earlier were sturdy enough to cross.

Assistant Chief Anthony Calzerano looks as though he should be rocking in a chair, leisurely discoursing on the serenity of the world around him. But as commanding officer of the entire block of precincts the police department calls Patrol Borough Brooklyn South, he has been at the center of some of the most potentially lethal conflagrations in New York. His quiet demeanor and seemingly easy-going personality mask a tough street cop endowed with savvy, cunning, and professionalism.

The combined resources of community relations, intelligence information, and deployment of manpower were all components of the tapestry Calzerano, under the supervision of Chief Robert Johnston, had to weave carefully if the march in Bensonhurst was to be kept from escalating into a riot. It was Calzerano's decision to use police motorcycles as moving barricades while the march was in progress, a strategy first deployed in 1988, during civil rights demonstrations in Canarsie, that had worked well.

Calzerano greeted Sharpton and the two men huddled with some of the Community Relations people, joined by representatives of the U.S. Department of Justice.

Calzerano had disturbing intelligence. One of the most popular foods at the feast is zeppole, and the little balls of dough are cooked in huge vats of boiling grease. Word that the marchers would be showered with boiling zeppole oil was not confirmed, but the threat was real enough to insist that the marchers make alternative arrangements. It was not Calzerano's wish to order compliance with a change of plans. Rather he hoped that Sharpton, Maddox, and the other march leaders would see the wisdom of planning a different route.

"He told us right out that they had information they were going to throw the hot oil if we marched over there. Some of these people came with babies in strollers. We couldn't risk that and we decided to cooperate," Sharpton said.

A new route might have been construed as capitulation to the authorities by some members of a group that numbered among its standard chants, "They say get back, we say fight back." Word that someone in Bensonhurst had effectively threatened to boil the marchers in oil could have incited the less forgiving to branch off on a march of their own, so no announcement was made.

In the schoolyard the marchers were ready, four abreast, women on the inside and men on the outside. Sharpton, Moses, Freddy, and Amir locked arms with Bishop Anthony Monk, a Bedford-Stuyvesant cleric and community leader. The motorcycle barricade moved out, the cops not looking left or right. Anyone foolish enough to cross their path would be run down or bumped. Cops on foot, helmeted and with sticks, walked in front of the line of marchers, several hundred strong, followed by patrol cars and Chief Calzerano on foot. Other police cars and the Department of Justice people along with Community Relations cops kept ahead, looking for signs of possible trouble. There were cops on the rooftops and plainclothes cops who began to circulate among the crowds forming on both sides of Twentieth Avenue.

The chanting of the marchers, many in African-style clothing, began to fill the air and mingle with the exhaust and the bike sounds until the entire avenue seemed to be an assault on all five senses. On the sidewalks stood hundreds of counterdemonstrators, some from other neighborhoods. Much of their ire seemed directed at Sharpton, on their signs that read GO HOME YOU FAT FUCK and chants of "Sharpton sucks! Sharpton sucks!"

Some of the marchers had bongos, and their rolling rhythm underscored the steady chant of "Yusuf! Yusuf!" The counterdemonstrators, mostly kids in bright-colored shorts who had stripped to the waist or wore T-shirts, chanted back, "You suck! You suck!" The marchers filed down the avenue and the neighborhood youth, anxious to see a celebrity, raced ahead, some tumbling over each other, to get to the next block for a clearer glimpse of Sharpton. The girls joined in, and at times those on the sidewalks picked up the marchers' chant of "Whose streets? Our streets!" trying to drown out the blacks and pointing to themselves on the word *our*.

There were two separate marches, actually, since the group of counterdemonstrators on both sides of the avenue swelled to the point they had to keep moving ahead. There wasn't enough room between the storefronts and the motorcycle cops, whose blank stares through tinted glasses meant nothing but business.

All the while, behind a phalanx of cops carrying riot shields, Sharpton kept his eyes straight ahead, his jaw set. Moses tried to do the same, but his eyes reflected rage at the thought that, after what had been done here to his son, these people would taunt and jeer a bereaved father. Some of the people on Twentieth Avenue had already formed their opinion. The grieving father wasn't grieving at all; he was hooked up with Sharpton and he must be getting something out of it.

One fourteen-year-old offered a most precocious observation:

"Look. Sharpton has to make money for his cause. So this shooting happened here, and now he comes and gets on television, and he makes more money for his cause. It's very simple."

At Seventy-third Street the taunters ran past the front of St. Dominic's church. A tall figure in a dark cassock stood on the steps. His eyes were tiny thunderclouds as he saw what was happening in his parish. Neatly styled hair and a youthful face gave Father Charles Sergio Fermeglia the look of a screen idol playing the role of priest in a troubled parish. His eyes caught those of Moses and of Sharpton as they passed the church. Later he would say that they seemed to look toward the church for something, he didn't know what exactly. But whatever it was, he knew they wouldn't find it in Bensonhurst.

Near where he stood, on the steps, was a statue of St. Martin de Porres, patron of the poor and disadvantaged.

Reporters tried to draw a comment from the priest, but he stood still and speechless as the statue, acknowledging no one. Particularly, he seemed intent on ignoring those of his young parishioners who ran by, their lips framing words of ignorance and hate.

"I thought the best response was silence," he explained later.

The chants of the demonstrators and counterdemonstrators were louder now on the avenue.

"Go home! Go home!"

"Yusuf, Yusuf!"

"You suck, you suck!"

"Who'd they kill? Yusuf Hawkins!"

At Seventy-sixth Street the marchers halted. They were going to make a U turn on the avenue. Middle-aged women looked out windows with thumbs-down hands; others extended their middle fingers in the air. Suddenly there was a scuffle as some of the whites tried to break through a wall of standing cops. Community Relations cops fought through a tangle of nightsticks, arms, and legs to get to the problem, an intoxicated young man screaming at the top of his lungs. He was hustled away by police and the marchers, flanked by the police on all sides, stood still and quiet. Even the white teenagers quieted down. The motorbike engines had been cut, which made it seem even quieter. There was a rumor on the street that this was where the marchers would break from the cops and begin to riot, ending up eventually at the feast. Some of the young whites looked genuinely frightened. Perhaps, some thought, this had all gone far enough. Once the tactical problem of the U turn was solved, the march continued. So did the jeering, verbal abuse escalating on both sides.

One young black man on the line of march gestured at a group of whites, his hands frantically waving toward himself as if to say "Come on and get me."

The whites gestured in turn.

"Yo, pizza boy! C'mon, man!"

"Wait'll the cops leave and stick around, ya nigger punk," was the reply. But Community Relations cops came to the rescue again. By the time the whites finished talking with the blue-jacketed cops, the black scrapper was way ahead with the march.

The march was progressing back toward the schoolyard, past more counterdemonstrators' signs. One said SUPPORT FRIENDS: KEEP MAYOR KOCH, BACK BENSONHURST.

A sign held by marchers passing Gina Shaughnessy, who has lived in the neighborhood for seventeen years, read BENSONHURST SAVAGES STILL FREE.

Shaughnessy had her own sign: WE ARE ALL GOD'S CHILDREN. DEATH HURTS US ALL.

"People aren't really taking a good look at themselves," she said. "This time I found a little corner to stand on with my sign, but the marchers are not marching with peace in their hearts."

On they went, still chanting, past the Caduti Superca Mola Soccer Club and the Perina and Sons Salumeria and Bakery. At Seventieth Street there was another scuffle. A middle-aged man yelled at the police: "What the fuck is this? I can't go on my own block?" A groundswell of neighborhood boys attracted to the trouble spot began to chant "Send the niggers home" while the police tried to reason with the man, who identified himself as Dominic DeFiore.

"You can go on your block in a minute," a lieutenant told DeFiore.

"Fuck this!"

"You're going to get locked up."

"The blacks can do it! They're walking where they want. Why can't we? They rape our women, they take our jobs, and this thing that happened, just an incident of jealousy . . ."

The marchers stopped near the spot where Yusuf was killed and Bishop Monk led them in prayer. Then, as police cordoned off the block, they filed back into the schoolyard and began boarding the buses. Some called out to the whites: "You are devils!"

One black woman, recognizing a group on the other side of a police barricade as kids who had been chanting while Monk was praying, said, "Why don't you devils learn how to pray?"

While the demonstration was winding down a small group of white kids started walking past the school on Twentieth Avenue, down toward Sixty-seventh Street. They wore the uniform of the day, multicolored shorts and T-shirts or no shirts at all.

One taller kid said, "Quiet, we'll go around this way. Let's pull the niggers off the buses."

In a chilling reenactment of what might have happened on the same block over a week earlier, the crowd of young men grew until there were almost forty. Somehow they all knew that they had to tread softly in their high-top-sneakered feet, that they couldn't run or they would attract attention.

The corner of Twenty-first Avenue and Sixty-eighth Street was barren of police. A group of about fifteen youths, joined by one or two older men, sat down at the intersection, hoping to block the buses.

A squadron of motorcycles appeared, aimed straight at the kids. One of the motorcycle cops, a black sergeant, wore a wide, sparkling-toothed smile as he revved his engine. He would have taken delight, it seemed, in running any one of them toward the sidewalk.

Blue-jacketed Community Relations officers appeared and one cop went to talk with the kids. Bending down, he spoke softly:

"What the fuck is the matter with you guys? I don't understand you! First you don't want them here. Now you don't want them to leave! C'mon, get up. I live here too, you know, and you're making me look bad and you look bad, and the whole neighborhood."

The sit-in ended abruptly as the buses moved out. They made a left onto Twenty-first Avenue and were escorted past the danger zone.

The group of kids had swelled, however, and as the private cars with headlights on turned the corner, some were pelted with pebbles and at least one egg. One white man jumped out into the avenue and began banging on the hood of a marcher's car. The black man got out, and it looked as if there were going to be blows. Cops moved in and separated the men. The cars continued on.

But the crowds of youths were getting larger still. A white-shirted ranking officer got into a confrontation with one heckler.

"What's with you guys?" the kid asked. His face looked like he had been betrayed by his best friend.

"What's this, you protect these crackheads and these junkies that come here to invade our neighborhood, and you've got your guys with sticks ready to beat on us?"

There was a shoving match between the boss and the kid and there were cops everywhere. Now they weren't fooling around. No longer concerned with two camps to keep separate, it didn't matter what the cops did. They just wanted the crowd dispersed.

"Move in!" the boss who had gotten into the scuffle ordered, and the cops, nightsticks at their breasts, moved on the kids, who tried to be brave at first but bolted and ran back down Sixty-seventh Street.

On the Eighteenth Avenue midway the normally packed rides stood motionless. Many of the food stands had not opened. But slowly, as word circulated that the marchers had left, the feast came back to life.

*   *   *

OTHER MARCHES, OTHER VOICES

To suggest that Al Sharpton welcomed the death of Yusuf Hawkins and the events that followed would be unfair, inaccurate, and totally inappropriate. To say that he and the movement he was trying to piece together in the New York of the 1980s benefited from the circumstances is another matter.

Bensonhurst's reactions to the marches made Sharpton's earlier branding of New York as the Birmingham of the North seem far from extremist rhetoric. The murder itself received national attention at the outset, but nowhere near the type of coverage given as a result of the marches. Stories appeared from New Jersey to Hong Kong, many with photographs of the white hecklers cursing those who said they came only to seek justice. And at the head of the parade was the man everyone loved to hate.

The more conservative elements of the black community refrained initially from criticizing Sharpton's marches. More than anyone else in New York's power structure, they were keenly aware of the frustration that had mounted long before the Hawkins murder, although the Bensonhurst case was certainly, in the words of Inspector Sanderson of the Bias Unit, "the icing on the cake."

There were marches besides those led by Sharpton immediately after the shooting. Some were led by the established black leadership. The Reverend Calvin Butts, a well-known New York activist, led one demonstration, and even Morton Downey, Jr., then a talk-show host, led a walking tour of the neighborhood with Roy Innis, director of the Congress of Racial Equality.

Bensonhurst did not react as strongly to these events as they did the Sharpton forays, perhaps confirming for better or worse Sharpton's own description of himself as a lightning rod for the hatred of bigoted whites. But as the day of the Democratic primary drew near black leaders were becoming more vocally critical of Sharpton's tactics. They understood the marches and couldn't totally condemn them. But they also felt that the only way for true change to be effected was for Ed Koch to be defeated. If the injustices of government were to be rectified there would have to be a change of leadership, and there were fears that a white backlash sparked by the marches could cost David Dinkins the election.

"What we need to do now is concentrate on the election, on making positive change," the Reverend Herbert Daughtry said. Although black leadership felt that the Hawkins murder could aid Dinkins in his primary bid if only because it might motivate more blacks to get out and vote, there were also concerns that the reaction to it could have the opposite effect.

Al Sharpton had only run for public office once, a state senatorial bid derailed because he didn't live in the district, and he firmly maintains that he holds no political ambitions. He believes that the quid pro quo of the political system inherently denies the disenfranchised equal representation, and so he harbored no hopes of major changes in the plight of the poor and disadvantaged merely because of a black-led administration in City Hall. If anything, Sharpton felt that Dinkins was courting other constituencies at the expense of those who were his greatest supporters.

"That nigger's been to so many synagogues wearing so many yarmulkes he's getting a bald spot on the back of his head," the activist said during dinner at Junior's Restaurant in Brooklyn, one of his frequent haunts. "Dave is like the man who goes out and spends all kinds of money on his mistress while he leaves his wife home in rags."

There was nothing unusual about Dinkins actively seeking support from the city's Jewish community, however, especially if he was to live up to being the healing force his supporters claimed him to be. It was no secret that Jews figured heavily in the numbers of organized labor leaders, and that large segments of the Jewish community voted as a bloc. The relationship between Jews and blacks had been deteriorating before Ed Koch became mayor, and any bonds that still held the two groups together continued to fray throughout his administration. In the city's Hassidic communities especially, tensions between those Jews and neighboring blacks and Hispanics had in the past erupted into violence.

The invitation of Louis Farrakhan, who had been quoted as calling Judaism a "gutter religion," to the Hawkins funeral and the knowledge that Moses Stewart had embraced his teachings frightened many

New Yorkers, especially the Dinkins camp, because of the anti-Semitic implications.

In light of these unfortunate rifts, a little-publicized march of black students and professionals from Prospect Park, where the ill-fated Brooklyn Bridge march began, proved especially poignant.

Approximately fifty men and women, most of them black, marched on the Saturday before primary day. They claimed they were not followers of anybody and that they hoped their demonstration could heal the wounds that had already been inflicted on the city.

A tall, older black man said his name was Johnny Appleseed and pulled out a driver's license to prove it.

"I been to them all," he said. "Been to Montgomery with King. Got to march today. It's just the same thing all over again. People have to be taught to love."

Another marcher said he was a college professor. "I have it all, I guess. I've got my degree, I've got a good job. But then something like this happens and you realize that for all your degrees or what job you have it doesn't make any difference. You can still die on the streets just because of your color."

Yet another marcher was asked why he had come.

"Because of my son," he said. "I want him to be able to grow up."

With uniformed police escorts in front and behind them the marchers proceeded, and soon they were in the Borough Park section of Brooklyn, which has a formidable Orthodox Jewish population.

Women wearing kerchiefs peered out of windows, and men wearing prayer shawls and yarmulkes crowded on the stoops of neat brick houses. The marchers had gone a block when suddenly the Jewish men were on the sidewalks, walking as the marchers walked, parallel to them on either side.

The Jewish men walked silently and slowly. Some shooed little boys back to the safety of their mothers' skirts, and a rabbi walked near a police captain who was in front.

One of the Orthodox men was asked whether this was a show of solidarity or an escort to make sure that marchers left the neighborhood. He walked slowly, a little boy holding each of his beefy hands.

"We are walking with them to show support," he said, explaining that he should not be speaking because it was still the Sabbath and that he did not wish to identify himself by name. He said that he and his neighbors thought the slaying of Yusuf Hawkins a terrible thing, that his community identified with it.

"After all, when the bigots go after everybody else, when they are done they come for the Jews," he said. "These Italian kids from Bensonhurst, they're not that far from here. They drive through sometimes, they holler from their cars 'Hey Jew boy,' this or that. We are used to it and we know how hatred like that, so blind, so stupid, leads to something senseless like this."

The man continued with his two sons after most of the other Jews had fallen away, stopping at Fiftieth Street as if it were a line of demarcation. In a sense it was, being the place where the Jewish community borders Bensonhurst. A phalanx of police officers in riot helmets with the clear plastic shields drawn down over their faces, looking like space aliens, were in place for this stretch of the march.

"It's not safe here," the police captain said to the Jewish man. "You should go back."

The man was determined to continue.

"I know what racism is," he said, and held the hands of his two little boys aloft. "And I want them to see what this terrible thing is."

He walked for two more blocks before he bade a good-bye and headed back toward home.

Now fully in enemy territory, the leaders changed the chant.

"Join with us, Bensonhurst, join with us!" they chanted as they clapped hands.

"We know that everyone here in Bensonhurst is not a racist," a leader said into the megaphone. "So come on, walk with us to prove it to the world! Join with us!"

The bullhorn was passed to different group members who voiced similar sentiments, and suddenly they were at the schoolyard on Twentieth Avenue, where it had all started less than a month before. The school building was open and under the watchful eyes of police officers the marchers used water fountains and bathroom facilities.

There were no razzings, no racist slogans and slurs. Some white kids watched with curiosity.

"Where's Sharpton?" one kid asked another.

"He's not here," the second boy said authoritatively. "He got the day off."

Both shrugged and they parted company.

The marchers continued back the way they came, to the subway station on Twentieth Avenue from which Yusuf and his friends had emerged the night of August 23. As they filed into the station they chanted in unison:

"Thank you, Bensonhurst, thank you!"

A UAM march down the usual route, held within the hour, also proceeded without incident. The Reverend Sharpton was not present, having gone to Chicago with Moses Stewart for a rally held by Louis Farrakhan.

Bensonhurst was becoming accustomed to invasions by strangers. A week later on a drizzly Saturday a handful of demonstrators headed by white supremacist Roy Barringer met a police guard at the schoolyard.

The van that bore the demonstrators had Alabama plates, and a white supremacist flag (white field with red arrows) was unfurled from the back of a rented Chevrolet. Barringer played John Philip Sousa marches from a cassette tape recorder into a bullhorn.

It was a ragtag group of brown-shirted young white men wearing jackboots and close-cropped hair.

"Where are you from?" a reporter asked one teenager.

"Brooklyn," he said with an unmistakable Southern drawl.

"God bless Bensonhurst!" Barringer shouted into the bullhorn above the strains of the band music.

"God bless Bensonhurst!" the young troops chanted back.

"God bless the Bensonhurst police department!" Barringer called.

"God bless the Bensonhurst police department!" the brownshirts responded.

Apparently the out-of-towners were so unaware of local geography that they thought Bensonhurst a separate place from New York altogether, with its own law enforcement body.

There were curious looks from the windows, but the residents didn't seem to like the brownshirts any more than they had the black faces.

"Who the fuck asked them to come here?" one man asked a police officer, who smiled and shrugged.

As the group marched a grapefruit-juice bottle plummeted earthward, narrowly missing a young marcher who bore a large American flag.

The group reached the 62nd's station house without any other incidents except for some occasional catcalls. Barringer made a speech about how important it is for a neighborhood to stand up for what it believes in, and then the marchers, all six of them, piled into the van that had followed them down the street.

The driver was a man who identified himself as Hank Schmidt and said he was from northern Florida. He was not dressed in the military style of the others, but looked more like an East Village biker. On his leather cap was a gold swastika.

"People are learning not to take any shit from these niggers anymore," he said, affecting a German accent as he spoke clipped words through rotted teeth.

The station house is located a mile from where Yusuf Hawkins was shot and killed. It is a different neighborhood from the Twentieth Avenue locale, even though both places are considered part of Bensonhurst. As word spread through the neighboring blocks that Nazis had come to praise the neighborhood, a group of the locals, mostly youngsters, assembled on the other side of a schoolyard where the van was parked with the marchers piling in.

They began to question their visitors in true Brooklyn style.

"Who the fuck are yez?"

"Who the fuck axed you to come here? We don't need you! Get the fuck out!"

The crowd grew larger and surrounded the van as police tried to clear a path for it, and with a squeal of rubber it was gone, with Barringer's Chevrolet behind it.

"Nazi bastards," one kid muttered as he left. "I woulda liked to had a piece of 'em. Fuckin' racists and troublemakers," he said, and joined some friends around the corner for a game of tag football.

While the marches and protests continued the wheels of the justice system moved on in Brooklyn. By mid-September a total of six arrests had been made in connection with the case. Fama, Mondello, Raucci, and Patino had been indicted on murder charges, and grand-jury proceedings were continuing against Stressler and Curreri.

Each of the defendants, had he wished to, could have testified on his own behalf before the grand jury. Lawyers for the first few indicted complained that since their clients had been arrested for assault and then charged with murder, their right to make an informed decision on whether they should give such testimony was infringed upon.

The District Attorney's office countered that lawyers should have known that the possibility of murder indictments existed since the crime that had taken place was, after all, a murder.

Defense lawyers continued to charge that the murder indictments were secured in order to placate an angry black community, and if that were the case then the strategy seemed to be working. The intensity of the community's anger did seem to be slowly ebbing. But Holtzman's office appeared to have been intent on bringing murder charges from the very beginning, even before the increased tensions brought on by the case.

The bulk of the evidence came from statements made by the defendants themselves to police, and even those could not be used at a trial against others, since it is unlawful to use testimony from one indicted co-conspirator against another. The prosecution's case at trial, therefore, especially against Joseph Fama, was circumstantial at best. The only people who had admitted seeing Fama fire the shots, or even have a gun, were Mondello and Stressler. One had been indicted and the other soon would be.

Prosecutors received a phone call in mid-September, however, that gave new life to a somewhat shaky collection of cases. John Vento, who fled Brooklyn after his meeting with crime capo Sammy Gravano and was being sought by police for his role in the Hawkins murder, telephoned prosecutors from upstate New York and said he was willing to cut a deal. Sources in Bensonhurst said that Vento fled with Fama and that the gunman had turned himself in after having some kind of an argument with his friend, possibly over Vento's willingness to "turn" for authorities, but prosecutors and Fama's attorneys dismissed the talk as "mere speculation." Vento has relatives in the Oneonta area, however, not far from where Fama surrendered.

In any event, prosecutors were willing to make a deal with the fugitive, and attorney Gerald DeCiarra, representing Vento, worked out the arrangements for his return to New York.

The agreement was simple. Vento would give full, complete, and truthful testimony before the grand jury and at his friends' trials. There would be no charges brought against him in connection with the Hawkins murder, and he would remain at liberty. Gleeful prosecutors thought their case was sewed up. As soon as he returned Vento was debriefed by detectives and began telling his story to several grand juries. It was the most graphic description of the events of August 23 authorities had been given to date and included a positive identification of Fama as the trigger man.

Even though indictments against some of the defendants had already been voted before the reappearance of Vento, superseding indictments continued to be issued based on his testimony and that of others.

The Hawkins family was not informed of Vento's status as a suspect, nor were they told that he had eventually agreed to cooperate. Al Sharpton had a reputation for leaking information to reporters, and his involvement may have been one reason for the decision to keep mum, even though an agreement with the family had been made to inform them of any deals. Moses Stewart, however, might not have been pleased.

"I wanted everyone responsible for the murder of my son to go to jail. If the police were doing their job they wouldn't need anyone to make a deal with," he said later.

Stewart and Sharpton became close during the weeks of marches and press conferences, and each man owed the other a debt. Sharpton had certainly kept the spotlight shining on the case, and Stewart felt that without the street-level pressure the marches exerted murder indictments might never have come about. Sharpton was providing other assistance as well.

At the time of Yusuf's death Moses was unemployed, and although he said that he would have preferred to find a job, it would have been impossible for him to hold one down while the murder case was active.

"How would I be able to get a suit dry-cleaned to go to court in? How could I just take off to go to the trials of those who murdered my son? There is no way I could do that. Reverend Sharpton and the UAM helped us to get by so we could do all that," Moses said.

Sharpton also became used to the ringing of the telephone late at night, when there were problems in the Hawkins household.

"People say I'm using Freddy," Sharpton (who always called Moses Freddy in private) said. "They don't see what's going on in that house. I spend more time with those kids than I do with my kids. I've got to go over there whenever he beats on his wife."

There had been problems in the Hawkins household before Yusuf's murder; the pressure on both parents afterward did nothing to improve matters, and the situation became worse. Still, the couple remained together and Sharpton seemed to act as a calming influence when things got tough.

Moses became a regular speaker at the UAM Slave Theater rallies, and Sharpton took him on the road when he had speaking engagements in other cities.

Diane, although grateful for the assistance given by Sharpton and his organization, did not have the same tolerance for many of the public activities. She behaved, however, like a dutiful wife, and would rarely speak out publicly about her anger.

As for Freddy and Amir, Yusuf's brothers, the marches and other UAM activities kept them busy, and they seemed to adjust well to

175

the loss of their brother, although Amir confided in an interview, "I miss him a lot."

Perhaps because of the murder indictments, especially Fama's, the case slowly began to recede from the front pages of the daily newspapers to occasional briefs on how the case was developing as the public furor and initial shock over the incident waned. Another developing story had replaced it.

David Dinkins defeated Ed Koch in the Democratic mayoral primary and would face Rudolph Guiliani, the former federal prosecutor and Republican nominee, in the November election. The new political developments seemed to have a soothing effect on portions of the city's black community. There were more protest marches in Bensonhurst led by Sharpton, but the numbers of the marchers began to dwindle and they were less representative of the professional, upper-middle-class people who initially swelled the ranks of the activist's camp.

Elizabeth Holtzman, as expected, won her primary race and was as good as elected to the office of comptroller, although she faced Republican opposition. Charles Hynes won his primary as well, and was regarded as the heir apparent to Holtzman's office.

Sharpton's critics accuse him of "profiteering" from racial disharmony. Sharpton deliberately injects himself into controversial situations involving race, they say, so that he can rack up more time on television and keep his name in the public consciousness. They have accused him of receiving money from the Brawley family, for one, and also feel that, like some television evangelists, his activities keep a constant flow of donations coming in.

He denies such accusations forcefully. He asserts, however, that even when public attention is not drawn to the problems poor blacks face in a white-dominated society those problems continue to fester, and so he uses whatever means he can to keep attention focused on those problems.

"Who's profiteering?" Sharpton retorts. "Dave Dinkins wants something, to be mayor. But nobody says he's profiteering. Hynes prosecuted Howard Beach, wrote a book about it, and they made a movie. So who's profiteering?"

Much of the public interest in the Bensonhurst marches arose from fears that they would result in violence, and when the expected riot failed to materialize the television cameras did the same. The black political establishment of the city, fueled by the Dinkins primary victory, was grabbing the spotlight from Sharpton and, he reasoned, from the movement. A new type of march was in order. But without the threat of violence present in the confrontational Bensonhurst marches.

On a warm night in late September Sharpton held a joint press conference with activist comedian Dick Gregory across the street from the Cemetery of the Evergreens, where Yusuf Hawkins was buried.

"It is wrong for us to merely protest what whites did in Bensonhurst, when there are people of color in Yusuf Hawkins' own neighborhood who are responsible for the deaths of other young black men," Sharpton said. He announced a month-long fast, something that brought snickers from some reporters, who sometimes joked about his weight. He would live in a van, he said, in front of an East New York high school, and each night of the fast he would lead an antidrug march through the streets.

The community drug patrols, which Gregory had organized with some success in Shreveport, Louisiana, and other cities, would be launched in the name of Yusuf Hawkins, and his brothers Freddy and Amir would participate.

On the first night of the Yusuf patrol, as it was called, more than three hundred people gathered and marched through the streets of the black neighborhood, chanting "No more drugs." They walked through the crack-ravaged schoolyards and parks, singing and chanting through dark streets where confused drug addicts hid in crack houses as they tried to figure out what was going on.

At the all-night tobacco stores where drug paraphernalia was sold members of the UAM youth arm, including Freddy and Amir, purchased crack vials and cocaine vials and brought them to Sharpton. He then marched in and demanded that the store stop selling the items, with the threat that protesters would remain singing and chanting outside the store until the sales ceased.

A week into the Yusuf patrols a homeboy with gold in his teeth, a baseball cap on his head, stood leaning against a blacked-out streetlamp on Saratoga Avenue, near a group of abandoned buildings frequented by addicts. He shook his head as he saw Sharpton and the others pass.

"That motherfucker's gonna get hisself killed," the young back man said and, still shaking his head, walked into one of the buildings.

The Yusuf patrol declined after about two weeks, and Sharpton claimed inadequate media coverage as part of the problem.

"If we go to Bensonhurst and they think somebody's going to get killed they cover us. But I find it ironic that when we try to do something to improve our own neighborhoods the media is nowhere to be seen," he said.

At the same time, at the state's intermediate appeals court in Brooklyn Heights, attorneys for Joseph Fama argued before a panel of judges that bail should be permitted for their client.

Fama's scrapes with other children and teachers throughout his school career were well known by those familiar with him, but problems seemed to be following him to the Brooklyn House of Detention as well, a fact noted to the judges by one of Fama's attorneys, Stanley Meyer.

Only a few weeks after his incarceration Fama suffered a black eye and other minor injuries in a scuffle with guards. An investigation by the city's Corrections Department indicated that Fama had been taking a shower late one night and that when he reached for his towel it was gone. A guard told him the towel had been locked inside his cell, and a dripping-wet Joey Fama returned there. As he shivered outside the cell door, a guard refused requests by Fama for it to be unlocked, so he returned to the shower and removed a shower curtain, covering himself with it. When he was finally admitted into the cell it had been soaked with liquid from a fire extinguisher, and Fama then began shouting and banging against the cell door. The injuries occurred as guards tried to force him into the drenched cell.

The incident was not determined to be racially motivated, since a white guard was involved.

"It could get bad, real nasty for him in there because of the notoriety of the case," Stanley Meyer said.

The decision came down later that afternoon, denying Fama's bail application. Moses, Diane, and Sharpton watched as reporters crowded around Fama's lawyers, Meyer and Dave DePetris. There seemed to be little interest on the part of the media in getting comment from the family or their adviser. The threesome, accompanied by some UAM volunteers, slowly walked back to their blue Buick sedan.

Moses jerked his thumb back at the television cameras and said, "You see? None of them people wants to talk to us when we're happy."

The relative calm of the city was not universal, however. There was still palpable anger, especially among young blacks who feared that they could have just as easily been the victims on Bay Ridge Avenue. A potentially violent demonstration of those emotions occurred on October 21, when Charles Stressler was formally indicted for murder.

Michael Santangelo, a short, bespectacled attorney, initially represented Stressler and, like the other Bensonhurst lawyers, harshly criticized the indictment as "political" and "unjust." He told reporters that he was going immediately to State Supreme Court, a few blocks away, to file papers opposing the indictment.

Resplendent in a pin-stripe suit complete with carnation, Santangelo and his gangly twenty-one-year-old client left the Criminal Court building shortly after noon. During all of the other Bensonhurst proceedings schools had not been in session. But this was October, and just down the street a large number of black high school students had just gotten out on a lunch break. Attracted by a WWOR television camera crew that was tailing Santangelo and Stressler, the students drew closer; somehow they realized that the tall young man was involved in the Yusuf Hawkins murder. Curiosity turned to anger, and soon the students were walking behind the pair, who tried not to notice. A bottle was thrown as they cut through a parking lot, and suddenly they were surrounded by more than a hundred young black men and women. They formed a circle around Stressler and his lawyer, raising their fists in the air and chanting "Fight the power," drawing ever closer.

Stressler said nothing, but his face was a mask of fear. His eyes darted first left and then right, looking for a way out until he realized there was none. Police sirens filled the air, and a squad car broke through the crowd. Stressler and Santangelo were hustled inside and the driver hit the gas as rocks and bottles began to fly.

A ring of police officers had circled the group, and an assistance call for what the police department calls a "rapid mobilization" of reinforcements went out. The street in front of the Criminal Court was a sea of riot-helmeted cops who tried to pen the angry blacks in. There were fears that if serious trouble started it could spread to the downtown business district, and the cops wanted to avoid that at all costs.

With Stressler gone the tempers cooled, and eventually the students returned to classes without further incident.

"I couldn't believe it," Stressler said later. "I saw hate in these people's eyes; these people all hated me and wanted to hurt me, and they didn't even know me. They didn't know anything about me."

In the Supreme Court building on Cadman Plaza just a block away, the Hawkins family's attorney, Alton Maddox, was making closing statements on behalf of a client charged with a drug-related murder, one of the more common crimes in Kings County and the kind that generates little publicity. The jury was composed almost entirely of black men and women, who listened to the lawyer's Georgia drawl as he concluded his case. The judge presiding over the courtroom was also a black man.

The Honorable Thaddeus Owens knew from close experience what racial prejudice was all about, because it had tragically touched his own family when an uncle was murdered by an Arkansas lynch mob. And when this murder case was over he would face one of the most formidable challenges of his judicial career. Owens had been specially selected by the New York State Office of Combined Court Administration upon the recommendation of the chief administrative judge of Kings County to preside over what would become known as the Bensonhurst murder trials.

HALLS OF JUSTICE

HE New York City Criminal Court is the lowest rung on the city's judicial ladder, and after defendants are indicted there for felonies their cases are brought to the next step in the system, New York State Supreme Court. Supreme Court proceedings in Brooklyn are held in a long and sleek six-story building on Court Street located in front of a wide promenade that is alive with colorful flowers in the spring and summer, giving Cadman Plaza (its official name) the look of a large village green.

Cadman Plaza is a busy place even when a high-profile case is not being heard, with lawyers, police officers, jurors, and defendants constantly trotting up and down the wide steps of the courthouse. On October 14 television vans were lined up for the length of the street and police barricades were set up as the first of the pretrial hearings was held before Judge Owens.

On the fourth floor of the courthouse security was tight, and everyone exiting the elevators except attorneys, credentialed press, and police officers had to walk through a metal detector. The reporters were lined up outside the door to Owens' courtroom and told that numbers would be assigned to them for seating. On the other side of the wooden barricades a large contingent of UAM people was waiting for the arrival of the Hawkins family and Reverend Sharpton, who emerged from the elevator and, as instructed, placed all of his change and the large Martin Luther King medallion in a plastic tray before walking through the metal detector.

The medal, by then a Sharpton trademark, was a gift from the

Reverend Hosea Williams, who led marches through segregated Forsythe County, Georgia, in 1986. It was forged of steel in Africa and depicted a likeness of the slain civil rights leader. Only a half-dozen of them had been made.

The waiting black men and women grew silent as Sharpton and Moses, each wearing a suit and a bow tie, escorted Diane to the courtroom door. Defendants and their lawyers swiftly walked down the hallway into the clerk's-office door at the end of the hall.

"Look at this," one black man said. "They pen us up here like we're doing something, and they got killers walking right in to the judge just like that." The use of the clerk's office was a security procedure, since the defendants and their families were still receiving death threats.

The press was invited into the courtroom, and Diane stared blankly at the reporters as they filed in. She looked strangely small and vulnerable. One reporter stopped to speak with Sharpton and asked him why he was there.

"Why am I here? We are all here today to see that justice is done, and we are going to ask the judge to jail all of these young men who are charged with the murder of Yusuf Hawkins," he said.

The courtroom was small, incapable of accommodating all those who waited outside. Blond wooden benches ran the entire width of the paneled chamber, and there was no center aisle. The first two rows were reserved for the press, as were the seats in the jury box, with priority given to sketch artists. (Judge Owens had already ruled that cameras would not be permitted in his courtroom.)

Strips of white masking tape had been placed down the center of each bench from the third row back, to separate spectators from the defendants' families.

"Please take seats on the far side of the tape," a court officer said as the spectators, including the Hawkins family and Sharpton, walked inside.

"What is this, Alabama?" one man said. "We got white seats and nigger seats in here?"

After the "black seats," those to the right, were filled, relatives and friends of the defendants walked in, looking nervously at the black spectators, who stared back at them. For Diane and Moses, however, the object of their attention was on the other side of the solid wood railing separating the well from the gallery.

The defendants sat at their table, looking straight ahead. Keith Mondello, Pasquale Raucci, Charles Stressler, James Patino, and Joseph Serrano still could not believe that they were facing murder charges. Steven Curreri was the only defendant not charged with murder; the top count of his indictment was assault, since even though he had had a bat, as others did, he never made it around the corner.

Realizing that the actual killers were seated in front of them, the black activists in the crowd started to hiss and some comments were passed among them.

"Look at that little skinny one," a woman said. "I bet he's a fag. He look like a little queer motherfucker."

"Shhhh," said someone else.

A door to the right of the vacant judge's bench opened and a court officer escorted a handcuffed Joseph Fama into the courtroom. He sat apart from his co-defendants—to the relief of most of their counsel, who preferred as little association as possible between Fama and their clients, even at this early stage in the game.

Fama rubbed his wrists absent-mindedly and then smiled at his father, Rocco, who sat in the third row. A serious look came over his face, then melted into a sneer. Dave DePetris, his lawyer, took a seat next to him and whispered in his ear, "You all right, buddy?"

Fama shrugged.

Diane Hawkins looked toward Joey Fama, turned away, and then locked her eyes on him again. She fixed him with a cold, hard stare and thought about how she was supposed to be forgiving because that's what the Bible says. But at this moment she could feel nothing close to forgiveness.

A short, gray-haired black man sauntered into the courtroom wearing judicial robes as a court officer said, "Remain seated."

Judge Owens took the bench and sat in a wooden chair, leaving the leather-upholstered judge's chair vacant. It was how he was most comfortable. He shuffled some papers and softly whistled a tune.

The special appointment of Owens to the Bensonhurst case raised a few eyebrows within the Brooklyn bar. There was significance, however undesirable or unintended, to the fact that a black judge would be presiding over a case of racial murder committed against a black teenager by white youths, especially considering the lynching of the judge's uncle forty years before. Sharpton was not pleased with the appointment, however, because only a year before Owens had been under fire for imposing what some considered a lenient sentence in a bias-related case. A Brooklyn teenager had been convicted of setting fire to a synagogue, resulting in the destruction of several torahs. The city's Orthodox Jewish community was livid at Owens' sentence of community service and his order that the boy write a paper on the Nazi Holocaust.

Matt Crossen, chief administrator of New York's courts, personally made the selection of Owens, bypassing the "wheel" system that is normally used to assign cases. According to Mary DeBourbon, a spokesperson for the state courts, the wheel procedure can be bypassed if a case is unusually sensitive or requires special expertise. "It has nothing to do with race," Crossen said, "but it has everything to do with the fact that he's an excellent judge."

The Owens selection came on the heels of another controversial Crossen pick, for the Central Park jogger case. Sharpton and other activists were critical of his choice, Judge Thomas Galligan, who had a reputation for tough sentences, although Crossen denied that was the reason.

"The Central Park defendants got the hanging judge, and for Yusuf's killers we get one who gives homework assignments," was Sharpton's assessment.

But Crossen knew that all eyes would be on the Bensonhurst case and felt that Owens could handle it fairly. "There are rare cases in which public attention is so intense that the proceedings will create a lasting perception of the criminal justice system by the way the case is handled," he said.

Bruce McIntyre, of outgoing DA Holtzman's homicide bureau, was the first to speak, bringing up the issue of Fama's bail once more. The gunman should remain in jail, he said, and made a motion that the other defendants should join him.

Owens said that Fama would remain jailed, not commenting on the other defendants. Then the defense attorneys asked for a change of venue. They felt their clients could not possibly get a fair trial in Brooklyn, a notion Owens scoffed at.

"What are you going to move this case for? Where are you going to move it to?" he asked. "China? The only place they probably haven't heard about this is China. You want to move it to China? Motion denied. Besides—" and the judge looked squarely at Murphy, who had given more than his share of press conferences during the preliminary criminal court stages—"you can't go talking to the press and using the media to advance your cause and then say it's not fair because of the publicity. You can't have it both ways. Motion denied."

Other administrative problems were worked out or postponed and a new court date set. Then Owens made his final announcement.

"The defendants with the exception of Joseph Fama are continued on bail," he said.

He arose from the bench and departed, leaving the courtroom in an uproar. Moses was on his feet, calling out: "Who does that hand-kerchief-headed nigger think he is—let my son's murderers go free on bail—"

Sharpton and a handful of UAM people walked Moses and Diane out of the courtroom as tears streamed down Diane's face.

On the courtroom steps Murphy told reporters that he was pleased but not surprised that Keith Mondello's bail had been continued.

"Why not? He didn't kill anybody. He's not going anywhere," Murphy whined. Then he said that he had a bombshell to drop. Keith Mondello, he said, had a black friend who was there on the night of the attack. "He's gonna testify," Murphy said, "that this was not racial. The black kid was there, and he's gonna testify."

*   *   *

Russell Gibbons had already spoken to a reporter several days after the murder, explaining what it was like to grow up black in Bensonhurst. "This is a good neighborhood," he said, "and everybody sticks together here. There's no racism here, not more than anywhere else." What Gibbons didn't mention was how well acquainted he was with the events of August 23, that he had helped Charlie Stressler bring the baseball bats, and that detectives were already interviewing him about the incident.

The families of many defendants knew Gibbons, and also knew that he was at the schoolyard the night of the shooting. They felt that the police were deliberately ignoring his presence to bolster their theory that the murder resulted from the actions of a crazed lynch mob.

"I don't want to say anything bad about Russell," Susan Mondello, Keith's mother, said. "But he was there, just like everybody else. How come they don't go after him? Because then everybody would know it wasn't racial, that's why. Russell is one of Keith's best friends."

Gibbons was already testifying before the grand jury when he tentatively told Murphy he would testify on Keith's behalf. But the information he had, especially regarding Stressler and the bats, was too valuable for prosecutors to risk losing, and detectives kept up pressure on Russell, threatening him with arrest if he did not cooperate.

"Russell's race had nothing to do with whether he was charged," a prosecutor said. "The dividing line we were using is not just who had the bats, or even who brought them, but what they were doing and where they were when Yusuf was on the corner and was shot."

Russell claimed that he was minding his radio in the schoolyard when the mob started to run, although one defendant who asked not to be identified later countered that assertion and said that Russell had indeed come around the corner. Elizabeth Galarza, the woman who looked out her neighbor's window, also said she saw Gibbons on the corner with a bat in his hand.

Although the defendants and their families were displeased by what they saw as yet another double standard in the Bensonhurst case, the boys who were charged remained curiously protective of Russell and did not volunteer any more information than was necessary about his actions to police or prosecutors. Gibbons also refused to confirm allegations about Vento's and Mondello's coke dealings, even though he was willing to testify against his friends in court to avoid arrest and prosecution. Russell still believes that the attack on Hawkins and his friends was not racially motivated.

When Al Sharpton was told that a black youth might have been involved in the murder, he didn't believe it possible at first.

"I personally don't believe that such a person exists," he said. "But if he did exist, and if a black youth was involved, then I would hope that he would be prosecuted as well. Being black doesn't make him above the law."

TIME OF TRANSITION

ROSECUTORS continued to take grand jury testimony as all of New York kept eyes turned toward the mayoral election. The morning after election day was chilly, and on Prospect Place and Underhill Avenue, not far from Al Sharpton's carriage house, a small black boy on his way to school walked into a bodega. He had to bang his tiny hand on the counter a few times for the clerk to see him, and he fished some change out of his pocket for bubble gum. As the boy turned to leave he glanced down at the milk crates where newspapers were stacked high and saw the face of David Dinkins on the *Daily News*, *Newsday*, and the New York *Post*. A look of joy spread across the little boy's face and he sported a broad grin.

"He won!" the boy said. Then he repeated the words as he skipped out of the store, elated.

David Dinkins had become the first African-American mayor in the history of the City of New York. The night before, in Harlem, Bedford-Stuyvesant, and other predominantly black neighborhoods there had been parties, prayers, and an overall sense of celebration.

In his victory speech, Dinkins had spoken of bringing the city together once again.

David Dinkins wasn't the only New Yorker with a new job that morning. Elizabeth Holtzman won the comptroller's seat and would no longer be the Brooklyn DA. Charles J. Hynes had also been victorious and was looking forward to taking over the DA job in January.

On election day Hynes held an impromptu news conference on the steps of Brooklyn Supreme Court. There was already a transition team in place, he said. He would personally be meeting with families of major Brooklyn crime victims to discuss their concerns, after the election. He also said that he would personally visit police precincts throughout the borough to discuss with officers what his office's specific policies would be on the use of force against suspects. The big question of course had to do with the Bensonhurst case.

Hynes said his office would be prepared to handle the case but was vague on what plans were already in the works. Those assistants who were in line for appointment to the Hynes administration were beginning to assemble data on their own, but some vital aspects of the case in progress only insiders could know, including the fact that John Vento, and not Gina Feliciano, would be the state's star witness.

The District Attorney's dealings with Vento would be far from trouble-free. For one thing, he was less than honest with investigators and did not inform detectives of the meeting with Sammy Gravano prior to his own flight from the city. And while Vento might have kept his word to the Brooklyn crime lords and followed their instructions about which names not to name to detectives, he was not as forthcoming with authorities in spite of his testimony. But after flipping for the prosecution, Vento flopped against it. In December 1989 Vento disappeared and was nowhere to be found. The Brooklyn District Attorney's office found that its star witness was gone, and perhaps their case along with him.

If the Hawkins family had known at the time of Vento's disappearance that the prosecution was seriously jeopardized they would have been furious. But they didn't know that he was a witness to begin with, and they had other concerns, including a budding disenchantment with the incoming administrations in City Hall and on Joralemon Street. A *New York Law Journal* article that purported to contain the names of new Hynes appointments made Al Sharpton, Moses Stewart, and Alton Maddox furious. Maddox was officially representing the Hawkins family in regard to a multimillion-dollar lawsuit against the City of New York, and along with Sharpton he sometimes served as their adviser. The activists (and Stewart by extension) were disturbed by the list because they claimed that few African-American attorneys appeared on it. They felt that Hynes had gained prominence and fame during the Howard Beach prosecution, deriving benefit from the black community's misfortune, but was not going to pay the community back in kind.

On a Saturday morning in December Sharpton and Maddox, along with the Hawkins family, met with Holtzman to express their concerns. The cooperation of Troy Banner, Claude Stanford, and Luther Sylvester would be withdrawn from the case unless the Brooklyn District Attorney's office evinced a willingness to hire more blacks. But the noncooperation threat, successfully employed in Howard Beach, was a paper tiger. The testimony of the black youths who were with Yusuf Hawkins was desirable, certainly, but not necessary. The threesome had been unable to pick Joseph Fama and other defendants out in line-ups, and the testimony of a witness like Vento would be far more essential to the case. The District Attorney's office had leverage against the activists as well. Pressure from Maddox and Sharpton to quell the seemingly cooperative bent of the boys could result in criminal charges for tampering with witnesses.

The activists also had another bone to pick with Holtzman, regarding Elizabeth Galarza. This mother of three had been termed "unreliable" by detectives and even top police brass, including chief of Brooklyn detectives Joseph DeMartino. The District Attorney's office sent out a letter, as required by law, to all defense attorneys. It stated that the office had a duty to inform them that this witness existed and that she had made statements which might prove "exculpatory"—that is, good for the defense. Such disclosures are referred to as "Brady material" by lawyers. But attorneys for some of the defendants, believing that Galarza's statements tended to clear their clients, said that the prosecution decision not to use Galarza as a witness was based instead on the mountains of information she knew about Gina Feliciano.

In a letter accusing Holtzman of "elevating politics over justice" Alton Maddox demanded the arrest of Galarza because of the conflicting statements she had reportedly given.

"Your office has converted the seemingly [sic] misconduct of Ms. Galarzia [sic] into good fortunes for some of the defendants. [This] has given the public the impression that some of the defendants are, in fact, innocent."

Both issues raised by Maddox and Sharpton died a slow death while the activists tried to regroup for more effective public relations strategies for UAM, and to keep the DA's office on its toes.

As authorities still desperately sought their missing witness, Joe Hynes assumed office as District Attorney and accepted resignations from a number of Holtzman aides and assistants who were the cartographers of the prosecution road map. In hindsight, some of those same key people said they were prepared for the possibility of a Vento turnaround. But such strategies, born of years of experience in the federal courts, which would have been used as a vise to squeeze Vento should he be found, were never discussed. Some Holtzman people, including Bruce McIntyre, remained in the Hynes administration. Paul Burns also decided to stay.

Several meetings were planned between Hynes and the Hawkins family in January but were canceled when word reached the news media. Hynes was not about to provide Sharpton with a photo opportunity if he could possibly help it.

Yet Sharpton was determined to generate interest in the Bensonhurst story again, for several reasons. For the moment, racial tensions had subsided in the city's neighborhoods. The same anger and bitterness existed, certainly, but it was not as prominently featured on the newscasts and in the papers. The focus was turning away from disharmony and toward a new unity under David Dinkins, who summarily dismissed Sharpton from his activities. On the day of Dinkins' inauguration Sharpton was nowhere to be found, and while he did not publicly express any negative sentiment, he seemed obviously miffed at the appearance of Herbert Daughtry right behind Dinkins on the City Hall steps.

Sharpton had another reason to keep himself in the spotlight in 1990. Late in 1989 he had been indicted on sixty-seven fraud and larceny counts by grand juries in Albany, the state capital, and New York City in connection with his old organization, the National Youth Movement. The New York indictment alleged that Sharpton had sought donations for NYM antidrug activities and pocketed them, and the Albany counts were charges that he failed to file state income tax. A previous federal grand jury probe had failed to result in an indictment on federal tax charges, but Robert Abrams, the state Attorney General who had been publicly embarrassed by Sharpton and Maddox during the Tawana Brawley case, had his own ideas about how the activist should be dealt with. Sharpton was unimpressed by the indictments, at least in public: "Martin Luther King was investigated for taxes. Every major civil rights leader there has ever been they've tried to bring down with tax charges," he said.

On January 15, 1990, Martin Luther King Day, Sharpton planned to confront Bensonhurst once again in an attempt at a massive public relations coup. Green-and-white street signs, just like the ones on lampposts all over Brooklyn, were made up with the words YUSUF HAWKINS BOULEVARD, to be placed on the corner of Twentieth Avenue and Bay Ridge Avenue.

The signs were unveiled at a rally inside the Slave Theater, attended by the UAM membership and (to its dismay) a new group of faces that were the product of a recent Sharpton alliance.

Dr. Lenora Fulani, former presidential candidate on the New Alliance Party ticket, had promised buses and marchers to Sharpton, and she had delivered. The decidedly left-wing NAP had been represented at the marches before, but without any accompanying fanfare.

Sharpton, wearing a long suede coat, arrived at the theater shortly after twelve and was hustled inside by bodyguards. Sharpton was unusually concerned about what kind of press coverage the King Day march on Bensonhurst would receive for a number of reasons. A few weeks earlier a state appeals court had reversed some of the lesser convictions in the Howard Beach case, and a protest march through the white enclave not only received a total media blackout but was ignored by residents as well. This was not good for the morale of the troops.

Although constantly vilified in their reports, the media still needed the rhetoric-spouting Reverend. As Sharpton noted in conferences with aides, they would need him when the Central Park case went to trial. He had access to several of the defendants, for whom he had arranged a bail campaign. Moses Stewart and Diane Hawkins were also under Sharpton's total control, and any media access to them as the Bensonhurst trials progressed would have to be obtained through him. Victims and alleged perpetrators of crimes were his bargaining chips, and reporters who gave what he deemed was "fair" coverage of UAM events were given "exclusive" interviews by desired subjects. The Reverend would be making a list of who covered his Martin Luther King Day march and he would be checking it more than twice when time came for payback, especially with pretrial hearings in his own case set to begin within a month.

Martin Luther King Day was also important to Sharpton because of the sincere admiration he had for King himself. "I wish I could be more like him," he once said, "but I don't have his patience and I don't have his forgiveness."

The game plan for the King Day march was to bank on expected hostility of white residents to the holiday itself and their already well-known dislike of Sharpton. "If they act up at this thing, then they're not just acting up against us, they're acting up against Dr. King," Sharpton said.

Morning drizzle was finally giving way to some sun, although the air outside was cold. Stragglers hurried into the theater since the show inside was about to begin. But there was a brief show outside when Moses and Diane, who had just arrived, continued a raucous argument that had begun as they left home. The tight circle of UAM people who protected them from outsiders would not answer questions about the tiff; neither would Moses, who came into the theater alone, appearing slightly intoxicated.

In a few minutes he was standing alone on the Slave's broad stage, his toes seeming to hang over the edge. He looked like a lost little boy. Everyone in the theater knew who he was, and there was silence after he raised his hands.

"I just want to say one thing," he said. "Me and Diane just had a little problem and some of you saw it." Moses looked at the few reporters who were seated in the front row on the right. "Anybody wanna make something out of that you go on ahead, but you'll have to deal with me. I *love* Diane! Diane is my life!" Stewart began to sound like a preacher exhorting the congregation to give witness to his profession of love and faith. "I would *kill* for Diane," he said, and the audience broke into applause.

Stewart still held the stage and the crowd's attention. Because of the difference between Moses' and Diane's last names and the fact that Yusuf's last name was Hawkins, just like his mother, there had been some quiet questions raised from time to time about the boy's paternity. At one point early in the court proceedings when an angry and exasperated Moses kicked out at a WNYW cameraperson and a still photographer there was even open speculation in some media circles that the publicly militant "father" wasn't the father of the Hawkins boys at all, but a plant by Sharpton. Stewart prepared to lay that rumor to rest.

"Some of y'all been questioning my relationship with my son," he said, pointing to the picture of Yusuf on the sweatshirt he constantly wore, the one that said above the picture A TOUCH OF CLASS. "Well, I am here to tell you that I am that boy's daddy!"

There were wild cheers from the seats, and Moses then offered anyone who was interested audiotapes of Louis Farrakhan speeches that he had for sale.

"Only six dollars each," he said.

Now the time had come for the main event, and as Al Sharpton strode briskly down the aisle the crowd once again had cause to go crazy. The top of his head was just barely visible above the caftan-clad guards. He mounted the stage and raised his fist.

"No justice!" he roared.

"No peace!" the crowd roared back.

"No justice!"

"No peace!"

The litany continued for just over a minute and when the crowd was good and worked-up Sharpton broke the cadence.

"Now shake the hand of the person next to you and wish them a happy King Day," Sharpton said, and the audience chuckled.

Almost immediately, his voice booming off the walls, Sharpton launched into an attack on the establishment and their method of celebrating the day.

"If Dr. King was here with us today he would not be in some

194

church. He would not be on the steps of City Hall with some bunch of Negros!"

There were calls from the crowd of "Amen" and "That's right."

"If Dr. King was with us today King would not be at some black-tie dinner acting pious."

"No, no," a woman said.

"If Dr. King was with us today, King would be marching! He would be on the streets in Bensonhurst today, where there were only seven arrested for killing a black youth when there was thirty that did the killing!"

The crowd whooped and cheered. Sharpton wiped his brow and continued. After introducing the assemblage to a new victim family, that of Wayne Kemp, a black man who died while in police custody, Sharpton advised the New Alliance people present to head for their buses so that he could address the UAM crowd exclusively, but not before explaining the mostly white group's presence to the blacks.

"Some people say this is an African movement, so why are there white people here today? I am a black nationalist. I don't even own white sheets. If you want to march with me, if you respect me and respect this movement, then I'll respect you too. It doesn't mean I have to like you. But I'll respect you."

With that the white reporters were kicked out as well, and within half an hour all of the buses outside the Slave Theater were loading up with marchers.

There were many differences on this January day from the marches during the summer besides the fact that the marchers now wore coats.

In the summertime, shortly after the shooting, there was a sense of foreboding among those who came on the yellow buses. But this time there was no tension even approaching the summer's level. Nonetheless, just as a precaution, a security man ordered the windows on his bus closed as it began to travel on Bensonhurst's streets. Some white residents walked by, staring at the black faces behind the glass, but their expressions seemed to say, "Oh no, they're here again," more in annoyance than in dread.

There were no armies of helmeted police officers this time, although a contingent of uniformed cops awaited the marchers in the schoolyard so many of them had come to know so well.

A sniff of the air told of something else missing, the exhaust from the police motorcycles. Bensonhurst, in fact, looked like a ghost town.

As the marchers lined up, Sharpton took his place in front, his left arm linked to the right arm of Moses, who was linked to Diane (she had not gone to the Slave rally after the argument with Moses, but later joined them in Bensonhurst). As if it were a shield, Sharpton held the green-and-white street sign that said YUSUF HAWKINS BOULE-VARD in front of his chest. The parade marshals gave their final instructions: "Brothers on the outside, sisters on the inside, five abreast. Brothers on the outside, sisters . . ."

Just as they had done over the summer, the marchers began to chant as they moved forward.

"Whose streets! Our streets!" was the first chant, and it took a few moments for the momentum to pick up. Then suddenly there were a few young whites running alongside while undercover cops kept a close eye on them. But there were no chants of "You suck" in response to "Yu-suf" this time. Just a lot of people looking out of windows and the handful of young people, the vociferous Bensonhurst welcoming committee.

"Who'd they kill?"

"Yu-suf!"

"Who'd they kill?

"Yu-suf!"

Amir and Freddy Hawkins broke the ranks of the march along with some of the other young men. They began slapping on the shuttered storefronts white stickers that read WELCOME TO YUSUF HAWK-INS BOULEVARD. Some residents began ripping down the stickers as soon as they went up.

One of the neighborhood white kids who walked briskly to keep up with the march muttered, "Why don't they go home? They don't belong here."

He was talking more loudly, trying to keep in step with a uniformed cop.

"I got a right," he said for the cop's benefit. "I got a constitutional right to shoot 'em," he said, and the cop tried to ignore him. "Hey, come on," the kid said to the cop. "You got a gun, why don't you just shoot them?"

"Why don't you just go home?" the cop retorted, and the kid disappeared.

The marchers did an about-face at Seventy-seventh Street and headed back for the schoolyard. At Bay Ridge Avenue it appeared that Sharpton, the YUSUF HAWKINS BOULEVARD sign still in his hands, was veering toward the lamppost. Some cops ran in front, forming a human barricade around the pole. The sign stayed in the Reverend's hands and did not go up.

Sharpton later said that he did not attempt to place the sign over the one that read BAY RIDGE AVENUE because "everybody was worked up and the crowd would have gone wild if there was trouble," but Chief Calzerano told a different story. He said Sharpton told him personally that he would not hang the sign after all because of the respect he had for Calzerano's handling of the marches.

There was a brief news conference in the schoolyard during which Sharpton said: "We are going to go to the community planning board and officially request that the corner be changed to Yusuf Hawkins Boulevard."

"Don't you think the people will be opposed?" he was asked.

"The people of Bensonhurst say they are not racist. They are telling us there are good people here who care about what happened. So if that's the case, then I think I'm giving more credit to the people of Bensonhurst than you are. If they are not racist and are sincere, then they will change the name of the street," he said matter-of-factly.

Then Sharpton made an announcement.

"We have heard from incoming District Attorney Hynes that some of the indictments will have to be dropped because of the sloppy work done by Elizabeth Holtzman," he said.

"Do you have faith in Hynes?" someone asked.

"I have faith in God and the Reverend Doctor Martin Luther King" was Sharpton's reply.

Then Moses spoke.

"Well, they've only got seven and there were thirty. I heard someone saying the other day about how when people seek redress nonviolently, and they are suppressed from what they want that movement can then become violent," he said as Diane stared at the ground. "If they're not going to give us thirty, then do they want us to come here and get the thirty? Because we will come here and get the thirty."

Sharpton was asked if he thought progress had been made with the King Day march.

"We have made some progress, I believe. Last time we were here we were called nigger a hundred times, and now it was only fifty times. Is that progress? I guess so."

Sharpton got into his car and his driver guided it to the schoolyard exit. The buses were boarded and the rest of the marchers followed Sharpton's car out under heavy police escort. The streets of Bensonhurst were empty once again.

On the corner where Yusuf Hawkins was killed some teenaged girls who looked like they'd been sent from Central Casting for a Cyndi Lauper video were tearing down the YUSUF stickers from the lampposts and the store gates.

"Why are you taking them down?" they were asked.

"Because they don't belong here," one girl said.

Another jerked her thumb at the departing buses.

"*They* don't belong here," she said.

A light rain fell and the girls continued ripping stickers, laughing as they ran down Twentieth Avenue.

The information Sharpton had about the Bensonhurst cases falling apart came direct from the new District Attorney himself, according to Sharpton, and defense attorneys later confirmed that, indeed, there was talk of dropping charges against some defendants. But Sharpton's assessment of the reason for the difficulties, the "sloppy" work done by Holtzman, was only part of the story.

The disappearance of Vento, of course, severely damaged the prosecution's case. What they were left with was Gina Feliciano and a lot of loose ends that they would have difficulty tying up to the satisfaction of a jury, if they could at all.

Several attorneys who represented defendants in the case said they would have preferred that Hynes had been District Attorney at the time of their clients' arrests, because they would have gotten more of a fair shake. Deeply entrenched in the backstage politics that dictate how the Brooklyn criminal justice system at the prosecution level was run, Hynes might have accepted pleas from one or more defendants or cut some other kind of deal in order to secure the convictions of Fama, Mondello, and Serrano, seen as major players in the scenario according to Feliciano, which was really all prosecutors had to work with.

There were other difficulties, too, stemming from what can only be described as hubris on the part of Hynes and his staff. According to Holtzman staffers who laid the foundations of the Bensonhurst case, the outgoing District Attorney realized that problems might develop for the prosecution further down the line, and an effort was made to include Hynes and his key people early in the planning of the case, immediately after the September primary. But Hynes wanted no part of it, they said. "We were told, 'It's your problem until January,' " one high-ranking Holtzman official said in later interviews. If this was true, then such a communication failure between the two prosecutors may have had devastating results, since the acting-in-concert theory developed by Holtzman's people was complex and in many ways a novel application of law.

Moral indignation at the senselessness of the act, the political and social climate at the time of the shooting, and a host of other factors (including difficulty selecting who would or could testify before the grand juries without jeopardizing the core of the prosecution) all pointed to the path Holtzman chose. If the Holtzman camp's allegations that Joe Hynes wanted to handle the case "his way" were true, then the decision by the incoming administration to build a new case so far down the road was a serious error.

But Holtzman also took a tremendous risk by giving carte blanche to Vento, who was free to flee at any time he wanted—and did.

When Hynes constructed the Howard Beach case he was able to secure the cooperation of Robert Riley, one of the mob responsible for the death of Michael Griffith. But there were almost airtight assurances of Riley's cooperation, including charges already lodged against him.

Holtzman had no such safeguards to ensure that Vento would keep his word, even though her top people thought they could use the federal courts to secure his cooperation. Federal indictment on violation of civil rights charges as well as possible action regarding Vento's alleged drug ventures could be successfully employed, they thought. The possibility of cooperation from Andrew Maloney, the U.S. Attorney for the Eastern District of New York, however, seemed highly unlikely.

Maloney, appointed by President Ronald Reagan, didn't like bringing civil rights actions in his district, preferring to concentrate the energies of his staff on mob prosecutions and growing Asian drug cartels. It was Maloney's office that was responsible for the prosecution of John Gotti each time he faced charges in federal court.

A Maloney staffer was asked in September 1989 whether a federal prosecution might be brought in the case of Kevin Thorpe, the mentally retarded man who died of asphyxiation while being restrained by police officers in Brooklyn's Gowanus Houses. "You've got to be kidding!" the high-level staffer said. "You know better than that. Those cases don't go anywhere." An official explanation was offered by an aide to Maloney, Ann Driscoll: "Mr. Maloney does not like intruding on the local prosecutor." Maloney's jurisdiction, which includes Queens, Brooklyn, Long Island, and Staten Island, was the site of many of the city's racial homicides as well as questionable police-custody deaths that occurred in the late 1980s. Families of victims sought help from his office on many occasions, but prosecution under the title of the United States Code that includes civil rights violations and violations when civil rights are impeded "under color

200

of law," as in the case of misconduct by law enforcement personnel, was never instituted.

George Daniels, a black assistant U.S. Attorney who is now a New York City Criminal Court judge, was given the responsibility of following up on civil rights actions and complaints. When Daniels left the office in 1989 to assume the bench, the same source from Maloney's office was asked about another potential civil rights case and for information on whether action was taken or entertained in the Thorpe matter.

"We don't know who's handling George's cases right now," was the answer from one staffer. "They're here somewhere; I think a few of them were given to everybody."

One New York State elected official, commenting on Maloney's performance as U.S. Attorney in such matters, said, "The best I understand it is that he has what they pretty much call a cop mentality"—meaning in this context that Maloney did not have much faith in the brutality claims.

The court of last resort throughout the civil rights movement had become a warehouse for cases that received perfunctory review by the FBI and then gathered dust in filing cabinets somewhere in the federal courthouse down the street from the state courts on Cadman Plaza. Perhaps Holtzman's people didn't realize that Maloney's office might well have resulted in a dead end.

If the case was falling apart, the responsibility would have to be shared equally by Holtzman and Hynes. Holtzman for permitting a grandiose experiment in the law to be used for the prosecution of what could have been a simple murder case, with the emphasis on making the case first and foremost against the young man directly responsible for firing the fatal shots and those who most immediately shared the responsibility. There is no doubt that the emphasis at the time of the arrests was on rounding up the largest number of individuals possible using the acting-in-concert theory, something Holtzman loyalists themselves admit was relatively untried, and certainly without a test in the appeals courts of the state.

As for Hynes, early intercession during the transition period, an invitation which Holtzman's staff claims was rejected, could only lead to an ineffective finish of the job. If the Bensonhurst prosecutions were not successful, it was because they were crippled from the start by either Holtzman's political ambition or her reckless acquiescence to public sentiment that flew in the face of established legal practices and given the death blow by the arrogance of the new administration.

Fears that the case was in trouble led Sharpton and Maddox to communicate directly with the United States Attorney's office, asking for a federal probe into the shooting of Yusuf. Maloney's terse reply through a spokesman was that such an action would not be entertained until the cases had been run through the state system.

"It's what we expected," Moses said. Yusuf's father, who knew that the murder cases might not amount to much in the way of convictions, was becoming more certain that he would not receive justice to any measure of his satisfaction in the courts, but said he still believed in the system. While Moses' outspoken nature did not endear him to the public as a whole, especially the white public, his inflammatory image was created in part by the media that reported on him. One question asked of Moses in particular was telling in this respect.

"If you could take the law into your own hands what would you do?" he was asked by a CNN reporter.

"We're seeking justice, not vengeance," was his reply.

TRIALS AND TRIBULATION

OPE sprang back briefly for Charles J. Hynes' staff in March when John Vento surrendered to authorities in Columbus, Ohio, where he had been staying since his disappearance. But upon his return to New York Vento refused to cooperate with prosecutors and was himself indicted for murder. Citing threats and fear of reprisal from Joseph Fama's family, Vento opted to stand trial rather than risk harm to himself or others close to him. Once indicted, Vento was useless as a witness, and the vivid description he had given of the events on Bay Ridge Avenue would be used against him personally.

Neither Hynes nor his assistants would have rested their case solely on a co-conspirator against whom charges had not been lodged. But the road map for the prosecution had already been drawn long before Hynes assumed office. Attempts to alter the course of events were unsuccessful. One was a try at turning Charles Stressler into a witness.

As the time drew near for the first trials to begin, Stressler was no longer represented by Michael Santangelo. There had been mounting dissatisfaction with the lawyer, who seemed to the Stressler family to be long on accommodating the press but short on preparing the kind of case Stressler and his family would have preferred. Tensions between attorney and client mounted when Santangelo insisted that Stressler plead guilty to lesser charges. In a disturbing scene in Santangelo's inner office, Stressler was told that he would without a doubt go to jail as a result of his decision.

The family turned to Jacob Evseroff, a former assistant district attorney who had represented a number of high-profile clients, including a Queens cop accused of murdering a young black teenager and one of a number of white Queens men charged in connection with the torching of a black family's home in an effort to drive them from a predominantly white neighborhood. Evseroff had a reputation for being an ace trial lawyer, and one who did not compromise easily.

Shortly after being retained by Stressler, Evseroff was approached by the District Attorney's office with a deal. Prosecutors would permit Stressler to plead guilty to any charge he wished, so long as he could testify that he saw Joseph Serrano pass the murder weapon to Joseph Fama shortly before the shooting. Such testimony would almost guarantee a conviction when Serrano came to the dock. But Stressler couldn't deliver, because he had simply not seen the alleged event take place. Stressler did not know Joseph Fama by sight, and only identified him during his interrogation when he was shown pictures of him. Undoubtedly Stressler could have been used as a witness against Fama as well, but no deal was cut and he remained charged with murder.

Attempts had been made to turn Steven Curreri and Pasquale Raucci as well, but they had never made it around the corner and hadn't seen anything of real value to the prosecution. Although Jimmy Patino had been there, he would in no way consider testifying against the others. Prosecutors were also less inclined to cut a deal with Patino, since they believed he had a gun earlier in the evening of August 23.

When zero hour came, the prosecution had Frankie Tighe, a teenager from the neighborhood who suffered from hallucinations and had been hospitalized for mental disorders in the past; Cyndi Hamburger, who could identify the people in the mob and testify as to what she saw and heard after the shooting; Irene DeSerio, the nurse who, along with Elizabeth Galarza, tried to help Yusuf as he lay dying; and Phyllis D'Agata and her daughter Gina Feliciano.

The fact that Hynes and his staff did not accept offers of early transition and cooperation from Holtzman's staff didn't mean that they were asleep at the switch. The veteran prosecutor had a profound personal distaste for racial violence, which he saw more clearly than ever before the evil that it was when he spearheaded the Howard Beach prosecution. Hynes appointees, particularly Ed Boyar and James Koehler, got to work on their own as soon as they were able, wading through boxes of DD-5s, police follow-up reports of interviews with witnesses and defendants, as well as reams of grand jury testimony in an effort to map their own strategy. But they had few tools to work with.

Koehler, a sixty-year-old warhorse, had for years been one of Hynes' closest personal associates, eventually acting as his chief assistant in the Special Prosecutor's office. He made invaluable contributions to the Howard Beach prosecution. Boyar, forty-eight, never knew the other side of the table in court, working as an investigator and then a prosecutor during his entire legal career, which included a significant role with the Howard Beach prosecution team.

The two holdovers from the Holtzman regime, Bruce McIntyre and Ed Burns, were both familiar with the cases from the very beginning. Burns, thirty-three, had been an assistant district attorney since he was twenty-seven. McIntyre, who had sat in on many of the strategy sessions, was a lawyer for whom many in the DA's office had great personal respect. But he would not remain on the case, or for that matter within the District Attorney's office at all, for very long.

McIntyre resigned after it became clear to him that he would play a minimal role in the prosecution. There were disagreements with the Hynes people over strategy, and the coup de grâce came when McIntyre, reassigned to a different unit and placed further and further away from any pivotal prosecutorial role, learned that he was being counted on to give opening and closing statements in the case. According to published reports in *New York Newsday* by Patricia Hurtado, from information attributed to high-ranking prosecution sources, and in the *City Sun* by Utrice Leid, which included an interview with McIntyre himself, his displeasure was based on the idea that he would be a "token" in the prosecution, "trotted out at showtime" for the presentations, while his real role kept rapidly diminishing. He was quoted in the *City Sun*, the black New York weekly, as saying that if he was to make opening and closing statements he would have a difficult time of it since he really didn't know what the Hynes office theory of the prosecution was all about.

Jeanne Hammock, a fifty-two-year-old black woman who had been an assistant to Hynes in the state special prosecutor's office, would be assigned in McIntyre's stead.

During pretrial hearings there were many attempts by defense lawyers to have their trials severed from Fama's. The key to the defense of many of those charged was that Fama acted alone when he shot Yusuf Hawkins and that his act was separate and apart from the gathering in the schoolyard. To have their clients tried in the same courtroom with Fama, even with separate juries, could prejudice their cases. Scheduling glitches added to a complexity of calendar-marking that resulted in Fama and Mondello being tried first. But they would have to have separate juries, since Mondello made statements to police that implicated Fama, and Fama's jury could not be permitted to hear them.

A videotape of Mondello's confession was disallowed by Judge Owens at a pretrial hearing, but a signed statement in which Mondello admits to having a bat would be permitted at the trial. If his client was going to be cleared of the highest charges, murder and manslaughter, then Stephen Murphy would have to hammer away at the statement's veracity in an attempt to prove that it had been coerced.

Mondello's family and many observers were critical of one decision the feisty Queens lawyer made on behalf of Mondello—the desire to go in first, rather than wait until some of the dust settled around other trials. There were rumblings that Murphy's desire for the limelight might be indulged at the expense of Keith Mondello's freedom, something that Murphy, who claims he has no interest in the publicity he has attained, vigorously denies.

Mondello's family and the lawyer had a bumpy relationship, stemming in large part from the family's inability to pay Murphy his agreed-upon fee.

When Murphy met with Keith's father Michael Mondello to discuss the lapses, the attorney asked how the family planned to take care of the obligation.

"We're trusting in God to help us through all of this," Mondello, Sr. replied.

"God?" Murphy shrieked. "God? Is God going to go up there and tell Thaddeus Owens not to send your kid to jail? Tell God to do that!"

In April 1990, as the date for jury selection approached, the silver-haired leprechaun with the acid tongue made no secret of what his strategy would be. Gina Feliciano was the state's star witness, and Murphy was going to eat her for breakfast.

"It was all because of her. She called black and Hispanic drug dealers to come to the neighborhood and she told everyone she was doing it. She's the one who should be prosecuted," Murphy said. The lawyer was well aware of Feliciano's drug problems and planned to make full use of them in an attempt to discredit her.

David DePetris, Fama's lawyer, was low-key and meticulous. He lacked Murphy's abrasiveness and penchant for discussing strategy publicly. At one point he had entertained the possibility of an insanity defense for Joseph Fama but decided against it. The prosecution, minus its most damaging witness with the charging of Vento, would have to prove every step of the way its allegations that Fama fired the shots. They had no murder weapon, and they had a witness, Frankie Tighe, who could be made to appear less than credible.

The selection of jurors began on April second, from a pool of four hundred potential panelists. Prosecutor Edward Boyar himself received a notice for jury duty. He was excused.

During a process that lasted nearly two weeks, potential jurors were interviewed until two panels were finally seated. In a case that had this high a profile, special problems developed. As Stephen Murphy put it, "If the guy knows about the case you've got to figure as best you can if he'll be fair. If he doesn't know about it you don't want him either because he's an idiot."

Both juries represented the racial and ethnic mix one might expect from the Kings County jury pool. The forewoman of the Mondello jury, Mimi Snowden, was a black letter carrier. Sandra Kipnes, a white Flatbush woman, worked for a brokerage house. Collette Murphy, an office worker, was from the Marine Park section. Preston

Williams was black, lived in Bedford-Stuyvesant, and worked for the New York City Transit Authority. Jose Cepeda, a cafeteria worker, was Hispanic. Elizabeth Luquis, also Hispanic, was an office clerk. Alice Quinn, a white woman, lived in the heavily Hispanic Williamsburgh section. Iris Roman, an Hispanic, was an office clerk. Christine Porter, like forewoman Snowden, was black and worked for the Postal Service. Michael Kaufer, a Caucasian, worked as a bank treasurer. James Enright and Theodore Simmons were both white.

The Fama jury was a similarly mixed bag of backgrounds, gender, and ethnicity. Forewoman Tonya Roberts was a white Southerner, originally from Lynchburg, Tennessee. She was part of a panel made up of eight women and four men. Six were white, three were black, two were Hispanic, and one was Asian.

The courtroom where Judge Owens usually presided was too small for the expected public turnout for the trial, so a larger chamber down the hall was used instead. Blue-and-white police barriers were set up outside the courtroom door for media representatives, some of whom had reserved seats inside. Those who did not have reserved status were assigned numbers by patient court officers who often bantered with the press before the day's proceedings began.

At the end of the hall near the elevator bank, just past the walk-through metal detector, other barricades corraled spectators. Most were black, many were angry, and all had to take a number.

Both juries sat in the courtroom, and the Fama jury was excused during those times when evidence necessary for the Mondello trial would have prejudiced them against Fama.

As the juries listened intently, Assistant District Attorney Ed Boyar opened the case against Fama by painting a picture of the night of the attack, how young white men armed themselves because they believed blacks were coming to Gina Feliciano's birthday party. "With callous disregard for human life Joseph Fama took out a pistol and fatally shot his victim through the heart . . . he fired the gun repeatedly into the heart of Yusuf Hawkins."

"The bullets struck him in the chest, striking his heart, literally blasting it apart," Boyar said, and Diane Hawkins began to sob quietly.

Dave DePetris quietly and calmly told the jurors that they would have to look at the motives of some witnesses who might testify, and try to figure out whether they gained their information firsthand or from other sources, such as the newspapers.

"I am asking you to keep an open mind," DePetris said.

Mondello was described as the ringleader of the attack, who gathered his friends together to teach Gina Feliciano and her black friends a lesson.

"He stood there with a bat in his hands," Boyar said of Mondello.

Both defendants sat calm and still. Rocco Fama, Joey's father, shook his head.

The first prosecution witness was Troy Banner, who was gently led through questioning about the events leading up to the incident and finally to what happened on the corner. The courtroom remained hushed as Troy told the jury about the white mob surrounding them on the corner. "Then the shots were fired," Banner said. "Yusuf yelled, and then he fell down."

Court officers carefully monitored the Hawkins family as well as the Mondellos and Famas, escorting them in and out of a special reserved elevator in order to prevent untimely confrontations between them. When court was not in session the Mondellos, including Keith, were kept in a small room at the extreme far end of the hall near Owens' old courtroom. The room, used for conferences between attorneys and clients, had a small table, several chairs, and a plate-glass window through which the Mondellos could see the reporters and other people who passed by trying not to appear as if they were looking.

Joseph Fama was still in custody, so during recesses he was reshackled and led away through a courtroom door behind the bench. His family congregated in a hallway behind a fire door at the opposite end of the building from the Mondellos.

During her direct testimony, Feliciano told the jury that Mondello had been bragging earlier in the day of the shooting of having five guns and that she saw a bat-wielding Mondello along with Joseph Fama chase Hawkins, Banner, Sylvester, and Stanford at the head of the mob of white youths.

It became apparent early in the proceedings that Judge Owens was not going to permit outbursts in his courtroom. The septuagenarian jurist listened to testimony with his chin resting on his fist, always alert, and always ready to accommodate objections raised by counsel on either side, at least for the Mondello trial. He was neither patient nor courteous toward DePetris, who believed that the judge was firmly disposed against his client.

Objections to lines of questioning by the prosecution were something heard often during Murphy's jackhammer cross examinations of Feliciano.

During questioning about her drug problems Gina, who had recently entered Phoenix House, a drug rehabilitation center, protested to the judge.

Owens had already warned Murphy several times, and he took the lawyer to his chambers to discuss just how far he was going to permit courtroom decorum to be stretched.

Murphy's grilling of Feliciano was almost anticlimactic, considering his boasts about what he was going to do to her on the stand. She was the kind of witness Murphy could sink his teeth into, as he sneered and gave sidelong glances to a jury that patiently listened.

"The two of you were there together?" he asked, wire-rimmed glasses perched on the tip of his nose, referring back to her testimony that she and her mother watched from their window as Yusuf and his friends passed.

"The two of you were there together, both of you?" he asked in a loud voice.

"No, I'm making it up," she snapped.

"It wouldn't be the first time," Murphy sneered.

Phyllis D'Agata, Gina's mother, also testified against both defendants, saying that she saw Mondello with a gun and that when Joey Fama (who she said begged Joseph Serrano for a gun) was at the head of the pack holding his side, she saw what appeared to be the outline of a gun in his waistband or under his shirt.

Irene Deserio was another witness who corroborated portions of that testimony, as did Cindy Hamburger.

Some of the most damaging testimony against Mondello came from Russell Gibbons, the black youth who admitted helping bring bats to the schoolyard. But one topic of Gibbons' direct examination, potentially damaging to Fama's defense, was something he later said never should have been.

At one point Ed Burns of the prosecution team referred to a portion of Gibbons' grand jury testimony. Before he took the stand, Burns had asked Russell to remember specifically the portion of his grand jury appearance where he said that Frankie Tighe called out to him, "Joey Fama shot a black kid." That is what Gibbons testified to at the trial, although he recalled testifying differently before the grand jury. "Somebody shot a black kid" was what he remembered. But the jury at Cadman Plaza had heard differently in the spring of 1989.

"Burns tricked me," Gibbons said later. "He just asked it so fast, and I answered before I knew what I was saying, it was like he put it in my head."

Claude Stanford, handled gently by both DePetris and Murphy, recalled what happened on the night of the shooting and identified Mondello as having a bat. There was little reason for DePetris to be concerned about the East New York youth's testimony, however, because at no time had he ever been able to identify Joseph Fama.

One decision made by Murphy could have backfired into a tool for the prosecution, but it proved in many ways helpful to the defense instead.

Mondello's police videotape could have been damning evidence, considering its content and context. But there was another tape, made with Murphy's permission, that was aired on WABC-TV. Reporter Sarah Wallace had interviewed Mondello and he got to tell his side of the story, including statements that he had no negative feelings toward blacks. Prosecutors subpoenaed the tape and used it in lieu of the confession, which was precluded from evidence. Although the Wallace interview was introduced by the opposition, it may have worked to Murphy's advantage. His client got to tell his side of the story in a nonthreatening atmosphere. The viewing by the jury gave Mondello the benefit of taking the witness stand without the rigors of cross-examination or the attendant waiver of rights against self-incrimination that accompanies such a decision.

One of the detectives who had interrogated Mondello, Darcy Callahan, was questioned as to the voluntariness of Mondello's signed statement, but the veteran detective held up well under Murphy's counterattack. Out of hearing of the Fama jury, the statement had been entered into evidence.

Not all of the witnesses against Fama were as cooperative at the trial as they had been during the grand jury, however. Chris Lomuto, the Paul Revere of Twentieth Avenue, was to have testified that Mondello told him at his house, after the shooting, that he was afraid he would be recognized. Under direct questioning, he could not recall the conversation. He was one of several witnesses who suffered from "Bensonhurst amnesia."

Prior to the trial, Joseph Fama had talked to several other inmates at the Brooklyn House of Detention. One, Charles Brown, described by some attorneys as a "professional rat," said he befriended Fama behind bars and that Fama confessed the killing to him. Brown admitted that he would have been willing to frame two innocent men in the past in order to free himself from jail. During his direct testimony Brown said that he heard Fama say "I capped him" and that he shot Hawkins because he was black. Rocco Fama, the stoic father who sat stonelike throughout the trial, began to move his lips when he heard Brown's testimony. "He's a liar," the elder Fama said. Another jailhouse confession was recalled by Robert Russo, a career criminal who asked Dave DePetris during his cross-examination if he was the one on trial. When DePetris went over Russo's long criminal record the witness asked the lawyer, "Did you expect them to have an angel up here," bringing chuckles to the courtroom.

The final witness was Frankie Tighe, whose psychological maladies included both visual and auditory hallucinations. "He sees helicopters," DePetris said outside the courtroom when describing how credible a witness he thought the young man would make against his client. Tighe gave an unembellished account of the shooting, placing the gun in Fama's hand, and was easily forthcoming about his four hospitalizations between 1987 and 1989.

On Monday, May 7, after closing arguments by Dave DePetris and Ed Boyar, the case against Joseph Fama went to the jury. Judge Owens gave lengthy explanations of criminal culpability and the meaning of "acting in concert," and the twelve men and women began the task of deciding the fate of the short young man with the pocket handkerchief.

The case against Mondello went to the jury the following day, with similar instructions, and an explanation by Owens of the jurors' choices of homicide convictions.

"If being a jerk is a crime, then he's guilty of being a jerk," Murphy told the Mondello jury in his summation. Although the charges against Fama were more serious because of the intentional murder count, the Mondello jury had far more to work with than the Fama panel. There were no intentional-murder charges against Mondello, and they only needed to find that he acted in concert with others to bring back a verdict of guilty to depraved mind murder (meaning that "evincing a depraved indifference to human life," he had contributed to the death of Yusuf Hawkins).

During the course of the trials demonstrators had begun appearing in the plaza in front of the courthouse, arguing issues of politics and racism with each other, denouncing the acts of the Bensonhurst mob in unison, and expressing their desire for verdicts of guilty on all counts. As word spread that both juries were out, the crowd in front of the courthouse grew, reaching numbers in the hundreds during lunchtime.

Although the racial tension that gripped New York City in the wake of the murder on Bay Ridge Avenue had abated with the election of David Dinkins, as the juries deliberated apprehension again grew citywide over what would happen if, indeed, there were acquittals of the alleged ringleader and the shooter.

Moses Stewart, uncharacteristically reserved, spoke to the press, along with Sharpton, after the juries began their work and urged motorists to shine their headlights as a show of support for convictions and maximum sentences.

"We ask all the people who want to see justice for Yusuf to turn their headlights on," Sharpton said, his sentiments echoed by Moses as Diane stood by mutely.

"I want everyone involved in this crime to get life," Moses said. "They took a good, innocent life, but I don't believe we're going to get the justice we deserve or ask for."

Upstairs, twenty-four men and women considered the evidence while spring flowers blossomed on Cadman Plaza, and the city held its breath. The weather was getting warm, and the talk on the street was that if there were acquittals somebody would be made to pay. With each passing day violence in New York seemed like more than idle speculation.

During the first days of jury deliberations there were a few false starts as reporters and courtroom watchers adjusted to the rhythms of justice. In the family room on the fourth floor Moses Stewart and Diane Hawkins received the reporters they had become familiar with throughout the preceding year, and Al Sharpton showed up often.

The juries were putting in long days, and with each note passed to the judge hopes would spring up momentarily that a verdict was near. In the other windowed room, on the far side of the courthouse, the Mondellos sat and tried not to notice the never-ending parade that passed by them. Finally, tired of being stared at (in the words of Susan Mondello, "as if we were in a fishbowl"), the Mondellos placed a huge piece of cardboard over the glass to ensure their privacy.

Outside the courthouse the atmosphere fluctuated from tense to near-carnival. A coffin with the name of Yusuf Hawkins lay upright against a tree, and several protesters burned American flags. Most of those who stayed outside were from the Revolutionary Communist Party or were drawn elsewhere from the flotsam and jetsam that wandered the streets of downtown Brooklyn. Pamphleteers pamphleteered, the deranged made speeches to nobody except themselves, and streetcorner debates became the rule of the day. It is possible that never before in the history of Brooklyn had the First

Amendment privilege been exercised so freely and openly, with white lunchers debating issues of racism with black activists as interested crowds looked on. The scene would have been amusing if the job being done by the jurors inside had not been so serious and the consequences so grave.

People walking the crowded Brooklyn streets were stopped by reporters who asked them their opinions on what the reaction would be if Mondello or Fama were acquitted. Many said they believed that there would be violence, a hint of which was undeniably in the air.

The first eruption occurred when Murphy ventured to his favorite restaurant and watering hole for lunch. Although Dave DePetris' client was accused of being the trigger man, the Manhattan attorney was never molested by anyone. He did not have Murphy's vitriolic tongue or presence, nor had he won a Howard Beach acquittal, something some members of the black community would never forgive Murphy for.

On the third day of deliberations Murphy had left the courthouse and was sauntering down the street when a group of demonstrators began to follow him, calling him names and shaking their fists. Suddenly, near the Republic National Bank on the corner of Cadman Plaza across from the courthouse, a fist flew and glanced Murphy's face. Stunned, the lawyer turned around and raised his fists, all composure gone.

Television camera crews and foot cops raced to the scene, not sure of what had just happened but certain that it did not bode well. Murphy, his fists clenched, called after his assailant.

"Come on, you want to do it here? Come on, let's do it right now!" he hollered, and then he was hustled away by a human blanket of police officers into the safety of Peter Hilary's Pub.

Shaken from the ordeal, Murphy ordered crabcakes and a double vodka while the crowd outside grew, chanting, "Fight the Power" and "No justice, no peace," shaking their fists in the air and attracting even more people.

The crowd spilled out onto the street but was contained by police officers who formed a ring around it, keeping even journalists from getting too close. Some words were exchanged, but there was no further violence that day. Shunning a suggestion that he leave through Hilary's basement, Murphy walked back to the courthouse under heavy police guard.

At Cadman Plaza the television vans were lined up with their poles extended for live broadcasts on the news shows. The weather had been pleasant, and crew members, happy with the overtime they were receiving, camped out on top of their vehicles and got early suntans. There was a barbecue one afternoon, and the appearance of smoke brought a response of nervous firefighters to the scene. That same day Al Sharpton had spoken at length with a New York *Post* reporter about the tension in town and how the black community might react if Mondello and Fama were freed.

"If they come back with less than murder you are lighting a match to the end of a powder keg and telling us to burn the town down," Sharpton was quoted as saying. The words were no different in substance than those spoken by Herbert Daughtry a month before the Hawkins murder. But it was a different time and place, and the papers were running out of Bensonhurst stories while readers waited anxiously for more trial news. Sharpton's words echoed back from the pages of the *Post*, which featured a cartoon of the preacher with a gasoline can in his hand.

Mayor Dinkins was critical of Sharpton's comments, which he said could be a self-fulfilling prophecy. He had characterized Sharpton in a television interview as "one who fans the flames of racial hatred." Sharpton, Moses Stewart, and attorney C. Vernon Mason were later critical of the mayor himself.

"We have not called for slaughter," Moses Stewart said. "We have called for justice. You kill our children, we are hurt. We get angry."

Dinkins also said that he didn't see much sense in reaching out to Stewart—or Sharpton, for that matter: "I don't know if I can communicate with him, and certainly not with Mr. Sharpton," the mayor said.

The media did not escape Dinkins' criticism either, for highlighting the remarks: "The media must seek out persons who have different attitudes than those speaking the loudest at this point . . . most people do not agree with Al Sharpton, period."

Pressed for further explanation of his controversial words about violence, Sharpton noted that at all times he and the family had called for calm and never once advocated violence.

The UAM contingent had not been to the courthouse in force, but on May 12, with the juries still out deliberating between requests for clarification of the law from Owens, they came as a group in buses to Bensonhurst.

Both Diane and Moses led the march with Sharpton, marching for about a mile as angry whites lined up behind police barricades, chanting, "Not guilty!" One sign held up by counterdemonstrators said FREE THE BOYS OF BENSONHURST. The march was more tense than any of the UAM visits to the troubled neighborhood had been, with the exception of the first few, and there were several scuffles between angry white residents and police, resulting in some minor injuries.

After leaving Bensonhurst the marchers came to the courthouse, where the demonstrators who had remained in front throughout the deliberations and the trial were massed near the steps, behind police barriers. The chanting could already be heard coming from the windows of the arriving yellow buses, cries of, "No justice, no peace," and "Yusuf, Yusuf."

As the UAM marchers carried placards and walked in a circle behind other barricades that had been set up, the courthouse contingent, excited at seeing Sharpton, began to surge toward the barricades that held them from the steps. Police on either side of the plaza were ready to move in, and riot-helmeted court officers on the steps added a tense note to the scene.

"This is a nonviolent demonstration," Sharpton said to the crowd at the steps. "If you want to join us you are welcome to, but if you are here to start shit, then you can go home because we don't want you here."

There were some surprised mumbles among the crowd, and soon the UAM marchers left the chastened RCP recruits, heading back for the Slave Theater. Sharpton and the Hawkins family entered the courthouse as still another day went by with no decision.

The Fama jury especially seemed confused on the issue of acting in concert and expressed their concerns to the judge once again on

217

Mother's Day, along with a request for clarification of other issues. The note the judge had been handed during a lunch recess indicated that the jury was having problems expressing themselves adequately with the presence of the media, and asked if the press could be excluded.

When court was to resume again, reporters shuffled nervously as court officers barred them from entering the locked chamber. The media and the public were locked out for over an hour, and none were happy.

Once the doors were opened again William Glaberson, who had been covering the trial for the New York *Times*, rose to address Judge Owens. Glaberson expressed indignation both personally and on behalf of the *Times*. It was incomprehensible to the seasoned reporter that a public trial during such a sensitive time in the city's history would become a closed-door affair. An attorney for the *Times* came to the courthouse at Glaberson's request and also addressed the issue.

However, Owens released transcripts of the "secret" meeting with the jury, and there were no further repercussions. There were still problems for the jury to sort out, the most notable whether mere presence at the scene of the crime was enough to convict someone of acting in concert.

Owens tried once again, this time with the press in the courtroom, to explain. Using the example of Mozart's *Requiem*, although possibly not sure how knowledgeable the jurors were in classical music, Owens told them that at the end of the work there is a single, barely audible drumbeat.

"But he is part of the orchestra," Owens said. What he tried to put across (and did with more clarity to the Mondello panel, according to some observers) was that if the defendant shared the state of mind of whoever committed the crime, then he was guilty as charged.

Dave DePetris, who had been having a hard time of things with Owens from the very beginning, voiced objections to the way the judge explained the law. According to Owens' instructions, any person on the corner of Bay Ridge and Twentieth avenues could be found guilty of murder, and although the judge mentioned that the person on the corner would have to share the intent of the actual

218

killer, DePetris felt that the distinction was not made clearly enough. "He already had my guy tried, convicted, and sentenced," DePetris said later.

A brief spat ensued between lawyer and judge that almost resulted in a contempt citation against DePetris.

As a new week wore on, Stephen Murphy also found himself at odds with Judge Owens, who chastised him for public comments he had made, predicting an acquittal for Mondello.

"That's adding fuel to the fire, Mr. Murphy," Owens said, as he warned the lawyer against making any further comments of a similar nature.

On Wednesday, the sixteenth of May, David Dinkins appeared live on the local television stations. Seated in the Board of Estimate chamber, the mayor addressed a city that both feared and eagerly anticipated the verdicts that could come at any hour or day. With the flags of the City of New York and the United States of America behind him, Dinkins gave a brief, dignified talk appealing for calm no matter what the verdicts might prove to be. To those in front of the courthouse and in the deep inner-city neighborhoods of Brooklyn, the chant of "Fight the power" took on a new significance. They had seen the power on their television screens, and it had a black face. They were not impressed.

The next day, May 17, the Fama jury sent a note down to the judge. Court officers were called in to the fourth floor from other sections to beef up security. Out on the street, through a prearranged plan, police reinforcements stood ready to respond to any trouble that might result. Harry Ryttenberg, a field producer for WNBC-TV, got the first word and then it went out to the city. There was a verdict.

The New York City Police Department had already quietly notified commanders of special units that had been waiting unobtrusively for word, including a contingent of eight or so cops who were to remain at City Hall in case violence came to David Dinkins' doorstep. The police did not want to add tension to tension, however, so the units stayed away from potential trouble areas, ready to respond if necessary.

On the fourth floor DePetris told Rocco Fama, who was accompanied by his wife Josephine, that the time had arrived. Josephine looked frail and nervous as she took her seat on the right side of the courtroom, across the aisle from the Hawkins family. Her brother-in-law Joseph, other relatives, and a young friend of her son Joseph's named Vito sat next to her.

In the middle aisle of the courtroom a line of court officers stood, ready for any confrontations that might occur. Rocco Fama bit his lip, and his son Joseph, seated at the defense table, looked blankly at the jury as they filed in.

Tonya Bailey stood straight and still, grateful that nobody could see her quavering knees. The emotions that had run rampant in the bright room lay dormant, waiting like crouching demons in the silence: "As to the first charge of murder in the second degree we find the defendant Joseph Fama not guilty."

There was a stifled cry from the Hawkins side of the courtroom as the intentional-murder charge, like Bailey's words, drifted away, and a few *sh*s as Bailey continued, not waiting for the reactions to cease as she read the second charge, depraved-mind murder, which carried the same sentence as the first, twenty-five years to life.

"We find the defendant guilty," she said. There was a silence, and then a "Yes," with hard emphasis on the *s*, sliced across toward Fama. It may have come from Diane Hawkins, who sat still as people around her gripped the backs of the benches in front of them listening for more.

On the Fama side of the courtroom Rocco, his head back, tried not to react, but the tears in his eyes spoke for him. Josephine shook her head, and the pained woman's voice squeaked, "Not my son!"

Joseph Fama looked toward his family with the realization that he would not be a free man for many years to come. He made a weak attempt at a lopsided smile.

The litany of charges continued, each punctuated with the word *guilty*, and then suddenly the Fama family was gone as the ratchetlike sounds of the handcuffs were heard clamping around Joseph's thin wrists before he was led away, giving one more brief backward glance.

The jury, tears streaming down the cheeks of some, were ready to leave after being thanked by Owens.

Dave DePetris, bitter and resigned, spoke briefly with reporters. He believed that the judge's explanation to the jury was unfair to his client, that the law had not been explained in a way that could make them understand.

"What else could I expect from this guy," DePetris said. "He was out to get my guy, period. We were ready for this."

Out on the street there was joyful pandemonium in the gathering Brooklyn dusk as the crowd at Cadman Plaza heard the news, but they weren't seen or heard by Rocco Fama as he walked silently out the back door of the courthouse, his wife next to him, while reporters thrust microphones into his face and camera flashes went off. Nearby, choking back tears, was Joseph's friend Vito, who could no longer contain himself and charged the cameras. Michelle Agins, a black New York *Times* photographer, tried to get a shot of the rampaging young man as he flailed out with fists and feet until she and her camera were in the way and she was doubled over in pain from a punch to her breast. Vito continued on, a triumphant teenaged Sonny Corleone in a crewcut who had struck a blow for justice by assaulting a black woman. The Famas got into a car and sped off as police responded and sought aid for the photographer.

Upstairs the reporters scrambled for telephones as arrangements for the jurors to make statements were made. A courtroom farther down the hall had been selected for that purpose.

The jurors generally believed that Joseph Fama had been the gunman, but that the state had not proved the case beyond all reasonable doubt. Based on Owens' explanation of acting in concert, they were able to convict on the second murder charge. No matter how many witnesses there had been, no matter how many people who saw the shooting might claim that they saw Joseph Fama fire the fatal rounds, as far as the criminal justice system was concerned Joseph Fama was not guilty of the actual murder, but had acted in concert with others to cause the death of Yusuf Hawkins.

Those technicalities aside, there was relative peace on the streets that night. The justifiably angry and those who will use any excuse to perpetrate violence did not care about the difference between "intentional" and "depraved-mind" murder. Joseph Fama had been convicted of homicide, and that was all that mattered.

In Bensonhurst, on Seventy-first Street and Eighteenth Avenue, the young men crowded around the television cameras poised near the empty Fama residence, where the curtains were drawn. Dave DePetris had stopped by earlier, after Rocco, Josephine, and the others first arrived, and then everybody left for a family retreat upstate.

The reaction on the block was bitter.

"He was a good boy," a next-door neighbor said, remembering the times she saw him leaving for work in the mornings with his father. "They are good, hard-working, family people. This is a shame."

"It was political," another woman offered. "It was all about the politics and they were afraid the blacks were going to riot, so now he pays and his parents pay."

Their work completed, the television vans packed up to leave. One moved forward just past Eighteenth Avenue as its pole antenna was nearly retracted and brought down a huge tree limb onto somebody's parked Oldsmobile. The cugeens appeared from everywhere and began to pursue the van, cursing in Italian and English, but it was gone.

A divided city remained calm in the wake of the Fama verdict, but there was still Keith Mondello to worry about. There was no way to know how many hours or days it would be before his jury reached a decision. And so the city and the young man from Twentieth Avenue slept uneasily. As it turned out, neither had to wait very long.

Courtroom veterans say that a happy-looking jury is less likely to convict, and if that was the case the Mondello panel certainly seemed less threatening compared with Fama's. The Fama jury often covered the back window of their van as they headed toward the hotel where they were sequestered, and on one of the few occasions they did not do so a juror waved his middle finger at journalists and cameramen watching their departure from the garage beneath the courthouse.

The Mondello jury was more whimsical. One night as they left there was a sign in the back of the bus that said WE'RE GOING TO DISNEYLAND.

The witnesses against Mondello placed him not only at the scene but also at the center of the arguments that led to the shooting of Yusuf Hawkins. Mondello further tightened the noose by virtue of his statement to police, signed in his own hand, even if, as his attorney argued, it had been coerced.

Mondello's parents, Susan and Michael, had tried valiantly to bear up under the pressure of the trial. They had absolutely no understanding of why their son had been charged with murder and comprehended even less some of the other charges, as well as things that were being written and broadcast about Keith. Few teenagers are apt to admit to their parents that they are dealing drugs, and Keith Mondello certainly was no exception. There is no reason to believe that, to his parents, Keith was not the sweet and considerate young man they claimed him to be.

The Mondellos glared at reporters when they walked through the hallway toward the courtroom, and after the Fama verdict their icy demeanor did not change. They felt used by the media and believed that the characterization of their family as a crazed collection of Neanderthal crackpot racists was unfair. Both Susan and her husband were highly excitable, especially Michael, who suffered from a nervous condition and was on medication.

On the evening after the Fama verdict, a Friday night, Stephen Murphy walked into the "family room" and nodded. Prepared for the absolute worst and hoping for the best, they trooped into the courtroom and took their seats in the third row. Michael Mondello leaned his head back and looked up at the lights in the courtroom ceiling. Across the aisle, past the court officers who stood at near-attention, Moses Stewart and Diane Hawkins, flanked by Al Sharpton and other UAM people, breathlessly took their seats.

The Hawkins family had suffered yet another tragic loss that morning when word was received that Moses' sister, who had been ill, had died. Sharpton had been attempting to help them make arrangements for burial when word of the verdict reached them and they returned to court as quickly as possible.

The courtroom was packed and the doors were locked. Susan and Michael Mondello held hands tightly on one side of the room while Moses Stewart and Diane Hawkins did the same on the other. Mondello, with Murphy seated next to him, adjusted the eyeglasses he had worn all through the trial, then fidgeted with a pen. Reporters with scorecards of the charges had pens in hand as well, ready to write the news as it was announced. Downstairs, in front of the courthouse, the congregation of verdict-watchers waited. They believed that there would be guilty verdicts for Mondello, their hopes heightened by the Fama conviction of the day before, which seemed so long ago to those seated in the fourth-floor court chamber.

The prosecution team turned toward the jury as they entered. Judge Owens, poker-faced as usual, surveyed the scene before him.

Forewoman Mimi Snowden announced the first verdict, murder in the second degree.

"Not guilty."

A scream that could have come from a wounded cat issued from the Hawkins side of the room as Michael Mondello began to shake and tremble.

"Hallelujah, Jesus has risen!" he said, as Snowden continued reading the panel's findings. Snowden answered the second murder count.

"Not guilty."

Blacks leaped up from their seats, ringed by the white-shirted court officers. One large black officer turned toward the side of the room.

"Sit down!" he bellowed. But the racking sobs of Diane Hawkins filled the room as she collapsed into the arms of Moses, who held her and stared in disbelief, even more crestfallen after the high hopes spawned by the day before.

Manslaughter first degree.

"Not guilty."

The cries of anguish reached to the ceiling and filled the courtroom as Michael Mondello, beside himself and hugging his wife as she sobbed, kept repeating, "It's God's will, thank you, God!"

Manslaughter second degree.

"Not guilty."

Keith Mondello looked on woodenly at first, confused by the scene behind him and then appeared to be crying as he lay his head down on the defense table. Diane Hawkins' whole body shook and she screamed as if cut in half and the tears still didn't stop.

First-degree riot.

"Guilty."

There were shouts and screams; then a tall black man in yellow stood shaking a fist and then pointed at Snowden.

"You're through, you're finished!" he hollered as court officers surrounded him and whisked him through the double doors out to the hallway while Al Sharpton stood up waving his arms and telling the family's supporters to shut up and sit down, and another person was ejected from the courtroom as insults and slurs spun through the air between blond wood panels. And then suddenly, like dust clearing from a battlefield, the words and the shouts had disappeared and lying on the reporters' scorecards were the totals. Sharpton and the Hawkins family were gone, storming out of the courtroom before the final tally was in. Keith Mondello had been found not guilty of murder and manslaughter, guilty of riot, unlawful imprisonment, menacing, discrimination, and fourth-degree criminal possession of a weapon.

Mayor David Dinkins, informed of the verdicts, said, "Keith Mondello is guilty of racism in the first degree."

Word quickly reached the streets below and exploded up and down the streets of Brooklyn. In front of the courthouse there were chants of the verdict, "Not guilty! Not guilty!" in the twilight. Somebody unfurled an American flag and set fire to it as a small group of black youths headed for Fulton Street, where a trash can was thrown through a coffee-shop window and where another group tried to pull a motorist from his car. They charged through the streets, followed by police officers with orders to keep their actions to a minimum. Knocking into pedestrians, turning over trash cans, and setting fires in blind rage and anger, they were joined by others who heard the news. Shopkeepers began rolling down their window gates, and at least one Korean fruit store was trashed as the marauding bands continued, not stopping at Flatbush Avenue but continuing to the Fort Greene section, where more fruit stores were vandalized.

Back on the fourth floor of the courthouse, Keith Mondello was handcuffed by court officers who took him away as his mother wept, over the objections of Murphy, who asked that bail be continued. Judge Owens looked at Murphy with an expression that seemed to say, "You must be kidding."

"Motion denied," he said flatly.

From the courthouse Michael Mondello called the 62nd Precinct station house. After telling the desk officer who he was, he said he wanted protection for his family when they arrived at their home.

"Is there a problem, there?" the desk officer asked.

"Not yet there's not, but who knows?" Mondello said.

"If there's no trouble there now then I really can't send a car—"

Mondello's face was flushed as he gripped the receiver with one hand and Susan with the other. The events had been bittersweet for him and his family. Although Keith had been acquitted of the top counts, he would still be going to jail and was still even now separated from them.

"Listen, my son is going to jail because everyone said he should have stayed home when he was threatened!" Mondello's high-pitched voice transformed itself into a thundering wail. "And he didn't call the police. Well, I am. I am asking for help so that there's not another goddam tragedy over there!"

Mondello hung up the phone, slamming it in its cradle. When he and Susan arrived home a blue-and-white police car was parked outside the house.

The mood on Twentieth Avenue was one of jubilation as neighbors of the Mondellos hugged each other and said to reporters, "We finally got some justice ourselves."

Not far from the corner where Yusuf Hawkins had been killed someone had painted a graffito on a wall. It was a circle, within which was the word NIGGERS with a slanted line through the word.

On the other end of Brooklyn the downtown terror spree had

transformed itself into an impromptu march, and by nine-thirty a group of about a hundred people were at Hegeman and Georgia avenues, where Yusuf Hawkins' grandparents lived.

Squads of police officers in riot gear responded to the scene as the marchers were joined by the curious, the sorrowful, and the angry of the dead youth's neighborhood. The camera crews were there as well, hoping to get reaction from the family. But they were with Sharpton, making funeral arrangements for Moses' sister.

One of the television trucks parked on Hegeman Avenue idled its engine while a growing assembly of neighborhood youths surrounded it.

"Hey man, you put me on TV?" a kid asked the driver. Meanwhile three or four kids, perhaps ten years old, tried to climb into the back of the vehicle and the driver panicked. The van lurched forward, its mast still extended, and suddenly there was a shower of sparks and there were screams as people ran for cover, not knowing what had happened. A power line caught on the mast fell to the ground, and suddenly the van was surrounded. Rumors flew up and down the street, that a kid had been hit, that the television truck had tried to run someone down, and then the cops stood by as the van was rocked and turned over on its side. The downed electric line was a power feed, and the entire block, now jammed past any capacity with people, was plunged into darkness.

The police did not want to restrict free movement, but the people had to be protected from the power line and an area was roped off while some bands of youths, now angry at the television people, began looking for trouble and found it.

WPIX reporter Ed Miller was punched in the nose and his crew car's window broken by rocks. There were other peltings, and a WCBS reporter, Lisa Rudolph, was punched in the nose.

Suddenly there was a stir within the crowd as a familiar form appeared. Al Sharpton arrived with Moses and Diane. After speaking briefly with police officials, Sharpton addressed the throng.

"What do you want to do this here for? There are other places for this, not in a black neighborhood, not where Yusuf's grandparents live," he began. They listened with rapt attention. He didn't chastise, he didn't preach. He was not in French cuffs and a fine suit in some City Hall room. Al Sharpton was talking to the children of the streets in the language of the streets. The master showman in Sharpton suddenly burst forth, and like a carnival huckster trying to hold the crowd he briefly dangled a carrot.

"Moses, Yusuf's father, is here and is going to speak to y'all. And Sister Diane, Yusuf Hawkins' mother, she's going to talk to all the sisters here, and you all have to listen to what she has to say."

Moses spoke first. He was comfortable here, and the cocky tone of bravado in his voice that people loved to hate reached out to the souls of those who stood in the darkness of Hegeman Avenue.

"We appreciate your support. We are angry today at this verdict, but we don't want to see anyone else get hurt! There is a live power line down, so everybody's gonna have to be real careful. Everybody's got to be cool and intelligent," he said, and then launched into a few words of UAM-style rhetoric.

Diane spoke as promised, although her words were brief and her tiny voice, issuing from a body already weak from the hellish day, could barely be heard. But whatever was said, the combination of speakers worked, but not before Sharpton got in a swipe at David Dinkins.

"The healers are resting comfortably in Gracie Mansion," Sharpton said. "I'm the one out here trying to stop the mayor's riots."

Slowly the crowds began to drift off. The police, who had been visibly nervous, relaxed a bit and took their helmets off. As the case has been with most racial violence in the United States throughout its history, the only real victims had a riot broken out on Hegeman Avenue would have been people of color, although there could have been others. Mark Kriegel, a streetwise *Daily News* staff writer, was one of the few journalists to follow the demonstrators all the way from downtown. He had been threatened by a stick with nails at the end of it.

But catastrophe had been averted, in part because of police restraint and also the fortuitous appearance of Sharpton, whose smooth street style belied an intense nervousness.

Violence on the night of the Mondello verdict reached far beyond the streets of East New York and downtown Brooklyn. In the Canarsie section a gang of between ten and fifteen blacks beat and robbed two Hispanics in a subway station, making mention of the Bensonhurst case. In the Times Square area of midtown Manhattan a group of as many as twenty blacks combed the streets after midnight, shouting, "This is for Yusuf," and "Take this, white boy," as they randomly pummeled and punched as many as six white passers-by at different locations. Arrests were made in the Manhattan attacks, which were classified as bias incidents.

Those who engaged in violence had either not heard or decided against heeding the words of the mayor, who spoke earlier in the day when the Mondello verdict became public:

"The memory of Yusuf Hawkins would be defiled if those disappointed in the jury's action use it as an excuse to rend our spirits further and cripple our future."

FOR THE COLOR OF HIS SKIN

O NLY a few days after the Mondello verdict, Gina Feliciano was in the news once again, arrested by transit police for possession of crack cocaine and fare-beating in a Brooklyn subway station. The arrest drew snickers from Mondello's family and others in the neighborhood. But the young woman's misfortune was not unexpected to people who knew her.

Shortly after May turned into June the courts in Brooklyn were the focus of attention once again, although the blister of tension in the city had seemingly burst. Even Al Sharpton had agreed to lay down his arms, or rather his picket signs, and a truce was reached between the activist and the Hawkins family and the community where the murder had occurred. At St. Dominic's church, where a priest had watched the marches—that seemed so long ago—in silence because he thought it the most appropriate response, Sharpton and Mayor Dinkins met with parish priests, a local assemblyman, and other Bensonhurst community leaders. The last march had been on the weekend after the acquittal, and the jeering reaction of Bensonhurst, old news because the marches failed to draw blood, were even criticized by the Mondello family.

"We've agreed to suspend the marches, based on their agreeing to call for justice, and it is a two-way agreement," Sharpton said.

On June 11, the day after Sharpton made peace with Bensonhurst, the time came for Keith Mondello and Joseph Fama to make their peace with the people of the State of New York.

"He caused the whole thing," Judge Owens said of Mondello, whose parents watched anxiously as their son was sentenced to five and one-half to sixteen years in prison. The reaction from Moses Stewart, also seated in the courtroom, was a simple and exultant "Yes."

Mondello simply shook his head.

Later that day a larger group of Hawkins family supporters arrived, and Moses exclaimed "Yes" again as Owens, without comment, sentenced Joseph Fama to thirty-two and one-half years to life. That was when the Fama family exploded.

"Fuck you, I hate you!" one Fama cousin shouted at the judge as other family members joined in and another cousin lunged toward the Hawkins family, body-blocked by a court officer.

As Fama was handcuffed and led away the blacks began to call after him, "Bye bye, Joey."

On the way out of the courtroom there was pushing, shoving, and cursing and Rocco Fama, in his broken English, cursed Al Sharpton.

But the case was still not over, and it would become clear that, in this particular homicide, the acting-in-concert theory envisioned by Elizabeth Holtzman and her staff was doomed from the beginning and then, according to high-level Holtzman assistants, mishandled by the Hynes prosecution team.

John Vento, the next defendant to be tried, was a special target of prosecutors who felt that his flip-flop had ruined their chance of getting an intentional-murder conviction against Fama. Some believed that the loss of Vento's cooperation turned the Bensonhurst cases into a house of cards that came tumbling down on top of the Brooklyn District Attorney's office. Even though his own grand jury testimony was used against him, Vento's jury was unable to reach a decision on the murder charges, convicting him only of lesser offenses for which he received four years. Retried on the murder charges in 1991, he was acquitted of them.

Charles Stressler's first trial resulted in a mistrial, after a juror yelled at Moses Stewart and accused him of staring at her. Stewart had complained the day before that the woman had been staring at him, and that it was his intention to stare back just as hard.

"She wants to stare, I'll stare right back at the bitch," Moses said in the private "family room" on the fourth floor of Supreme Court.

If there was any doubt of how doomed the cases were, it disappeared with the Stressler trial. Justice Owens had already informed prosecutors that if the jury convicted Stressler on anything more than weapons-possession charges he was going to set the verdict aside. Douglas Nadjari, the assistant who prosecuted the Stressler case, informed Moses and Diane of the possibility before the shouting match that led to the mistrial.

The flaw in the concert theory may have been identified by Jacob Evseroff in his summations during the Stressler trial.

"Nobody has ever been shot with a baseball bat," he said. The jury believed him.

As the Bensonhurst acquittals came in one by one the fear that gripped the city immediately after the shooting and during the first trials was not evident. It is difficult to assess whether the relative lack of media attention to the case was a matter of cause or effect.

"I think people are starting to come to their senses," Dave DePetris, Joey Fama's lawyer, said. "This was a highly political case, with a lot of pressure on everyone."

The pressures mounted for the Hawkins family when their adviser left the Brooklyn carriage house he had occupied since they first knew him. Sharpton moved his family to a town house in the New Jersey suburb of Englewood, across the George Washington Bridge from Manhattan and a considerable distance from the Brooklyn streets. The move was sparked in part by another controversial case that the activist had involved himself in. A police shooting of a black youth, Phillip Pannell, in Teaneck, New Jersey, had sparked a night of rioting after a demonstration led by community activists, including the Reverend Daughtry.

Sharpton, who led later demonstrations in Teaneck, was criticized for involving himself in the affair by other black leaders who claimed he was not invited. According to Sharpton, the move to New Jersey was in part a response to that criticism.

Problems in the Hawkins home continued, however, and Sharpton's mediation skills, although desperately needed once again, were more difficult to come by once he had moved. This is cited as one

FOR THE COLOR OF HIS SKIN

reason why, during the first Stressler trial, Diane called New York City housing police to the apartment during a fracas there.

"Why don't you people go find who killed my son instead of throwing me out of my own house?" a visibly intoxicated Moses said to the officers. He was arrested and charged on Diane's complaint, but police will not release full details of the incident, claiming that they cannot do so in "domestic situations." Diane Hawkins had to be afforded the same rights and considerations as any other domestic-violence victim.

An order of protection was issued against Moses, who was directed to stay away from the apartment in the Brevoort Houses. He violated it a few weeks later and was arrested once again.

But in spite of the difficulties between them, husband and wife both attended court proceedings together, at least for a while.

The jury did not accept the prosecution's claims that Joseph Serrano had passed a gun to Joseph Fama, and convicted him only on a weapons charge. He was sentenced to community service.

For James Patino, the defendant about whom little was known from the beginning, it appeared at first as if things might not go so smoothly. Prosecutors believed they could prove that the murder weapon, or some other gun, had been stashed in his car earlier in the afternoon. But the claims were groundless in the eyes of the jury. Patino was acquitted on all charges.

Steven Curreri, the only defendant not charged with murder, was also acquitted.

"We weren't surprised," said his attorney, Matthew Mari. "He was innocent and we knew he was innocent. The surprise was that he was charged with a crime at all."

Al Sharpton fared far better in court that year as a defendant than did the Hawkins family as complainants. It took a Manhattan jury four hours to dismiss every one of the sixty-seven fraud and larceny counts brought against Sharpton by Robert Abrams.

*   *   *

With each passing trial of each defendant the media coverage shrank. The daily papers had short spots when verdicts came in, but there was no perceived threat of violence, and public interest in the case declined.

The black community was far less vocal with each acquittal as well, something that can be attributed in large part to Dinkins' mayoralty. Problems continued to exist for blacks in New York and still do. But under David Dinkins there was a feeling that, even if those problems were not addressed in as timely or effective a fashion as the community would have preferred, they were at least not being ignored.

A turning point for many came in the summer of 1990, when a triumphant Nelson Mandela, leader of South Africa's African National Congress, came to New York for a celebration of his freedom after a quarter-century of imprisonment in his native land.

Speeches, parades, and other festivities were planned, with the Dinkins administration pulling out all the stops to give the freedom fighter red-carpet treatment. For the first time, the City of New York had given recognition and acknowledgment to an issue close to the hearts of its black citizens. The Mandela visit had a calming, soothing effect on the city at large, although there was some criticism of the tremendous sums of money that were spent on the welcome.

By 1991 another issue had taken over the headlines and nightly news shows, pushing the stories of the Bensonhurst trials further out of the public consciousness. Under Saddam Hussein, president of Iraq, the Iraqi Army had invaded the tiny neighboring country of Kuwait.

The world's eyes were turned as one toward the Middle East, as January 15, President Bush's deadline for Saddam Hussein to get out of Kuwait, drew near and war seemed imminent.

Al Sharpton's battle with Bensonhurst was not over yet, however, and two days before the Middle East deadline he had his own war to fight. The truce with Bensonhurst had been broken, he said.

"When we took to the streets and were marching we got some convictions. And now we have been quiet, and Yusuf's killers are walking free, acquitted of his murder," Sharpton said.

Al Sharpton once again came to Bensonhurst, on January 13,

1991, to protest acquittals, but all eyes were no longer on the schoolyard at Twentieth Avenue when the demonstrators got off the buses. The television cameras were for the most part absent, although there were a few still photographers and some print people. There was a crew from the British Broadcasting Corporation, doing a documentary on Sharpton and his movement, but that was about it.

Sharpton walked past some police officers to instruct marshals on how to space the marchers apart. Suddenly a young white man walked up to Sharpton and plunged a kitchen knife through his leather coat, narrowly missing his heart.

"I thought I had gotten punched," Sharpton later said. "Then I looked down and I saw this knife sticking out."

Moses Stewart and Freddy Hawkins, along with longtime Sharpton bodyguard Skawkee Mohammed, chased after the fleeing suspect and tackled him, assisted by stunned police officers. Sharpton was rushed to Coney Island Hospital, where he was found to have a punctured lung. New York *Post* columnist Mike MacAlary, who has had more than a few differences with Sharpton in the past, later wrote that he had often wished to see the minister silenced, "but not this way."

When he woke up after surgery, Sharpton saw Mayor Dinkins and Police Commissioner Lee Brown standing over him.

Although he was uncomfortable and in pain during his hospital stay, Sharpton pulled through easily, as newspapers and magazines began printing stories about how he had become mainstream because he issued a message calling for calm after he regained consciousness: "I have never called for violence, I have always called for calm. So I don't know what they're talking about."

A week after the ordeal he was released from the hospital, and as he was being discharged a young white doctor came and shook his hand.

"I'm very glad that you are well, Reverend," Sharpton says the doctor told him. The young surgeon said he had worked on Sharpton when he was first brought into the emergency room.

"It was particularly important to me," the young man continued.

"You see, I was one of the doctors at Maimonedes who worked on Yusuf Hawkins when he came in."

Six weeks later scant notice was paid to the final Bensonhurst trial. Pasquale Raucci, the short little teenager who liked to play rap records at parties, was acquitted of homicide charges in connection with the death of Yusuf Hawkins. His convictions on assault, civil rights infringements, and false imprisonment charges were set aside by Judge Owens, who sentenced him to probation on the single remaining charge, criminal possession of a baseball bat. Almost two years after the fatal shots were fired, only three of the eight young men convicted were given jail time for their crimes.

Participants in the attack that night have said in interviews that Joseph Fama was the gunman, although he was never convicted of it, and the murder weapon has still never turned up. He is serving his time at the maximum-security Dannemora prison in upstate New York, and his lawyers are appealing.

Keith Mondello was transferred from a correctional facility close to New York City and was ordered to finish the rest of his jail time at Attica State Penitentiary. His mother is still trying to raise money for his appeal.

"Keith is there in jail, and he doesn't know why. He didn't kill anyone; he never meant to kill anyone. He was a victim of politics," Susan Mondello said. As if to bolster her claims that Keith could not have possibly harbored racist feelings, Susan shows anyone who is interested a receipt signed by a black friend of Keith's, who brought him clothes while he was still jailed in New York City.

The signature belongs to Russell Gibbons, who brought the bats to the schoolyard with Charlie Stressler on August 23 and was never charged with anything.

John Vento continues doing his time, and neither his family nor his attorney, Gerald DeChiarra, wished to be interviewed at length. DeChiarra claims, however, that allegations of organized-crime connections leveled against his client are false, as well as claims that Vento and Mondello were in the cocaine business together.

The bitterness has not left Bensonhurst. Its residents still feel that their community was unfairly labeled racist and intolerant, in spite of the visible and vocal reactions of residents to the marches that took place there. But life is returning to normal. Young men who were subjected to unpleasant and allegedly unfair interrogation by the police now take a different view of such procedures. Their counter-parts in black neighborhoods have long known of such practices as the rough treatment afforded Keith Mondello. But such conduct is not often used against white suspects.

Even the Central Park jogger case, which resulted in convictions against all of those charged, was looked at differently by people in Bensonhurst who suddenly realized that the police aren't necessarily always right in what they have done. Attorneys for the Central Park defendants alleged that police pressured videotaped confessions out of their clients.

"If they treated Keith the way they did, then who knows if what those black kids are saying about the way they were treated might be true?" Keith's girlfriend, Sarina Scavone, said during that case. Mondello's parents agreed.

After the Raucci acquittal, Sharpton was asked what his next move would be.

"This isn't over yet," Sharpton said. "Some black congressmen are trying to put pressure on the U.S. Attorney to bring civil rights cases against these young men. We will still go after them in the federal courts."

An attorney for one of the acquitted defendants said he had no fears that any attempt at federal charges would be successful. "They just don't do those kinds of cases," he said, echoing the sentiments expressed years before by Andrew Maloney's staff.

New York has not had another racial murder since the Hawkins killing, although some assaults are still under investigation, including the beating of two black men in Greenwich Village by a group of white youths. Attacks by whites against blacks have subsided.

"One of our biggest problems right now are crimes committed

because of sexual orientation," said Inspector Sanderson of the Bias Unit. The number of attacks against homosexual men and lesbians has skyrocketed in recent years, according to advocacy groups. But New York is one of the few cities in the country that keeps records of such crimes, even though there is now general recognition that hate crimes based on race, religion, and ethnicity must be tabulated by enforcement agencies at the local as well as the federal level.

In April 1991 the United States Justice Department announced that it would begin keeping records of bias crimes in every category except sexual orientation, a move that could be traced to the tremendous publicity the Hawkins case received, but due also to the tireless work of men and women who knew all along that it was the right thing to do and never stopped trying.

The long-standing claims of police brutality against blacks, which were partially responsible for the anger poor blacks and all fair-minded and informed Americans felt before the Hawkins slaying, are finally being looked at more seriously by authorities. On March 3, 1991, a black man was brutally beaten by Los Angeles police officers after a car chase, and what might have resulted in just another unsubstantiated complaint by a criminal suspect became national news because a bystander had videotaped the senseless attack. Even President Bush commented on the Los Angeles tape. "This made me sick," he said.

The New York State Senate is preparing a hearing on police brutality in its state. Some of the witnesses expected to testify are police officers who themselves have witnessed such crimes, even some who have committed them.

Although the police-brutality issue does not relate to the Hawkins case directly, it does in a broader sense. As mainstream political leaders begin to explore with open minds allegations made by the most disenfranchised in society, who before only had an Al Sharpton in their corner, then the need for such avant-garde spokesmen will disappear, perhaps resulting in greater understanding among all of us.

"If Yusuf hadn't been shot, and he and his friends called police because they were stopped by the young men with the bats, they might have been arrested themselves," Sharpton said.

The thought is shared by several defense attorneys from the Bensonhurst case, who maintain that there were two different incidents that night. One was the gathering of forces against Gina Feliciano's friends. The other was the crime of the gunman. One Bensonhurst defendant said that his participation in the schoolyard gathering was not motivated by race.

"But Fama wouldn't have shot him if he wasn't black," this defendant, who has asked not to be identified, said. "The killing was racial. But none of us knew that was going to happen. I cried when I realized what he did."

Was the Hawkins murder merely a case of mistaken identity or a vicious urban lynching? The many acquittals in the case would seem to lead to the first answer. But that is not necessarily true. The credo that "in Bensonhurst trouble means get out the bats" is wrong, and yet is tolerated by parents and police officers who made no move to stop the initial gathering. And if Gina Feliciano's friends were white, would there have been such a showing from so many different neighborhoods in Bensonhurst area? Probably not. Bensonhurst's racial troubles, especially at John Dewey and New Utrecht high schools, are well documented.

If anything, the Hawkins murder and the arrests of the defendants have caused some residents of such areas to give pause to what they say, what they think, and what they teach their children about those who are different from themselves. It is yet doubtful, however, whether bigotry so deeply rooted can be so easily weeded out.

From the time of his burial in September 1989 until the first anniversary of Yusuf Hawkins' death his grave was an unmarked plot in a pine-tree-shaded corner of the Cemetery of the Evergreens. On August 23, 1990, a tombstone was finally laid, paid for by the United African Movement and chosen, Al Sharpton said, by the Hawkins family.

The unveiling of the monument drew a respectable representation from the media, as well as Charles Hynes, who was not welcomed by the family. His decision to announce publicly that he would personally prosecute the alleged murderer of a Williamsburgh rabbi was seen as a slap in the face by the Hawkinses, because his personal advocacy was not offered for the Bensonhurst cases. There was also bad blood between Hynes and Moses Stewart because the District Attorney's office did not provide transportation for them to and from court, as had been done in the Howard Beach case for Michael Griffith's family. Moses also received a small stipend from Hynes' office, from funds for a witness and victim program. Along with help from Sharpton, it was all that kept his family afloat throughout the trials, he said. He was angry when that was cut back.

The prosecutor stood off to the side with some staff members and watched as the family joined in a prayer circle and the Reverend Alfred C. Sharpton delivered an invocation, and did not participate.

The tombstone was polished granite and in its center was carved a raised fist that appears to be reaching up from the grave in anger and defiance. The epitaph was miscarved, and has yet to be corrected: "In death is the struggle that cause change."

The stone and its fist seemed so heavy a weight to rest upon the grave of a gentle young man who would be sixteen forever.

Yusuf Hawkins was the last person anyone might have thought would become a symbol of the intolerance and racism that still exist in society. It was certainly not a role he would have chosen. Like the wounds that resulted in his death, the role of martyr and symbol had been thrust upon him simply for the color of his skin.